THE RISE AND FALL OF THE EUROPEAN ⌣

The Draft European Constitution was arguably both an attempt to constitutionalise the Union, re-framing that project in the language of the state, and an attempt to stretch the boundaries of constitutionalism itself, re-imagining that concept to accommodate the sui generis European Union. The (partial) failure of this project is the subject of this collection of essays. The collection brings together leading EU constitutional scholars to consider, with the benefit of hindsight, the purportedly constitutional character of the proposed Constitutional Treaty, the reasons for its rejection by voters in France and the Netherlands, the ongoing implications of this episode for the European project, and the lessons it teaches us about what constitutionalism really means.

The Rise and Fall of the European Constitution

Edited by
NW Barber
Maria Cahill
and
Richard Ekins

·HART·
OXFORD · LONDON · NEW YORK · NEW DELHI · SYDNEY

HART PUBLISHING
Bloomsbury Publishing Plc
Kemp House, Chawley Park, Cumnor Hill, Oxford, OX2 9PH, UK

HART PUBLISHING, the Hart/Stag logo, BLOOMSBURY and the Diana logo are
trademarks of Bloomsbury Publishing Plc
First published in Great Britain 2019

First published in hardback, 2019
Paperback edition, 2020

A catalogue record for this book is available from the British Library.

Library of Congress Cataloging-in-Publication Data

Names: Barber, N. W. (Nicholas William), editor. | Cahill, Maria, editor. | Ekins, Richard, editor.

Title: The rise and fall of the European constitution / edited by Nicholas Barber,
Maria Cahill, Richard Ekins.

Description: Oxford, UK ; Portland, Oregon : Hart Publishing, 2019. |
Series: Modern studies in European law

Identifiers: LCCN 2018038072 (print) | LCCN 2018038551 (ebook) |
ISBN 9781509910991 (epub) | ISBN 9781509910984 (hardback)

Subjects: LCSH: Treaty Establishing a Constitution for Europe (2004 October 29) |
European Union—Constitution. | Constitutional law—European Union countries. |
European Union countries—Politics and government.

Classification: LCC KJE4443.32004 (ebook) | LCC KJE4443.32004 .R568 2019 (print) |
DDC 342.2402—dc23

LC record available at https://lccn.loc.gov/2018038072

ISBN: HB: 978-1-50991-098-4
PB: 978-1-50994-523-8
ePDF: 978-1-50991-100-4
ePub: 978-1-50991-099-1

Typeset by Compuscript Ltd, Shannon

To find out more about our authors and books visit www.hartpublishing.co.uk. Here you will find
extracts, author information, details of forthcoming events and the option to sign up for our newsletters.

ACKNOWLEDGEMENTS

The conference on which this collection is based was held under the auspices of the Programme for the Foundations of Law and Constitutional Government. The editors have reason to be grateful to a great many people for their support of this project. We are grateful to the contributors who have written a set of stimulating essays. We are grateful to Achas Burin, who provided expert editorial assistance. And we are very grateful to Graham Child who generously funded the project.

TABLE OF CONTENTS

LIST OF CONTRIBUTORS

Giuliano Amato was twice Prime Minister of Italy and is presently a judge in the Italian Constitutional Court. He was also vice-president of the Convention that drafted the European Constitution.

Nick Barber is Professor of Constitutional Law and Theory at the University of Oxford, and a Fellow of Trinity College Oxford.

Gunnar Beck is a barrister and a specialist in European Law at SOAS, University of London. He also acted as legal advisor to the UK parliamentary delegates to the Convention.

Maria Cahill is a Lecturer in Law at University College Cork.

Paul Craig is Professor of English Law at St John's College, Oxford.

Erin F Delaney is Professor of Law at Northwestern University Pritzker School of Law.

Richard Ekins is an Associate Professor of Law at Oxford University and a Fellow of St John's College.

Dieter Grimm is a Professor at Humboldt University and was a justice of the Federal Constitutional Court of Germany from 1987 to 1999.

Dorota Leczykiewicz is an Associate Professor of Law at Oxford University and a Fellow of St Peter's College, Oxford.

Richard Mullender is Professor of Law and Legal Theory at Newcastle University.

Kalypso Nicolaidis is Professor in International Relations at Oxford University. She was a member of the Greek delegation to the Convention.

The **Rt. Hon. Gisela Stuart** was a member of the UK Parliament from 1997 to 2017. She was one of the UK parliamentary delegates to the Convention.

Neil Walker is the Regius Professor of Public Law and the Law of Nature and Nations and Edinburgh University.

Stephen Weatherill is the Jacques Delors Professor of European Law in the University of Oxford and a Fellow of Somerville College.

1

Introduction

The Draft European Constitution could have been, and almost was, one of the defining constitutional events of the early part of the twenty-first century. It was certainly amongst the most ambitious. It drew elements from the constitutional traditions of the nation state, and applied these features to the European Union. Though the extent of its ambitions is debated in this volume, it can be seen both as an attempt to constitutionalise the Union, re-framing that project in the language of the state and as an attempt to stretch the boundaries of constitutionalism itself, re-imagining that concept to accommodate the *sui generis* European Union. The (partial) failure of this project is the subject of this collection of essays.

The launch of the project of the European Constitution is often considered to be the speech given by Joschka Fischer, the then German Foreign Minister, at Humboldt University on 12 May 2000, almost exactly 50 years after Robert Schuman, the then French Foreign Minister, delivered his famous Schuman Declaration on 9 May 1950.[1] While Schumann had insisted that 'Europe will not be made all at once, or according to a single plan',[2] Fischer, speaking in a private capacity, presented a grand plan for 'the completion of European integration'.[3] He wanted a federation based on a constituent treaty, with a European Parliament and a European government grounded in a division of sovereignty between those institutions and the institutions of the nation state. Fischer was aware of the need to placate the Eurosceptics 'on this and the other side of the Channel', insisting that it was a long-term vision, and noting that there were 'procedural and substantive problems' which would need to be resolved before a federation could be realised.[4] In particular, Fischer argued that 'it would be an irreparable mistake in the construction of Europe if one were to try to complete political integration *against* the existing national institutions and traditions rather than by involving them. Any such endeavour would be doomed to failure ...'.[5] Instead, his recommendation

---

[1] J Fischer, *From Confederation to Federation: Thoughts on the Finality of European Integration* (London, Federal Trust, 2000); P Norman, *The Accidental Constitution* (Brussels, Eurocomment, 2005) 12–14.

[2] M Burgess, *Federalism and the European Union: The Building of Europe 1950–2000* (London, Routledge, 2000) 64–65.

[3] Fischer, *From Confederation to Federation* (n 1) 9.

[4] Ibid, 16.

[5] Ibid, 17, emphasis added.

was that the federal project would be workable '[o]nly if European integration takes the nation states along with it ... only if their institutions are not devalued or even made to disappear ...'.[6] The tensions between the push towards federalisation and the conflicting sovereignties of the Member States, tensions that were later to be played out in the Convention and the referendums on the Draft Constitution, were prefigured in Fischer's speech.

A few short months later, in December 2000, the Nice Intergovernmental Conference called for 'deeper and wider debate about the future of the European Union', a call that was formalised in Declaration No 23 annexed to the Treaty of Nice, which was signed on 26 February 2001.[7] The Declaration set out the aims of the upcoming Laeken European Council meeting, enjoining it to agree on 'appropriate initiatives' for continuing that debate, highlighting the need for a process which would address the allocation of competences in accordance with the principle of subsidiarity, the status of the Charter of Fundamental Rights, the need for simplification of the Treaties, and to reconsider the role of national parliaments.

Responding to these calls, the Laeken Declaration of 15 December 2001 announced the establishment of a Convention on the Future of Europe which would move 'towards a Constitution for Europe'.[8] The challenges facing the European Union were identified as (1) how to bring citizens, especially the young, closer to the European project; (2) how to organise politics after enlargement; and (3) how to develop the Union 'into a stabilising factor and a model in the new, multipolar world'. However, the mandate of the Convention began with a far more modest desire for simplification: there were too many treaties and too many powers and policies, the Declaration argued, and thus, for the sake of transparency, simplification was 'essential'. Immediately following this argument, however, the Declaration calls into question the distinction between the European Communities and the Union and the three pillars, moots the possibility of a basic treaty (with its own amendment and ratification procedures) and other treaty provisions, and raises the prospect of including the Charter in the Treaties and acceding to the European Convention on Human Rights, before going on to ask, with seeming restraint 'whether this simplification and reorganisation might not lead in the long run to the adoption of a constitutional text'.

The Laeken Declaration conceived that the Convention on the Future of Europe should debate 'as broadly and as openly as possible' in respect of the Union's future development and to identify 'various possible responses'. The Declaration noted that the European Council appointed Mr Valéry Giscard d'Estaing as Chairman of the Convention and Mr Giuliano Amato and Mr Jean-Luc Dehaene as Vice-Chairmen. In addition, the Convention was to be composed of 15 representatives

---

[6] Ibid, 17.

[7] Norman, *The Accidental Constitution* (n 1) 16–18.

[8] 'Presidency Conclusions of the Laeken European Council' EU Bull, No 12, Annex 1 (2001); Norman (n 1) 18–23.

of each of the Heads of States or national governments (one from each Member State), as well as 30 representatives of national parliaments (two from each Member State), 16 members of the European Parliament and two representatives of the Commission. The accession candidates[9] were to be represented in the same way as existing Member States (one government representative and two national parliament representatives) and allowed to freely participate in the discussions, without having the power to block any emerging consensus. Within this cohort of 106 Convention delegates, there was an inner circle, the Praesidium, which was composed of the Chairman and Vice-Chairmen as well as nine of the 106, the nine consisting of the representatives of the governments who held the Presidency of the European Council during the lifetime of the Convention, two national parliament representatives, two European Parliament representatives, and two Commission representatives. Three representatives of the Economic and Social Committee and three representatives of the European social partners, along with six Committee of the Regions representatives, and the European Ombudsman, were invited as observers. International experts were to be called to assist the Convention in its work as necessary. The inaugural meeting of the Convention was on 1 March 2002 and proceedings were to be completed after one year.[10]

Three of the contributors to this volume were directly involved in the Convention process. Giuliano Amato held the position of Vice-Chairman of the Constitutional Convention. Gisela Stuart was one of the UK parliamentary representatives to the Convention who was also a member of the Praesidium. Kalypso Nicolaidis, who served as chair of an international group of expert advisors to the Convention and as 'sherpa' to the Greek Foreign Minister before and during the 2003 Greek Presidency, which was the last Convention Presidency.

Following the Convention, the text was then reviewed by an Intergovernmental Conference, which completed its work in June 2004.[11] The IGC made a number of significant changes to the document, though it remained identifiably the work of the Convention. In the process, some of the provisions were renumbered, and two versions of numbering can be found in the literature: first, the 2003 text produced by the Convention, second, the 2004 text agreed by the Intergovernmental Conference.

A number of states either agreed to hold, or were legally required to hold, referendums on the Draft Constitution. In Spain and Luxembourg, the Draft Constitution was passed, but the votes in France and the Netherlands went against the proposal.[12] Proposed referendums in other countries, including the United Kingdom, were abandoned, as the Members States suspended the processes of ratification. In the aftermath of the French and Dutch referendums on 29 May and

---

[9] Bulgaria, Czech Republic, Cyprus, Estonia, Hungary, Latvia, Lithuania, Malta, Poland, Romania, Slovakia, Slovenia and Turkey.

[10] Norman (n 1) 19–21; PP Craig, *The Treaty of Lisbon* (Oxford, Oxford University Press, 2010) 1–2.

[11] Norman (n 1) ch 18; Craig, *The Treaty of Lisbon* (n 10) 16–20.

[12] J Dinan, *Europe Recast* (Basingstoke, Palgrave, 2014) 307–08.

1 June 2005, respectively, there was significant disquiet about why the referendums failed and, within weeks, a 'period of reflection' was announced following the European Council meeting in Brussels in June 2005.[13] Jean-Claude Juncker, the current President of the Commission, spoke then in his capacity as President of the European Council endorsing the position of those Member States who wished to suspend their ratification plans given the unstable position of the Constitution, saying that:

> I would like ... to have now a more extended period of reflection, explanation, debate and, if necessary, controversy throughout the Member States ... We need to discuss Europe and I would like the institutions of the European Union, the European Parliament, the Council, the Commission, the Member States, civil society, trade unions, political parties and national parliaments to take part in this vast debate. ... I would like the Commission, which is the guardian not only of the treaty, but also, and above all, of the spirit of the treaty and of the European ambition, to be at the centre of this debate, not to give the impression that everything is inspired and dominated by Brussels, but to provide us with a common thread characterised by wisdom and ambition, in this national and Europe-wide debate.

In political terms, the period of reflection began with the convening of the group of 'wise men', otherwise known as the Amato group, in September 2006 and ended with the decision to 'abandon' the constitutional project in June 2007,[14] a conclusion which paved the way for the signing of the Lisbon Treaty on 13 December 2007. The Lisbon Treaty contained much of the substance of the Draft Constitution, though with many of the more ostentatious resemblances to state constitutions removed.

Within academia, however, it is not clear that the period of reflection ever properly started. With a number of important exceptions, there is relatively little scholarship reflecting seriously and carefully on the failure of the Draft Constitution and suspension of the constitutional project, rather than simply the failure of the French and Dutch referendums. The episode of the rise, fall and partial resurrection of the Draft Constitution repays study at a number of levels. At the most abstract level, it speaks to constitutionalism in general. It raises questions about the nature and purpose of constitutions, and their relationship with the state. Did the labelling of the document as a 'constitution' have any significance, and, if it did, was this an attempt to import the structures of the state into the European project? As a number of the contributors argue, this could be seen as a challenge to the unique nature of the European project, a political structure that some see as having transcended the state tradition and others see as complementing that tradition. More specifically, what lessons are there to be learned from

---

[13] Full text of Jean-Claude Juncker's speech, current President of the Council of the European Union, at the European Parliament, on the outcome of the Luxembourg Presidency and the European Council held on 16–17 June, Brussels, 22 June 2005 available at www.eu2005.lu/en/actualites/discours/2005/06/22jclj-pe/index.html.

[14] German Presidency Conclusions, 21–22 June 2007.

the abandonment of the European Constitution and the inclusion of so much of its substance in the Lisbon Treaty? Did the decision to include so much of the Draft Constitution in Lisbon show sufficient respect for the votes of the French and Dutch peoples? Is there a case to be made that the rejection of the Constitution undermined the position of the European project more generally or, conversely, in the light of the Eurozone crisis, the immigration crisis and now the Brexit crisis, that the need for a constitution is greater than ever? If we once defended the theoretical possibility and sociological plausibility of a European Constitution existing alongside national constitutions, do we now believe that this view needs refinement, or do we contend that the constitutional moment simply had not arrived? These are conversations that need to be engaged in; the rejection of the Draft Constitution is not an episode that can simply be forgotten. Since there was such a heavy expense of academic time and expertise in the process of rethinking the traditional preconditions for a constitution in order to accommodate the idiosyncrasies of supranational constitutionalism in the first place, and given that that scholarship was characterised by great intellectual creativity, it seems that reflection on the lessons to be learned would be a worthwhile process. The contributions to this collection shatter that silence by engaging in the kind of explanation, debate and controversy that Juncker imagined. Our hope is that, in doing so, they revive a conversation that should never have been suspended.

The book opens with a contribution from one of the co-chairs of the Convention, Giuliano Amato. Amato recalls that the Convention was established in the context of the entry into force of the Euro and the imminent enlargement of the Union to the east, on the basis of the felt need for the Member States to agree a form of 'deepening' that would accompany that 'widening' in terms of the scope and membership. Yet despite the need for deepening, he notes that the Laeken Declaration did not give the Convention members a strong mandate to draft a constitution but only the much weaker invitation to consider possible avenues for the Union's future. The decision to write a Constitution was proposed by Chairman Giscard d'Estaing but it was one which, Amato notes, the Convention members were happy to endorse. Nonetheless, the Convention witnessed the perennial tension between those who wished to proceed to constitutional *finalité* and those who opposed federalisation; the desire to deliver a Constitution was ultimately frustrated such that the document was the compromised Constitutional *Treaty*, which Amato maintains fell far below the goals of Joschka Fischer's speech. Considering the current situation, and drawing on the functionalist perspective, Amato imagines an alternative series of thematic conventions each with mandates for institutional reform to be agreed sector by sector, a multi-speed Europe in which clusters of Member States could progress integration in monetary and fiscal matters but also security, defence and immigration, and only then a Convention to articulate a common framework for this 'multi-cluster Europe'.

The decision to use the label 'constitution' was controversial at the time, and the significance of this word remains a source of debate. Dieter Grimm reflects on implications of choosing to approach the reforms of the Treaties through a purportedly constitutional document. As Grimm contends, at least one of the motivations for the invocation of the word was the hope that some of the lustre of state constitutions would be cast on the European Union; the label would bring with it some of the legitimating function it plays at the national level. But, Grimm argues, there is a crucial difference. Whilst state constitutions are grounded, more or less convincingly, in the will of their people, the European Union is grounded in the decisions of its Member States. There is no 'European society' that has produced the Treaties. So was the Draft Constitution truly a constitution? Crucially, in the Draft Constitution the power to amend the document remained in the hands of the Member States; constitutional power had not shifted, and the document remained a treaty, even if given the title of a constitution. Furthermore, Grimm argues Europe's lack of a constitution in the state sense has led to a failure to divide constitutional provisions from ordinary legislation. There is an 'over-constitutionalisation' of the European project, with the structures of the Treaties rendering it hard for Member States to change European law where they believe too much power has shifted to the Union level. This over-constitutionalisation insulates many areas of European activity from the political supervision of the Member States and the European Parliament. Reconfiguring the Treaties to allow a distinction to be drawn between a small number of constitutional norms and a far larger number of ordinary laws – which would be easier for the politically account-able parts of the European project to modify – might help fill this legitimacy gap.

Kalypso Nicolaidis provides an insider's view of the workings of the Convention and subsequent referendums. Starting with the pressures that led to the Convention, Nicolaidis then examines the operation of that body and explores the tensions within the Convention, in particular the stresses that emerged between the smaller and larger countries. Nicolaidis is sharply critical of the leadership shown by Giscard d'Estaing, arguing that he was unwilling to accommodate the claims of smaller states, and, more generally, failed to run the Convention in an inclusive manner. The failure of the Convention to engage with those outside of the Chamber may provide one of the explanations for the rejection of the Draft Constitution by the peoples of France and the Netherlands. Whilst Nicolaidis concedes that these referendum campaigns were dominated by local issues – with the merits of the Draft Constitution pushed into the background – she contends that this lack of interest was, itself, a product of the failure of the Convention to involve the peoples of Europe. When the time came to vote on the Draft Constitution, few voters cared much about that document, and the referendums became dominated by other issues.

The failure of the Dutch and French peoples to engage with the Draft Constitution during the referendum debates is also considered by Paul Craig, but he draws a different lesson. For Craig, the Convention should not be regarded as a waste of effort. The bulk of the rules produced by that body found a home in the Treaty of Lisbon and, given that the reasons for the rejection of the Draft Constitution in the Dutch and French referendums turned on local issues, it would be a mistake to regard these aspects of the Draft Constitution as having been rejected by the Dutch and French peoples. Craig identifies a number of what he believes to be misconceptions about the Convention process. First, as he demonstrates, it is inaccurate to claim that the Draft Constitution was forced on Member States; in contrast, the process of the Convention was both animated by and dominated by the representatives of the Member States. Second, and contrary to some of the other contributors to this volume, he argues that the Draft Convention was not a step towards a federal Europe and did not embody statist ambitions. According to Craig, there is no reason why the label of a 'constitution' should be accorded this significance, and there was little of substance in the Draft Constitution that was truly novel; indeed, most of the new provisions in the Draft Constitution clarified and limited the competences of the Union, and enhanced Member State control of its institutions.

The Draft Constitution was an attempt to reshape the nature of the European Union. Erin Delaney and Nick Barber each examine that nature in light of the attempt to recast it. Delaney reflects on the nature of federalism and the ways in which the development of the European Union has moved that entity towards a federal structure. Starting with an examination of the philosophy of the founders of the European project, in particular Jean Monnet, Delaney examines the strategy of 'incremental federalism'. Rather than starting with an explicitly federal constitutional structure, incremental federalism aspired to move towards federalism in gradual steps – with social integration building on economic integration, and political integration then building on social integration. But, Delaney argues, there are limits to what can be achieved through this gradual process towards federation. The democratic structures needed to legitimate the project require a formal constitutional change, the production of an explicitly federal constitution, which cannot be brought about incrementally. For Delaney, the Convention and the Draft Constitution were the inevitable outcomes of incremental federalism, and – if Europe continues down this constitutional path – something like this process must, one day, be repeated.

Barber's chapter examines the contrast between federations and confederations, contending that, prior to the Convention, the European Union contained elements of each form of ordering. This permitted what Barber styles a 'Grand Bargain' between two rival visions of Europe – a vision of Europe as a federal state, and a vision of Europe as a new form of polity, a closely linked collection of sovereign states. The Draft Constitution unsettled this bargain by pushing the Europe towards the federal model. Barber argues this was unnecessary and counterproductive, dividing supporters of the European project by forcing upon them a decision that did not yet need to be made. Following the rejection of the Draft Constitution by the peoples of France and the Netherlands, the subsequent inclusion of much of the substance of that document in Treaty of Lisbon may have further weakened Europe's democratic credibility, giving the appearance that the elites of Europe were willing to ignore the results of these referendums.

The relationship between the Draft Constitution and the Treaty of Lisbon is a central theme in several of the contributions to the volume. Stephen Weatherill identifies 'competence creep' as those situations in which the European Union acts outside the scope of the powers conferred on it by the Treaties or where it unnecessarily interferes with decisions that should have been left to the Member States. Competence creep is, in part, the result of the vagueness of the rules that empower the Union, and the corresponding weakness of those rules, such as proportionality and subsidiarity, that are intended to regulate the exercise of these powers. The result is that the Union may sometimes act, or appear to act, beyond its proper reach, harming its legitimacy in the eyes of its people. The Draft Constitution was, in part, an attempt to tackle the problems raised by competence creep by clarifying the powers possessed by the Union. Weatherill compares the Lisbon Treaty and the Draft Constitution and concludes that, in substance, the two documents are very similar. The decision to enact the Lisbon Treaty without fresh referendums in France and the Netherlands (and those other states promised a referendum on the Draft Constitution) deepened alienation from the European project. Weatherill concludes by considering ways in which the European Union could be made more politically accountable. Like Grimm, Weatherill contends that too many areas of European activity have become insulated from political control. First, competence creep could be tackled by permitting change through a combination of majority voting and opt-outs; this would allow for a clear articulation of the rules governing the Union. Second, it could be made easier for the political parts of the Union to reconsider rulings of the European courts – enabling surprising decisions to be reversed.

One of the most celebrated aspects of the Draft Constitution was the Charter of Fundamental Rights, which although not retained in the text of the Treaty of Lisbon, was given legal recognition therein. Dorota Leczykiewicz argues that the inclusion of the Charter was an attempt to 'constitutionalise' the Union, tying it to deeper constitutional values. Examining the Charter's content and application, Leczykiewicz argues that it has failed in this aspiration, due to flaws in the text and in judicial interpretation. As a result, the Charter has done little to constrain the expansionist tendencies of the Court of Justice and instead broadened the Court's capacity to render national laws incompatible with EU law. Leczykiewicz points out that while the Court has interpreted the field of application of EU law broadly (in the *Fransson* judgment), it has interpreted the field of application of national constitutional law narrowly (in the *Melloni* judgment). Moreover, when the vindication of fundamental rights and the effectiveness of EU law come into conflict, the Court has consistently put its weight behind the latter rather than the former. All in all, as Leczykiewicz demonstrates, the Charter and its use by the Court are failing to produce the sort of limited government and the guarantees of individual liberties that are the hallmarks of a truly constitutional order.

Perhaps 'the most prominent casualty' of the abandonment of Constitutional Treaty argues Gunnar Beck in his chapter, was the primacy clause, which was subsequently relegated to a declaration annexed to the Treaty of Lisbon. On one reading, it is surprising that such a fuss should have been made of a clause that codified the existing constitutional position which had been laid down by the Court of

Justice 40 years previously. As the chapter argues, it is because the primacy claim has always been controversial that its codification, *viz* entrenchment, constituted a distinct threat to the self-understanding of (some of) the national constitutional or supreme courts of the Member States. Nonetheless, the chapter also demonstrates that the line of cases handed down by the German Federal Constitutional Court from the *Solange 1* case in 1974 through to the *Honeywell* decision in 2010 and the Court's 2016 response to the Court of Justice's preliminary reference in relation to the Outright Monetary Transactions programme are testament to the fact that the German Court has accepted, in all but principle, that it is subservient to the Court of Justice. This position is then contrasted with that of the Danish Supreme Court, in the *Ajos* case in December 2016, which asserted the non-application of European law in the face of a conflicting national measure. All in all, Beck concludes that the idea of a European Constitution is likely to be resurrected in order to deal finally with this vexed question of *Kompetenz-Kompetenz*.

The next two chapters aim, in different ways, to situate the Constitution in a wider philosophical and political context. Neil Walker's chapter presents the idea that the Constitutional Treaty was (only) an overture which sets the scene for a more fulsome performance which has yet to be heard. While, the current climate might seem bleak, since the Union has faced the sovereign debt crisis followed by the migration and security crisis followed by the Brexit crisis in the last decade, Walker nonetheless makes the case that the present moment may be a moment of ripeness for constitutionalism because, as a result of those various crises, 'the constitutional register' has become more familiar and more indispensable. In conceptual terms, Walker proposes that we abandon the statist mind-set, and realise that constitutionalism may be 'a layered achievement' based on mutual dependencies within and between its legal-institutional and socio-political dimensions. While Europe has tended to focus, from its earliest foundations through to the development of the draft Constitution, on the legal-institutional dimension at the expense of the socio-political dimension, the present moment – in which the status quo is generally thought to be unsatisfactory, irreversible and demanding of a common response – may present a more apt opportunity for listening to the entire symphony.

Richard Mullender's contribution to the collection reflects on how certain of Nietzsche's ideas find resonance in the process of European integration and, specifically, the European Constitution. In particular, he identifies echoes of 'the compulsion to grand politics' – the drive to rise above concerns about corrective and distributive justice and to re-imagine and recreate society and culture in a more fundamental way – in the Constitutional Treaty; for example, in its bold ambition that 'the peoples of Europe are determined to transcend their ancient divisions and … forge a common destiny'. Mullender highlights the Preface, the Preamble and the proportionality principle to support this argument. At the same time, according to Mullender, the Convention operated in a cross-pressured context because the compulsion to grand politics had to be balanced against practical political challenges that called for caution about integrationist ambition.

Thus although for Mullender the Draft Constitution was an expression and an appeal to 'good Europeanism', as Nietzsche describes it, it may have prioritised the pursuit of union at the expense of *politeia*: the use of law, politics and economics in ways that express a civilisational commitment to sustain the life of the community.

Having opened with Guiliano Amato's account of the Convention from the perspective of a co-chair, the collection closes with Gisela Stuart's account of the Convention from the perspective of a delegate of the United Kingdom Parliament. Stuart notes wryly that the delegates purported to draw inspiration from the example of the Founding Fathers of the US Constitution and yet singularly failed to achieve what the Founding Fathers did, namely, to create a system that promoted accountability through checks and balances and called forth 'a people' in whose name the Constitution was adopted. The problem, Stuart argues, is that the European Union systematically fails to inspire and motivate the people of Europe, which accounts for why the European *demos* 'stubbornly refuses to emerge'. The empowerment of the European Parliament has not ameliorated this situation at all and in fact has been an obstacle to the emergence of a European *demos*. Fittingly for the final contribution, Stuart's chapter ends by reflecting on the connection between the failure of the Constitutional Treaty and Brexit and on the post-Brexit position of the UK in Europe.

Irrespective of whether the failure of the European Constitution is judged to have been inevitable or contingent, reflection on its origins and unhappy fate helps illuminate the nature of the European project and, relatedly, the demands of constitution-making in an extraordinary context. The Constitution's legacy is disputed, as the diversity of this collection confirms, but it should have an important place in how scholars reflect on the EU's peculiar development. It may also be relevant, even if only as a negative example, to how Europeans reason about how best to respond to the EU's contemporary plight, whatever one's view is as to whether the main problem is an excess of constitutionalism, incomplete constitutional development, inadequate state capacity, or popular disengagement from the European project. In thinking through the shape and origin of these problems and about options for their resolution, the failure of the European Constitution may yet prove to be of use.

2

From the Years of the Convention to the Years of Brexit. Where Do We Go from Here?

GIULIANO AMATO

I. The Cautious Mandate to the 2002 Convention

At the turn of the century, the Community and the Union (we had both at the time) were supposed to prepare themselves for the two major events expected in the imminent future, namely the actual entrance into force of the Euro and the enlargement of the candidate states of Eastern Europe. Incredibly enough (under the light of the later difficulties in the governance of the Eurozone and of the last-minute rush in inventing new instruments to face them) nothing was planned, nor even discussed, for the euro. Our governments and the European institutions seemed satisfied with the unsatisfactory arrangement they had agreed upon in Maastricht, namely the coordination of national economic and fiscal policies, as a sufficient source of convergence and stability.

In relation to the enlargement there was, at least, a debate around the issue of 'deepening': was it, or was it not, an essential prerequisite of a successful 'widening'? It is a fact that our governments could not initially agree on any form of deepening, and the Intergovernmental Conference of Nice in December 2000 limited its efforts to the few innovations that were simply inescapable to make the enlargement possible: basically, the redistribution of the seats in the Parliament, and of the voting rights in the Council.

However, the demand for wider reforms of the Treaties was not utterly ignored. A Declaration was adopted (declaration n. 23, annexed to the Treaty), by which 'having opened the way to enlargement, the Conference' called 'for a deeper and wider debate about the future of the European Union ... with all interested parties', from national parliaments to universities and other representatives of civil society. Following a report to be drawn up for the European Council, in December 2001 the Council itself would agree on 'a declaration containing appropriate initiatives for the continuation of this process'. A short list of issues followed, but it is hard to find evidence in it that deepening was the real aim of the Conference. The list of issues included: more precise delimitation of powers between the Union and the States, reflecting subsidiarity; the status of the Charter of Fundamental Rights; simplification of the Treaties; and, the role of national parliaments in the European architecture (I added this final item by hand and it proved essential to gain the consent of the UK).

The Laeken Declaration of December 2001 contained a much wider list of questions, including the 'democratic deficit' of the Union and its possible remedies, but the prospect of a European Constitution was raised only in the final words and only for the long-run future: 'The question ultimately arises as to whether this simplification and re-organisation might not lead in the long run to the adoption of a constitutional text. What might the basic features of such a Constitution be?'. Furthermore the Convention that was convened was not conferred with the explicit mandate to write a text (constitutional or not), but just 'to consider the key issues arising for the Union's future development and try to identify the various possible responses'.

II. In the Convention the Lost Battle of the Federalists

The transparent cautiousness of our governments vis-à-vis a future of more deepening has to be taken into account also in assessing the developments that followed the Convention. The first moves of the Convention were the demonstration of an old truth: whatever your intent to limit their mandate, and whatever your wording in defining such mandate, do not rely on the readiness of state representatives to accept those limits (particularly when most of them represent parliaments, not governments, and when they meet in a hemicycle – as happens in the European Parliament). If a charismatic President like Valéry Giscard D'Estaing urges them to go beyond, they will enthusiastically do it.

This is what happened with the Convention on the Future of Europe. Since the beginning, its work was to be the writing, not of 'the various possible responses' to the questions of Laeken, but of a single and complete normative text. Furthermore, when Giscard proposed the writing not just of a consolidated text of the pre-existing Treaties, but of a Constitution, the plenary happily approved: making history is more gratifying than answering questions.

However, the eagerness of the Convention did not necessarily change the expectations of (several) Member States and of their governments. Did a Constitution necessarily mean more integration? Couldn't it be just a better definition of the relationship between the states and the Union, to the advantage of the former? Furthermore, Giscard had proposed the writing of a 'Constitutional Treaty', in other words an international act containing a Constitution, the force of which, therefore, was not expected to come from the citizens of Europe, but from the states.

The fact of the matter is that in the Convention two opposite points of view were confronting each other: on the one side, the position of the representatives of most of the governments, expecting from the Convention not more integration, but more clarity and more simplification. On the other side, the position of the representatives of the European Parliament and of the Commission, firmly in favour of more integration. The only surprise came from the representatives of national parliaments, who more frequently stood on the side of their colleagues from the European Parliament than on the side of their governments; quite likely on the assumption that, by doing so, they were better interpreting the will of their citizens rather than the interests of their governmental machineries.

The contest was very tight indeed. The arguments against a truly federal Constitution were more than robust, but it is beyond doubt that the momentum for the federal move arrived *with* the Convention, and neither before nor after. Here I have only mentioned the Conferences and the documents of the governments that led to the Convention, but behind the decision to convene it there were also the resolutions of the European Parliament and the positions which emerged in public debate, definitely in favour of more political integration. A turning point in the debate had been the speech delivered by the German Minister of Foreign Affairs, Joschka Fischer, at Humboldt University in May 2000 (well before the Intergovernmental Conference of Nice). Fischer had openly argued that the functionalist method by which the Community had grown step-by-step in the past had lost its vitality. The Union could survive and successfully cope with the challenges of the new century only by going federal. The Member States would lose some of their national prerogatives, but accepting such loss in favour of supranational governance was in their own interest.

When the word 'constitution' entered the Convention, a tail-wind was blowing behind it. Was the outcome consistent with this wind? Must we really blame the French and the Dutch referenda for the loss of the European Constitution? No, the final output of the Convention's work was far below the standards set out in Joschka Fischer's speech. There were some of the ingredients of a constitutional architecture: not only the flag, the anthem and the motto, as has been frequently pointed out, but also more substantial innovations, such as the reduction of the Commission's members to 15, the separation of legislative and non-legislative acts, the adoption of co-decision as the ordinary legislative procedure and the legal force given to the Charter of Fundamental Rights. But on other crucial issues, the traditional patterns prevailed.

In the text which the Convention submitted to the European Council in June 2003, there was a clause stating that 'The Constitution and law adopted by the Union's institutions in exercising the competences conferred on it shall have primacy over the law of the Member States' (Article I-10). The clause was included in the Constitution (but later deleted from the Lisbon Treaty). However the competences were conferred on the Union not by it, but by the states (Article I-9) on the basis of the principle of conferral, the first in the list of the fundamental principles on the allocation of powers and of the consequent acts. Not so the supremacy clause of a federal Constitution, which sounds much more clear-cut: 'This Constitution and the Laws of the United States which shall be made in pursuance thereof … shall be the Supreme Law of the Land'. Furthermore, a second and no less decisive difference should be noticed. The US supremacy clause continues by stating '… any Thing in the Constitution or Laws of any State to the Contrary notwithstanding'. Compare this final part of the US supremacy clause to Article I-5 of the Convention's text. By such article (now Article 4 of the TEU), the Union is obliged to respect a detailed list of features of the national identity of its Member States, and currently this is considered the main European legal basis of those 'counter-limits' that national Constitutional Courts are entitled to erect against Regulations and Directives, despite their supposed primacy.

No less significant was the chapter on amendment procedures. A federal Constitution is generally amended by majority voting and even when the approval of the Member States is required, such approval does not take the form of ratification, which is typical of international treaties. Not so in our case. Also the simplified procedures were to be concluded by the unanimous approval of the Member States, 'according to their respective constitutional procedures', which meant, in all of them, ratification. Only the so-called '*passerelle*' clause allowed an extremely simplified procedure. It only referred to the replacement of unanimity by majority voting in some specific cases. Here, upon a decision approved by the European Parliament by absolute majority and notified to national parliaments, that replacement (which formally was an amendment) could occur. It was something, but certainly not enough to satisfy James Madison.

Finally, and along the same lines, any decision on new financial resources to be assigned to the Union needed (as it still needs) approval by the Member States.

When we were approaching the conclusion of the Convention's work, I declared that my hope of delivering a female (the word for 'Constitution', in some of our languages, is a 'she', while the word for 'Treaty' is a 'he') was being frustrated and that we would need to accept the hermaphrodite it was becoming. This was realistic. What I did not say is that the federalists, when eventually called to the battlefield where they had the opportunity to measure their forces vis-à-vis the supporters of the intergovernmental Union, actually demonstrated their weakness and lost the battle. They tended to think they lost against the prevailing force of the governments, which, in the framework of the Convention, seemed to be true. However, it remains an open and quite sensible question whether the governments were representing only themselves (and their bureaucracies), or whether they were in fact representing the views of their domestic constituencies.

Taking this angle, the defeat of the Constitutional Treaty in the French and in the Dutch referenda is less important than it might seem, independently of the reasons that led to it (some of them were unrelated to the contents of the document, others were due to its absurd format – which included, in a continuous sequence, both the few articles of the Constitution and the 300 or more articles of the consolidated Treaties). The fact of the matter is that it was not a Constitution. As we have just seen, issues that were crucial as to the nature of our organisation were solved by opting, with some ambiguities, for an enduring union of states, not for a federal state. A union of states is what we have now, but it also is what we would have had, had our Constitutional Treaty been approved as it was – and not under the disguising structure of the Lisbon Treaty.

III. 15 Years Later is it Time for a New Convention?

15 years later, we cannot compare the developments that have actually occurred with the counterfactual history of a federal European Union coping with the same difficulties. For sure, the limits of intergovernmental coordination have emerged powerfully in the most delicate areas where coordination applies, such as the governance of the Eurozone, the governance of immigration and the preventive and repressive fight against terrorism.

During the preparatory negotiations to the Maastricht Treaty (when the decision to adopt the single currency was taken), many economists had already warned our governments that the governance of the Euro could not be effective without conferring economic and fiscal powers at supranational level; the latter aimed at supporting the overall stability of the Eurozone. But national governments refused to surrender their prerogatives. Monetary policy was centralised in the hands of the newly created European Central Bank but otherwise, the governments insisted, the coordination of national policies on the basis of common rules would be sufficient to support the Eurozone.

This has not happened. When the bad times arrived, the Member States burdened by heavy public debts respected (not always immediately, not always fully) the common rules and adopted measures of financial readjustment. However, such measures also had disastrous economic, social, and (consequently) political, effects. This was because the measures affected levels of social protection, the overall economy, and the sympathy of the electors for Europe and its stronger Member States. A still-ongoing, distorted, debate took place on austerity, with some Member States arguing that it is counterproductive for growth and others defending its reasons. The fact of the matter is that financial readjustment is essential when public debt is too high, but its cyclical effects should be counterweighted by anticyclical interventions that a multilevel system of government should supply. This is how it works in the federal US, where states take care of their own debts, and Washington intervenes with federal funds that keep the economy alive. By contrast, the lack of a centralised stabilisation function has been the root of our flaws.

Mutatis mutandis, the governance of immigration also suffers from the lack of central powers and more than one study has proved that the hostility of our citizens towards immigrants largely depends on the rate of efficiency of governance.

The more immigration appears to them as an uncontrolled invasion, the more our people are against it. But no individual Member State can adopt all the internal and external policies that are needed to reduce inflows and keep them under control. Nor can a single Member State solve the problem by closing its borders and therefore denying its position, as well as its obligations, as a member of the Union.

Only a few words are needed about the fight against terrorism. Everybody understands that not having an FBI to cope with an inherently cross-border criminal phenomenon is a liability; a liability that Europol, at the moment, is not removing.

In the developments I have briefly described above, a disturbing asymmetry has been growing. On the one side, it is manifest that the poor delivery of our European and national institutions can only be cured by more European integration. On the other side, such poor delivery has nurtured anti-European feelings, that, captured and amplified by populist political movements, give strength to their fight against European integration in the name of national sovereignty. Until last year, it seemed to be a sort of catch-22 and the referendum on Brexit was a shocking, although not unpredictable, confirmation of the support which anti-European feeling had gained.

However, the impact of the referendum outside of the UK has been exactly the opposite. Instead of paving the way for further anti-European moves, it has increased the number of people wary of the lonely future of the secessionists and therefore has promoted their renewed loyalty to the European destiny. The Dutch and French elections have been eloquent evidence of this new atmosphere, also testified to by polls and surveys in other Member States.

Having escaped the paralysing catch-22 trap, once more in our history the question is 'Where do we go from here?'. Is it time for us to go federal or shall we just refine our existing tools, by using more integration but holding back from aims that are more ambitious? One way or another, is it time for a Convention again?

IV. Again Federalist and Functional Views Facing Each Other

Some similarities are undeniable between the current condition of our Union and the situation from 16 years ago that I have described. Now, too, a widespread awareness exists that we have to face hard issues, whilst relying upon institutions and procedures that have already proved seriously inadequate. There are also differences, though. Now the Eastern states are in, and they share a common position that is opposed to any further integration. Most of the others, or at least the members of the Eurozone, are convinced that more integration is needed. It is upon this background that a 'two-speed Europe' is being advocated as the compromise between those who want to remain where we are and those who want to go further. However, independently of this new division, even 'going further' cannot be given a single and undisputed meaning. Once more, the dispute is between the federal view on the one side; and on the other side, further limited steps in specific areas.

The supporters of the federal view utilise the new attention of the citizens for what Europe does, or does not do, as a compelling argument against the enduring democratic deficit. (Europe was all but ignored in our public debates years ago.) The institutions of the Union have always been distant from the citizens, but such distance has become intolerable in times when decisions are taken (or not taken) that affect them all. Accountability is the missing link. In order for us to introduce it, we need a federal setting in which the Federal Executive, equipped with the necessary powers, responds either to the Federal Parliament or directly to the citizens (should we opt for the direct election of its Head).

Nor – supporters of the federal view also argue – could limited steps towards further integration be made without coming across this very problem. Imagine a new fiscal capacity were to be conferred onto our European institutions, with a view to redistributing resources for the benefit of any economies or citizens in a state of need. Is it conceivable that this could be done without the democratic accountability of the institutions concerned? So, one way or another, the need to go federal becomes unavoidable.

The supporters of the other view are convinced – they say – that sooner or later the functionalist step-by-step approach will have to be abandoned. But, as Robert Schuman said in his declaration of 9 May 1950, this abandonment has a prerequisite, namely the gradual formation of a platform of mutual solidarity among Europeans. Only a platform of mutual solidarity has the solidity needed to support federal integration. Joschka Fischer was convinced that in the year 2000 our mutual solidarity was adequately formed already, while the functionalist approach was exhausted. Whether it was really so can be disputed because of what happened in the Convention, where the federalists did not prevail. For sure, one can argue that in the following years the rate of solidarity has sharply reduced. Wouldn't Schuman himself suggest restoring it, before making the decisive, ultimate steps?

Furthermore, while it is true that our citizens are dissatisfied with the European institutions, it is open to debate whether they really want a paramount Europe or rather prefer, for the sake of democracy itself, an enduring balance between the supranational and the national levels of government. It is a fact that in recent years national parliaments have been considered more and more as the main defenders of the democratic needs of citizens. It might have been a reaction against the distant and intrusive Europe, but it might also be something more: namely, the symptom of an understanding of democracy according to which our citizens want to be represented by reason of their national identities and not only as Europeans.

Upon this background, finding remedies to the European democratic deficit does not necessarily mean giving our citizens the opportunity to elect the President of the Union. Perhaps this is not what they aspire to, nor is it what they are ready for. The democratic deficit exists, but the first and most urgent treatment is not on the side of the input, it is on the side of the output. By this, it is meant that what our citizens really resent about the European institutions is not their inadequate representativeness, but rather their inadequate delivery.

If this is the argument of the non-federalists, their being functionalists does not mean they are supporters of the status quo and consequently against institutional reforms. To the contrary, they have their own agenda. This agenda proceeds area-by-area, and each area has specific proposals of reform, on the whole aimed at more integration.

V. On Behalf of the Functionalist View

Having so described the range of the existing positions, let us return to the question of whether it is time for a new Convention. According to Article 48 of the TEU, a Convention can be convened to work out any kind of amendments, but the European Council, by simple majority voting and with the consent of the Parliament, may decide not to do it 'should this not be justified by the extension of the proposed amendments'. In the situation described, the Council would find itself deeply divided: on the one side, there would be the supporters of the status quo (as to the balance between the Union and its Members). On the opposite side, we would find the federalists. And in between them would be positioned the supporters of more integration within specific projects (such as governance of the euro, security and defence, immigration and terrorism). Is it likely that its members will agree on a substantial package of amendments or, at least, on sufficiently shared reformist intentions that may to be submitted to the Convention? In the absence of such preliminary agreement, would it be advisable for the Council to convene a Convention that would consequently have very uncertain prospects of success?

A counter-argument could be found in the experience of the first Convention. It was convened on the basis of a long list of questions, not supported at all by a solid consensus among the governments on any specific solution. For sure, no government expected the Convention to write a constitutional text. Yet, the Convention forced its mandate and wrote the Constitutional Treaty. Why don't we rely on a similar trigger for the success of a new Convention? Yes, it can be done, but it is quite unlikely that a new Convention will be more successful than the previous one – and therefore less affected by the ambiguities that prevailed at the time.

An optimistic dreamer could imagine that the Convention, by opening its works to groups and associations expressing the views of our societies, might receive by them a sort of de facto mandate to be bold and to pursue the only aim that nowadays can underpin such a solemn amendment process: the federalisation of the Union. Some Europeans would certainly welcome such a mandate. But I do not know how many others would be willing to concur. I have doubts it will ever happen. Therefore I do not find it conceivable that a Convention could today write the European Constitution that was not written 15 years ago.

There is a second potential proposal. Rather than having a single Convention, what about several thematic conventions, each with distinct missions of institutional reform by sector? Such an unusual solution would perhaps work more successfully than the previous one, for reaching consensus would be easier. Contingent institutional arrangements are all that would be seen to be at stake. Institutional reforms would be viewed as merely instrumental to the practical results that would be achieved; and not, therefore, wider projects, deeply marked by ideology.

However, on the basis of this, one might conclude that the traditional functionalist method could work better than any Convention: going project-by-project and thereby reaching agreement on the completion of the Eurozone, on the strengthening of the common defence and security policy, on the governance of immigration and on the fight against terrorism. Once such agreements have been reached, an intergovernmental conference may adopt the Treaty amendments that the agreements themselves require and the content of which they have necessarily defined. There would be no risk of failure nor of unexpected outcomes in an amendment procedure the result of which is largely predetermined. And the governments would embark on it with a high rate of confidence and a low rate of confrontational predisposition – two excellent prerequisites of a good result.

VI. The Case of the Eurozone and the Prospect of a Multi-cluster Europe

Is there a chance of similar agreements in all of these sectors, or in some of them? Here the first advantage would be procedural, for our institutions would work according to the patterns of their usual business and therefore focusing on the merit of the substantive issues to be solved. There would not be the special attention that is reserved to special events; nor would the playground foster intense and harsh confrontations between Europhiles and Eurosceptics, or populists and anti-populists, which would otherwise be predictable.

Take the case of the reform of the Eurozone, already under discussion and outlined in the recent 'Reflection Paper on the Deepening of the Economic and Monetary Union', delivered by the Commission on 31 May 2017. The document firstly says that many policies that are decisive for economic resilience have to remain primarily in the hands of the Member States; such as employment, education, taxation, the design of welfare systems and others. Therefore, further steps towards stronger convergence shall be made by coordination in the European Semester. However, there are other aspects of economic and fiscal policy as to which coordination will not be enough.

The Banking Union itself will not achieve its aims without a last resort common backstop. But, the Reflection Paper adds, even though the European Stability Mechanism (ESM) has lending capacity, its decision-making procedures should be streamlined if we want the backstop to be activated in time and also ensure maximum cost-efficiency. We all know that this means abandoning the intergovernmental unanimity and passing the ESM under a more centralised authority.

As to the wider governance of the Eurozone, the document advances two main proposals: the creation of a macroeconomic stabilisation function to be exercised centrally and a safe European asset 'on a par with US Treasury bonds'. The stabilisation function is proposed in relation to two main areas: the protection of public investments from the impact of economic downturns and the reinsurance of national unemployment insurance schemes. An exceptionally high level of unemployment may completely exhaust national unemployment insurance schemes, leaving the workers with no source of income. The European asset is proposed as an antidote to the current volatility of our financial markets and to the too-large exposure of banks to their national sovereign. It could also facilitate, the document says, the transmission of monetary policy. Of course, a crucial aspect to be agreed upon is whether the new asset should be based on mutualisation or whether it should not entail any joint liability.

Whatever the choice on this last point, both the European asset and the stabilisation function are technically conceivable only in the hands of supranational institutions. But neither the former nor the latter would be acceptable without adequate forms of democratic accountability of the institutions to whom they are conferred. To this effect, the Paper suggests initial arrangements and institutional agreements with the European Parliament, which are to be subsequently integrated into the Treaties as the necessary framework for the future Euro Area Treasury. The Treasury should be responsible for economic and fiscal surveillance over the Member States, the coordination of issuing the European asset and the management of the macroeconomic stabilisation function. It has to be added that, in this context also, the single Euro Area's voice is necessary in the international financial institutions (IMF first).

I appreciate that this digression on the content of the Commission's Paper has been long and detailed. However, only by entering into such details and therefore capturing the intimate relationship between the economic results to be achieved and the institutional innovations that are needed to achieve them can we appreciate the advantages of discussing and agreeing upon these innovations in the context of a project on the functioning of the Economic and Monetary Union (more than of an overall institutional project).

One of these advantages is that we would not face issues such as the question over a two-speed Europe, not only because such issues would be beyond our horizon, but because other areas – security and defence, and also immigration – could similarly be streamlined and generate further clusters of closer integration, the members of which not necessarily would be the same as of the Eurozone.

Quite likely they would have fewer members and, perhaps, a more accentuated integration. How could we speak of a two-speed Europe? It might rather then be a multi-speed Europe and our remaining problem would be how to give its clusters a common framework, granting the necessary standards of enduring uniformity for all the members of the Union.

At this stage, but only at this stage, summoning a Convention could perhaps be a sensible, final step for the purpose of designing both the common frame-work and the respective roles in it of the various institutional actors: the European Parliament, the Commission, the Council, the European Council, the new figures that will have emerged in each reformed sector and, in their specific and more limited responsibilities, national parliaments. At this final stage, two impediments which currently face a Convention would be absent. At present, a Convention would not be responding to a demand sufficiently shared by our citizens (who have other demands in their minds) nor could it receive a sufficiently clear mandate. However, ultimately, the Convention would have a task both very well-defined and conclusive; one which would be understood and (if not warmly supported, at least) appreciated by the citizens. It would not be the Convention for the Federal Constitution of Europe. However, assuming (as the European Court of Justice already did more than 60 years ago) that our Union of States has its own 'constitutional order', it could usefully re-define such order on the basis of the multi-cluster Europe.

I am well aware of the complexity of this sequence, with two or even (with the Convention) three tiers linked to each other. As I have argued in the previous pages, it is not necessarily a disadvantage, for splitting the overall task into pieces makes the handling of each piece simpler and easier. Is this wishful thinking? My arguments should reasonably demonstrate that it is not, but no answer – I know – is beyond any reasonable doubt.*

VII. Brexit and the Lost Benefits of a Multi-cluster Europe

A final issue requires due attention, namely the impact of the scenarios described upon the United Kingdom. As we all know, the opinion has been expressed that the final outcome of the two-speed Europe should be accompanied by the distinction between full members and associate members of the Union; and such distinction would be an incentive for the UK to return into the Union, precisely as an associate member.

---

* I wrote this chapter several months ago, after the Dutch and the French elections. In the meantime, other political developments have intervened in Germany, Austria and Italy. Due to them, the doubts surrounding the feasibility of what I am pleading for here are heavier than they initially were.

As we have seen, on the basis of the existing trends, we can expect the multi-speed outcome over the two-speed one. However, assuming the latter as the future prospect, I cannot see the benefits for the UK in re-joining the Union as a peripheral member. It would have all the disadvantages of the current position without the benefits envisaged from Brexit, namely domestic freedom in dealing with non-European and European immigrants. Associate members, unless foreign to the integrated market (which is quite unlikely), would be subject to the current obligations of the participants to it.

The multi-speed Europe, which should be more correctly defined as the 'multi-cluster Europe', might actually be a much more interesting prospect for the UK. Any form of European enhanced cooperation, or otherwise more integrated organisation in the area of security and defence, would draw incommensurable benefits from British participation in it. And the UK would share an experience of 'closer integration' in which it would certainly play a leading role, presumably satisfying its officials and its citizens.

However, it has to be made clear, such a role implies the enduring position of the UK as a member of the Union. This is the position it holds now, despite the intention it has expressed to withdraw. The future is not ours to see, but we could not agree more with Prime Minister May when she says that Brexit is Brexit.

3

Constitutionalisation without Constitution: A Democracy Problem

DIETER GRIMM*

I. The Treaty Establishing a Constitution for Europe – Treaty or Constitution?

In the beginning was the Treaty of Rome. In this Treaty, six sovereign states agreed, under international law, to establish the European Economic Community and to transfer public powers to it that were deemed necessary to establish and maintain a common market. The European Community was a creation of this Treaty. A prior social substrate, such as states used to have, was absent from the European project. However, the Treaty did not exhaust itself in creating the European Community and transferring powers to it. It also endowed the Community with organs that enabled it to act on its behalf and determined the conditions under which it was permitted to exercise these powers – all provisions that, within states, would be found in their constitution.

This parallel has led some observers to call the Treaties the 'Constitution' of the European Community. The European Court of Justice confirmed this view insofar as it did not interpret the Treaties like traditional international law, namely according to the will of the parties to a treaty, and narrowly wherever their sovereignty was affected, but like constitutional law, namely more or less detached from the will of the Member States and instead oriented at an objectivised purpose and unconcerned about their sovereignty. In two fundamental judgments of 1963 and 1964 the ECJ decided that, first, the Treaties applied directly within the Member States, and, secondly, that they enjoyed supremacy, not only over EU secondary law, but also over Member States' law, again a characteristic of constitutional law up to then alien to international law.[1]

---

* I used parts of previous articles for this contribution, especially 'Verfassung -Verfassungsvertrag – Vertrag über eine Verfassung' in O Beaud et al (eds), *L'Europe en Voie de Constitution* (Brussels, Bruylant, 2004) and 'The Democratic Costs of Constitutionalization – The European Case' in D Grimm, *The Constitution of European Democracy* (Oxford, Oxford University Press, 2017).
[1] Case 26/62 *Van Gend en Loos* [1963] ECR 1; Case 6/64 *Costa v ENEL* [1964] ERC 585.

The Treaties were changed several times, beginning with the Single European Act of 1986. European integration thereby proceeded further in terms of space, powers and structure. This development distanced the European Community more and more from a traditional international organisation and brought it closer and closer to a federal state, however, without transgressing the threshold to a state. All Treaty amendments took place in the form of treaties under international law, agreed upon by the Heads of State and Government with ensuing ratification in the Member States according to the provisions of their constitutions. This is also true for the transition from the European Community to the European Union in the Treaty of Maastricht of 1992.

The Treaty Establishing a Constitution for Europe of 2003 was a new step in this development as it created the impression, or even had the purpose, of using the form of a treaty to establish a constitution. This raises the question of whether a constitution can be created by a treaty. To be sure, this is not a common way to make a constitution. Normally, constitutions come into being by a decision of a constituent assembly summoned or elected for this purpose, or by a referendum on a draft constitution. However, a treaty is a proven means where existing states wish to unite into a new superior state in which they either dissolve or continue to exist as dependent member states. Thus, the German Empire of 1871 was founded by an agreement of the various sovereign German states on a constitution for the new federal state; so that the treaty was the means of establishing the constitution or, in other words, the constitution was the product of the treaty.

However, not every treaty among states that brings a new common political entity into being is a constitution. The term 'constitution' used to be reserved for the legal foundation of states; whereas the legal foundation of international organisations created by states were contractual in nature and called treaties, statutes, charters, acts etc. Only recently can a tendency be observed to call the foundational documents of international organisations their 'constitution'.[2] However, the name means little. There are legal documents that are undoubtedly constitutions but bear a different name, such as Germany's Constitution which is called the 'Basic Law'. Likewise, it is possible that there are legal documents called 'constitutions' without being one. Whether or not the legal foundation of a political entity deserves the name 'constitution' depends on the concept of a constitution.

A generally accepted or universally applicable notion of the term 'constitution' does not exist. Different purposes or research interests may entail different uses of the term. The call for a European constitution finds its explanation in two corresponding developments: the increasing power of the EU that brought it ever closer to a federal state, on the one hand, and the decreasing legitimacy the more that power shift came to the fore, on the other. The need for a revision of the European Treaties, which was motivated both by Europe's new role in world politics after the end of the East-West-divide and the arrival of a large number of new Member

---

[2] See among many J Klabbers, A Peters, G Ulfstein, *The Constitutionalism of International Law* (Oxford, Oxford University Press, 2011).

States, could have been met by amendments to the Treaties as in previous years. The idea that this time it should be a constitution was inspired by the experience that, in many Member States, the constitution was a source of legitimacy, and by the hope that a European constitution could render the same service within the EU.[3] Hence, it was the achievement of state constitutions that guided the reform process and the draft of 2003. This suggests the choice of modern state constitutionalism as it emerged in the American and the French Revolution as a yardstick.

A constitution in this sense is characterised by five elements.[4] It is, firstly, a complex of legal norms, not a description of the state of a polity as was the case with the pre-modern empirical notion of constitution. These legal norms, secondly, refer to public power. They constitute public power rather than merely modifying it and prescribe its exercise. Thirdly, the modern constitution regulates public power not only in this or that aspect like the older *leges fundamentales*, but systematically and comprehensively. In order to fulfil this function, it fourthly enjoys supremacy over all government acts. These acts are valid only insofar as they comply with the constitutional provisions. This is at the same time why constitutional law does not emanate from the government but, fifthly, antedates it and emanates from or is attributed to the people as the ultimate source of public authority. Thus, the constitution is an act of self-determination of a society with regard to the form and purpose of government.[5]

If one compares the legal foundation of the European Union to modern state constitutions, one will find a number of similarities. The Treaties are legally binding, they constitute the Union and establish its organs and regulate its powers and procedures. They do this in a systematic and comprehensive way, and they enjoy primacy over the legal acts of the European Union. In this way, one can say that the Treaties fulfil functions that, within a state, are fulfilled by a constitution. Different from a state constitution, however, the Treaties are neither adopted by nor attributed to a European people, or to a European society, as the source of all European public power. The legal foundation of the EU is, in contrast, created by states through the conclusion of treaties under international law. The citizens of the Union have no share in it, nor are they regarded as the holders of public power of the Union. This position is held by the Member States.

Hence, the Treaties are not an act of self-determination of a European society. No such society has given itself a constitution. Rather, the EU received its legal foundation from the Member States. Even after having concluded the Treaties, the Member States retained power over them; the Treaties could be changed only in the same way they were concluded. The fact that the Member States are themselves

---

[3] See D Grimm, 'Integration by Constitution' (2005) 3 *I-CON* 193.

[4] See D Grimm, *Constitutionalism. Past – Present – Future* (Oxford, Oxford University Press, 2016) 363.

[5] This is not to say that every state constitution shows all 5 characteristics. But, to the extent that they are missing, the constitution falls short of the *achievement* of constitutionalism; see D Grimm, 'The Achievement of Constitutionalism and its Prospects in a Changed World' in P Dobner and M Loughlin (eds), *The Twilight of Constitutionalism?* (Oxford, Oxford University Press, 2010) 3.

democracies and have to ratify the Treaty in a democratic way does not transform the adoption of the Treaty into an act of a European citizenry. If the citizens are involved directly or indirectly, they are involved as citizens of their state. In sum, the EU is as strongly developed as constitutional states with regard to the legalisation of public power. Regarding democratic legitimacy, however, it falls short of the requirements of modern constitutionalism. It is this difference that matters, not the name.

Would things have changed had the Constitutional Treaty been adopted? To be sure, although drafted by a Convention convoked for this purpose, it was adopted by way of an international treaty, not by way of a decision of a constituent assembly or a referendum. But this is not the end of the discussion. As discussed above, there are examples in history where the treaty concluded by sovereign states results in a constitution. What is necessary for a treaty to become a constitution? The character of a treaty must be consummated at the moment of its conclusion. From that moment on, its future fate must be put into the hands of the newly-created entity. To be more precise, the founding states must transfer the power of amendment to the new entity instead of retaining it. They may reserve a share in the amendment power for themselves, but in this case they exercise it, not as sovereign states, but as members of an organ of the new political entity.

Was this provided for in the Constitutional Treaty of 2003? The answer must be sought in the provisions concerning amendments of the Treaty. The amendment procedure was regulated by Article IV-7.[6] It determines, in section 1, the right to take the initiative. Section 2 concerns the preparatory stage of amendments. Section 3 is the centrepiece which regulates the amendment process. It reads:

> The conference of representatives of the governments of the Member States shall be convened by the President of the Council of Ministers for the purpose of determining by common accord the amendment to be made to the Treaty establishing the Constitution. The amendment shall enter into force after being ratified by all the Member States in accordance with their respective constitutional requirements.

Section 4 stipulates that, in case not all Member States have ratified the amendment within two years, 'the matter shall be referred to the European Council'. But it does not authorise the European Council to substitute the missing ratification of a Member State by a decision of its own.

This means that, even in the Constitutional Treaty, the Member States were not willing to transfer the amendment power to the EU but retained it for themselves. No transition from hetero-determination to self-determination would have taken place had the Treaty entered into force. The character of a treaty would not have been transcended. In its legal nature, the legal foundation of the EU would have remained a treaty. The Lisbon Treaty has not changed this.[7] If one nevertheless calls

---

[6] Renumbered IV-447 in the 2004 Treaty.

[7] For a detailed discussion, see D Grimm, 'On the Status of the EU's Democratic Legitimacy after Lisbon' in D Grimm, *The Constitution of European Democracy* (Oxford, Oxford University Press, 2017) 57.

the Treaty a 'constitution', one uses the notion in a way that falls below the requirements of modern constitutionalism. This is the error made by those who regarded the Treaty of Rome as a constitution, or at least saw the Constitutional Treaty as crossing the threshold from treaty to constitution. They give up a central element of modern constitutionalism, namely democratic legitimation, and content themselves with a watered-down notion or bridge the gap with fictions.

II. The Distinction between Constitutional and Ordinary Law as a Precondition of Democracy

However, there is yet another way to address the question of whether the Treaty of 2003, had it been adopted by all Member States, would have been a constitution. This way refers us not to the notion but to the function of constitutions. To be sure, constitutions have more than one function. But their principal function, that from which all the other functions derive, consists in regulating the establishment and exercise of public authority. They define the purpose of a political entity and the principles on which it rests; they determine how the powers that act on behalf of the polity are constituted and composed; they allocate their competences and regulate the way in which these may be exercised; and they set substantive limits to public power by defining the sphere of freedom of those subjected to public power in the form of fundamental rights. In sum, they define the conditions for legitimate rule and, by doing so, separate legitimate from illegitimate power claims.

A precondition for the constitutional norms to fulfil their functions is that they enjoy primacy over all government acts including legislation. Constitutions bring legitimate government into existence and formulate the conditions for the exercise of public power. They thus antedate government and are not at its disposal. The consequence is a distinction between *pouvoir constituant* and *pouvoir constitué* and, accordingly, the division of law into two parts: one that is attributed to the people and binds government – constitutional law; and one that emanates from the government and binds the citizens – ordinary law. The first part regulates the making of the latter whereas rule-making itself is left to the second part. This distinction between the rules for political decision-making and the political decisions themselves, ie the distinction between the level of constitutional law and the level of ordinary law, is crucial for constitutionalism.

As a consequence of this differentiation, everything that has been regulated on constitutional level is no longer open to majority decision. What is entrenched in the constitution is not an object but a premise of democratic politics. To the extent that constitutional law reaches, elections do not matter because the elected body is not above but below the constitution. It is not a constituent but a constituted power and therefore subject to the conditions determined in the constitution for the exercise of public authority. The only possible way to alter these conditions is by constitutional amendment. But because amendments change the rules of the game they are distinguished from ordinary legislation and usually require a referendum or at least a supermajority in the legislature, a procedural safeguard that is normally high enough to demand a consensus among majority and opposition, which will not be easily available.

However, this is precisely why constitutionalism may be in tension with democracy. To be sure, a constitution in the full meaning of the term is itself a product of a democratic decision. In this decision, a society agrees on the principles and procedures for political competition and political action. It forms a basic consensus for political actors who may otherwise be of different opinions about the common good. But this basic agreement is a consensus of the past and may collide with actual majorities in the present. This is why postulates exist according to which constitutions should only contain organisational and procedural rules and refrain from establishing substantive limits to government. The concern is not unfounded. As a matter of fact, democracy may undermine constitutional rights. Constitutional rights may overwhelm democracy. Carl Schmitt even assumes that there is not only a tension but an antagonism between democracy and rights.[8] Tension leaves room for accommodation, contradiction excludes it. This raises the question whether democracy and rights could each exist in the absence of the other.

Democracy, to begin with, has some preconditions. It depends on free elections that, in turn, require free citizens. They must be politically free to form and express their opinions, articulate their interests, and associate with others in order to invigorate their political influence. Free media are an indispensable condition for political freedom of citizens. But citizens must also be free in their private sphere, since political freedom will not thrive without private autonomy. Democracy itself cannot guarantee these preconditions. They depend on protection by fundamental rights. Rights also have preconditions. They do not enforce themselves. They are in need of being protected and they have to be limited in order to make the many liberties, or the liberties of the many, compatible with each other. In short, they depend on governmental power. Yet, governmental power is in itself a threat to individual freedom. How can the two be reconciled? Among the various forms of government, democracy seems to be the form that best serves the autonomy of the individual because it grounds public power on the will of the rights-bearers and rejects legitimacy principles that trump rights.

Therefore, Schmitt's asserted antagonism between rights and democracy exists only if they are pushed to extremes. Radical democracy is strictly majoritarian. It recognises only one fundamental right: the right of every citizen to participate in the formation of the general will. All other limits on government are incompatible with this notion of democracy. The minority is unconditionally surrendered to majority decisions. In a radical democracy, constitutions shrink to a number of rules that regulate will formation and execution organisationally and procedurally.

---

[8] C Schmitt, *Verfassungslehre* (Munich, Duncker & Humblot, 1928) 125, 200.

Majoritarian democracy is formal democracy. Substantive prescriptions are incompatible with it. But just as radical democracy tends to minimise legal rules that limit political action, rights foundationalism[9] tends to minimise democracy. The reason is just that all matters regulated on the constitutional level are not open to political decision. The constitution functions no longer as a framework and directive but as a blueprint for politics. In the end, all politics is reduced to executing the constitution. Public power shifts from the people and their elected representatives to the courts.

Both radical versions develop a self-destructive dynamic. Radical democracy may take the form of popular dictatorship. It cannot even defend itself against the abolition of majority rule by majority vote. On the other hand, rights foundationalism reduces the importance of elections and endangers the adaptability of laws to changing circumstances. It therefore risks the constitution hampering democratic change and becoming a barrier to coping with new challenges. The stronger the challenges are, the sooner politics will reappear on the scene and circumvent or suspend the constitution in order to achieve what is understood to be the requirements of the moment.

There may be, and often is, too little constitutionalism. But it may also be that there is too much. Both deviations disregard the crucial distinction between the rules for political decision-making and the political decisions themselves, each in its own way. In the first case, the tension is dissolved in favour of politics. The constitution will fail to fulfil its function of guiding and limiting governments effectively. Such a constitution will hardly be able to legitimate the exercise of public power. In the second case, the tension is dissolved in favour of the law. The democratic process is left in tatters; politics is reduced to the execution of constitutional prescriptions. The administration and the judiciary marginalise the legislature.

There are no universally applicable principles for determining what belongs in a constitution and what does not. New constitutions react to past experiences and seek to provide for a better future. Every country must decide for itself what it deems so important for a better future that it should be exempted from the wavering will of simple majorities. These questions are not uncontroversial. Agreements between different forces in a convention or a constituent assembly require compromises. Some can only be reached by leaving gaps where one would expect a rule, others may only be reached by accommodating many interests, and thereby inflate the constitution.

However, even if it is difficult to formulate substantive rules for constitution-making, the function of constitutions allows some generalisations that transcend the particular design of a political system, which may differ from country to country. The function of constitutions is to legitimate and to limit political power,

---

[9] The term appears in B Ackerman, *We the People* (Cambridge, Mass, Harvard University Press, 1991) 10.

but not to replace it. Constitutions are a framework for politics, not a blueprint for all political decisions. Where the distinction between a constitution and ordinary law is lost, one will not enjoy the benefits of constitutionalism. The constitution furnishes the basic structure and the lasting principle for politics. Politics concretises them and fills the space they leave according to changing preferences and circumstances. Constitutions thus provide a durable structure for change. They combine principles that enjoy a broad consensus with flexibility to meet new challenges or changing preferences and thereby enable a peaceful transition of power.

However, the text of the constitution is one thing, its interpretation and application to individual cases is quite another. Even if the text avoids the risk of radicalism, courts may interpret it in a way that increasingly narrows the space for political decisions. To the same extent, the power of courts will increase. Constitutionalisation of ordinary law by way of interpretation may have the same cementing effect. The more ordinary law is regarded as constitutionally-mandated, the less politics can change it if this is required by circumstances or by a shift of political priorities after an election.

This danger exists especially where courts have the last word in determining the meaning of constitutional provisions. It is true that constitutions are of little value without judicial enforcement. To be sure, courts should also have the power to adapt constitutional law to new challenges. But even though it may be difficult to define, there is a distinction between interpreting law and making law under the disguise of interpretation. When courts overstep this line, the only remedy for politics is to re-programme the judiciary by amending the constitution, which is easy in some countries, but extremely difficult in others. The more difficult constitutional amendments are, the less space remains for democratic re-direction of courts.

III. Constitutionalisation of the Treaties through the Jurisprudence of the European Court of Justice

How does this connect to the European Treaties and their qualification as a constitution? At this point, it seems necessary to take a closer look to the two seminal judgments of the ECJ of 1963 and 1964.[10] In 1963, the ECJ initially confronted the relationship between European and national law. The traditional answer to that question was clear: since European law is international law, it binds the Member States, but produces legal effects for the individual citizens only after having been incorporated into, or concretised by, national law. This was the position of several Member States when they argued the *Van Gend en Loos* case in court, and it was equally the position of the Court's Advocate General. In contrast, the ECJ declared

---

[10] *Van Gend en Loos* and *Costa* (n 1).

European law to be directly applicable in the Member States, to the effect that the Treaty obligations of the Member States to establish a common market and adapt their laws to the four economic freedoms were transformed into subjective rights of the market participants. They could from now on invoke these rights vis-à-vis their own state and claim them before the national courts without waiting for further concretisation by the national legislature.

However, the initial decision did not answer the question as to what would happen if European and national law conflicted. The case was referred to Luxemburg by a Dutch court, and according to the Dutch Constitution international law prevails over national law, so that there was no need to address the question of primacy in 1963. The answer followed a year later in a second case that originated in Italy whose constitution did not contain such a rule.[11] The Court declared that the Treaties, and European law in general, enjoyed primacy over national law, even over the highest national law, the constitutions of the Member States. National law that contradicted European law lost its applicability. No national court or other agency was permitted to apply it. In case of doubt, national courts had to refer the question of compatibility to the ECJ, whose decision was binding on them.

In hindsight, these judgments are perceived as revolutionary, but when they were handed down, they remained largely below the threshold of public attention. They appeared as decisions in singular and non-conspicuous cases, rendered by a court that went more or less unnoticed. Revolutionary they were, though, because neither direct effect nor primacy of European law were explicitly mentioned in the Treaties. Rather, they resulted from a purposive interpretation that was by no means without alternative. They were revolutionary also because, without them, the EU would not have become what it is today, namely an unprecedented political entity somewhere between an international organisation and a federal state, but because of the amount of its powers and the density of its organisational structure closer to the latter than to the former.

Yet, they deserve their characterisation as revolutionary for still another reason: they radically changed the power structure of the EU. Although remaining completely within the framework of its procedural limits, the ECJ enlarged its own power by the extensive interpretation of substantive law at the expense of the democratically-legitimised and accountable organs of the EU. By re-defining the legal nature of the Treaties, the Court gained a position that by far exceeded the powers of an international court and resembled more closely that of a constitutional court. Its judgments sought to establish the direct effect and primacy of European law, not only over secondary European law but also over national law. This is not to say that the Court's intent was to enhance its own power, it rather was the effect of the re-definition of European law, and by the same token the power of the Member States decreased.

American observers were the first to notice what had happened. The judgments endowed the Treaties with effects typical of constitutional law. The observers

[11] *Costa v ENEL* (n 1).

described this as 'constitutionalisation'.[12] 'Constitutionalisation' does not mean that the Treaties were transformed into a constitution. This is not within the powers of a court. It would have needed a unanimous decision by the Member States. Nor does 'constitutionalisation' mean the permeation of ordinary law by constitutional law through interpretation, as is characteristic for some Member States with strong constitutional courts. In the EU, 'constitutionalisation' rather means that, as a result of the two judgments, the Treaties function like constitutions. They withdraw everything that is regulated on Treaty level from the political process. Acts within the sphere covered by the Treaties are implementations of the constitution and thus not open to political choice.

Just because of these depoliticising effects, constitutions are, or should be, limited to the rules for political decision-making and refrain from regulating all sorts of policies. A comparison of constitutions with the European Treaties that were constitutionalised in 1963/64 shows, however, that this crucial difference is not respected in Europe. The Treaties, which were not written with the intention to draft a European constitution, are full of rules that would be ordinary law in every state. This explains the volume of the Treaties, which by far exceeds that of constitutions. As long as the Treaties were not constitutionalised, this did not pose a problem. The Treaty obligations had to be fulfilled by legislation. The Court was limited to ascertaining whether a Member State failed to comply with the Treaties upon an action by the Commission, but it was not in a position to take action itself. This changed with constitutionalisation.

Some observers overlook this difference and see the volume of the Treaties just as a blemish. But it is not a question of constitutional aesthetics. It is a question of democracy. All the policy matters that have been regulated in the Treaties are no longer open for democratic decision. They now fall within the competence of the judiciary. The political organs of the EU are barred from deciding upon these subject matters, but cannot correct the Court's jurisprudence either if they think that its rulings do not reflect their intentions when they concluded the Treaties or produce detrimental effects. The distinction between constitutional law and ordinary law which is crucial for democratic constitutionalism is levelled in Europe. It is not sufficient to state that the Treaties have been constitutionalised. Because of their sheer volume, the EU is over-constitutionalised.

The Treaty Establishing a Constitution for Europe did not change anything in this respect. In spite of the label 'constitution', the text did not limit itself to provisions of a constitutional nature. It retained all the provisions of the original Treaty that are of statutory nature. In this respect as well, the Constitutional Treaty would not have been constitutional. This situation continues to exist. Unlike the

---

[12] E Stein, 'Lawyers, Judges and the Making of a Transnational Constitution' (1981) 75 *American Journal of International Law* 75; JHH Weiler, 'The Transformation of Europe' (1991) 100 *Yale Law Journal* 2403. For an analysis why this became possible, see KJ Alter, *Establishing the Supremacy of European Law* (Oxford, Oxford University Press, 2001).

Constitutional Treaty, the Lisbon Treaty of 2007 is divided into three treaties: the Treaty on the European Union, whose norms are mostly of a constitutional nature; the Treaty on the Functioning of the European Union, whose norms are mostly of a statutory nature; and the Charter of Fundamental Rights and Freedoms. But all three share the rank of European primary law and thus participate in the constitutionalisation of 1963/64.

The question here is not whether the judgments were right or wrong from a legal point of view. What is relevant here is their consequences. As an immediate effect of the two revolutionary judgments, Member States were no longer needed in order to establish the single market. Direct effect and supremacy of European law allowed the Commission (as the organ charged with enforcing the Treaties vis-à-vis the Member States) and the ECJ (the organ charged with determining the meaning of the Treaties in concrete cases) to take the task of implementing economic integration in their own hands. If they declared that national law impeded the common market, the national law became inapplicable without the Member States having a chance to defend their own law in an effective way. Their view of the common market did not count, but rather the Court's view did.

Everything depended now on how the ECJ would interpret the Treaties, favouring uniformity or diversity of the law, market-friendly or regulation-friendly, liberal or social. As it turned out, the ECJ pursued the goal of market integration with considerable zeal, subordinating other concerns to this goal. It was a court with an agenda, as Rainer Wahl has put it.[13] Based on the methodological principle of *effet utile*, powers transferred to the EU were interpreted broadly, powers retained by the Member States narrowly. The same can be observed regarding the principle of proportionality. When applied to national laws, the ECJ submitted them to strict scrutiny; when applied to European laws, it used a lenient standard of review.

The main beneficiaries were the four fundamental freedoms, all economic in nature (free movement of goods, persons, services and capital) and their concretisation in the Treaties. These freedoms were transformed from objective principles for legislation into subjective rights of the market participants who could claim them against the Member States before the national courts, which, in turn, have to adhere to the meaning that the ECJ attributes to these freedoms. Their implementation thus became a matter of jurisdiction rather than legislation. The majority of cases that reach the ECJ are requests for a preliminary ruling by national courts where economic actors claim that national regulations violate their Treaty freedoms.

There is not enough space to describe the effects of this mechanism in detail.[14] Suffice it to state that the jurisprudence of the ECJ leaves deep marks on national

---

[13] R Wahl, 'Das Recht der Integrationsgemeinschaft Europäische Union' in C Franzius (ed), *Beharren – Bewegen, Festschrift für Michael Kloepfer* (Berlin, Duncker & Humblot, 2013) 233, 248.

[14] For a comprehensive account, see AK Mangold, *Gemeinschaftsrecht und deutsches Recht* (Tübingen, Mohr Siebeck, 2012).

law and politics. The Court's broad interpretation of the impediments to trade deprives the Member States of the possibility of upholding national standards of consumer protection, workers' protection, health protection, etc. The extension of the prohibition of state subsidies that distort the market from private enterprises to public services deprives the Member States of the power to determine the borderline between the public and the private sector. The privatisation of many public services finds its origin here. The jurisprudence on Directives narrows the space for national legislation. The expanded scope of Charter rights and the salience of the four fundamental freedoms impose the ECJ's preference for economic freedoms on the Member States, whose constitutional courts tend to prioritise personal, communicative, cultural and social rights over economic liberties.

IV. The Democratic Costs of Over-constitutionalisation

The integration-friendly jurisprudence of the ECJ is usually told as a success story. And a success story it is, at least insofar as the economic integration of Europe is concerned. In the years of political stagnation during de Gaulle's presidency in France and again from the mid-70s to the mid-80s, it was the ECJ that upheld and strengthened integration considerably, by recognising implied powers, attributing direct effect to Directives and the like. The consequence was a creeping gain of terrain for the European Community whose flipside was a corresponding loss of terrain for the Member States. But the economic perspective is not the only possible one. The economic success has a legitimacy drawback whose deeper reasons are still not widely noticed.

Due to the jurisprudence of the ECJ, there are now two paths towards integration instead of one. The original path, provided by the Treaties, consists in creating European primary law and in enacting European secondary law. This path can be taken by the Member States only – regarding the Treaties, by a unanimous decision in the conference of the Heads of State and Government, followed by ratification in each Member State; and regarding secondary law, by a decision of the Council of Ministers that also required unanimity until the Single European Act entered into force in 1987 and, as of then, requires the consent of the European Parliament. The new path consists in applying the Treaties as understood by the ECJ. This path is open to the executive and judicial powers of the EU.

The two paths towards integration differ considerably. On the basis of the first, powers are transferred by the Member States to the EU. This path is political and involves the democratically legitimated and accountable governments of the Member States and, to varying degrees, the parliaments of the Member States as well as – more recently – the European Parliament. On the basis of the second path, the EU restricts the competences of Member States by a broad interpretation of the Treaties. This path is administrative and adjudicative in nature. The democratically legitimated and controlled governments of the Member States, their parliaments as well as the European Parliament, have no share in it. The general public does not get a chance to intervene. It is integration by stealth.[15]

However, the non-political mode of decision-making in the second path does not deprive the decisions themselves of their political character. It only shifts the power to decide questions of high political impact from the political organs of the EU to non-political institutions. To the same extent, the political means to secure democratic legitimacy and accountability fail to work. In the field of Treaty application, the administrative and judicial organs of the EU are uncoupled from the democratic process in the Member States and the EU, and enjoy far-reaching independence. This has a number of consequences.

The difference between the political and non-political mode of integration is responsible for the asymmetry between negative and positive integration that was first identified by Fritz Scharpf.[16] Negative integration means deregulation on the national level; positive integration means re-regulation on the European level. As a consequence of the constitutionalisation of the Treaties, negative integration occurs in a non-political mode by a stroke of the pen of the Commission or the ECJ, whereas positive integration requires a political decision where the representatives of the Member States in the Council, the European Parliament and the Commission must find agreement. This has worked in some fields, such as protection of the environment, but has failed in other areas.

The asymmetry also accounts for the liberalising tendency of the ECJ's jurisprudence.[17] This is not to say that the ECJ pursues an agenda of economic liberalism. It rather pursues the Treaty goal to establish and maintain the single market. Yet, since the vast majority of requests for a preliminary ruling which reach the ECJ have their origin in actions by economic actors who see their interests threatened by national legislation, and since the ECJ can contribute to the establishment of the single market only negatively, the result is a structural bias in favour of liberalisation. This, in turn, affects social policy. Although reserved for Member States, social policy comes under pressure because of the liberalising effects of the ECJ's jurisprudence, as upholding a high standard of social security tends to weaken the competitiveness of the national economy.[18]

Why is all this a reason for concern? Are not Member States the 'Masters of the Treaties'? Are they not in a position to stop these judicially created tendencies if they are not happy with them? After all, they decide in the European Council

---

[15] See D Majone, *Dilemmas of European Integration* (Oxford, Oxford University Press, 2005).

[16] F Scharpf, *Governing in Europe: Effective and Democratic?* (Oxford, Oxford University Press, 1999) 43. See also Majone *Dilemmas* (n 15) 143.

[17] See V Schmidt and M Thatcher (eds), *Resilient Liberalism in Europe's Economy* (Cambridge, Cambridge University Press, 2013).

[18] See F Scharpf, *Community and Autonomy* (Frankfurt, Campus, 2010) 221, 353; F Scharpf and VA Schmidt (eds), *Welfare and Work in the Open Economy* (Oxford, Oxford University Press, 2000); C Joerges and F Rödl, 'Informal Politics, Formalised Law and the "Social Deficit" of European Integration: Reflections after the Judgments of the ECJ in *Viking* and *Laval*' (2009) 15 *European Law Journal* 1.

on the direction, extent and pace of integration and they are the main actors of European legislation in the Council of Ministers. This should give them the opportunity to re-programme the jurisprudence of the ECJ by explicit legislation if they do not recognise their intentions in the Court's interpretation of the Treaties or observe detrimental effects caused by that interpretation. Why don't they do it?

The answer is that they cannot, and the reason for their incapacity is over-constitutionalisation. First, the over-constitutionalisation severely limits the Member States' role as 'Masters of the Treaties'. Their 'mastery' continues to exist with regard to formal amendments. But it is undermined at the level of treaty application. The principle of conferral that limits the power of the EU to those competences that have been explicitly transferred by the Member States is undermined. The same is true for the *Kompetenz-Kompetenz*, which guarantees that only the Member States have the power to determine the allocation of competences. There is a creeping power shift from Member States towards the EU that blurs the borderline between treaty amendment and treaty interpretation, and particularly bothers the German Constitutional Court.[19]

Second, the lack of differentiation between the constitutional law level and the ordinary law level, combined with the constitutionalisation of the Treaties, immunises the Commission and particularly the ECJ against any attempt by the democratically responsible institutions of the EU to react to the Court's jurisprudence by changing the law. Likewise, they immunise the executive and judicial institutions of the EU against public pressure. As far as the Treaty extends, elections do not matter. The political actors who have to take public opinion into account cannot change anything. The administrative and judicial actors who could change things by reconsidering their practice do not have to pay attention to public opinion.

To be sure, the Member States are not without any means to defend themselves against the creeping power shift towards the EU. They can bring an action for annulment of decisions by the Commission if, in their view, they transgress the competences of the EU. And they can amend the Treaties. But the practical use of these instruments is limited. Given the pro-integration attitude of an ECJ that does not understand itself as an umpire between the EU and the Member States, there is little chance of success for an annulment action. Amendments to the Treaties are practically unavailable because of the extremely high hurdles Member States have to jump over to be successful. It seems almost impossible to mobilise this instrument in order to reach a seemingly minor goal such as the correction of a line of jurisprudence.

Thus, the example of the EU confirms the statement: 'the more constitutional law, the less democracy'. The confusion of elements of constitutional law with elements of ordinary law in the Treaties favours the unelected and non-accountable

---

[19] See *BVerfGE* 123, 267(2009); D Grimm, 'The Basic Law as a Barrier against a Transformation of the EU into a State' in Grimm, *Constitution* (n 7) 207.

institutions of the EU over the democratically legitimised and accountable organs. Much of the progress of European integration is the work of unaccountable actors. Decisions of great political impact are taken in a non-political mode, but are not open for political revision either. It went almost unnoticed, even in academic writing,[20] that over-constitutionalisation is a source of this situation.

The lack of acceptance by its citizens from which the EU suffers cannot be explained without taking this into account. Not driven by political actors, the development was not subjected to political debate. When its result became apparent long after the causes had been set, European citizens found themselves confronted with a degree and outlook of integration to which they had never had a chance to react to, but could not change either, even if they did not support it. Over-constitutionalisation shields it against political reforms. The costs appear now in the form of a withdrawal of legitimacy.

V. The Remedy: Re-politicisation by De-constitutionalisation

Over-constitutionalisation is not the only cause of the legitimacy problem the EU faces. But it is the most neglected one. Blindness about the de-legitimising effects of over-constitutionalisation means that the search for remedies is misguided. The reason for the democratic deficit of the EU is mostly thought to be in the European Parliament's lack of adequate powers. In fact, it does not possess all the competences that national parliaments used to have. Therefore, many believe that the democratic deficit would be repaired if only the European Parliament were endowed with the competences that parliaments in a parliamentary democracy enjoy. They call for a full parliamentarisation of the EU according to the state model.

The insistence on the importance of the European Parliament is by no means unsound. The European Parliament is needed as a counterweight against the dominance of national interests in the Council and the technocratic tendencies in the Commission. But it seems doubtful whether full parliamentarisation of the EU could solve the deeper problems of European democracy. The reasons are manifold. In general, parliaments are the losers in the growing internationalisation of politics. Everywhere, it plays into the hands of the executive. It would be surprising if it were only the European Parliament that was exempted from this secular trend.

But there are also specific European reasons which create doubts that parliamentarisation is a suitable means to solve the legitimacy problem. The European Parliament is much less representative for the European citizenry than the national

---

[20] But see now SK Schmidt, *The European Court of Justice and the Policy Process* (Oxford, Oxford University Press, 2018).

parliaments for the people of the Member States.[21] The main reason for this is that European elections are not truly Europeanised. The European Parliament is elected according to national election laws. The seats are allocated according to national quotas that do not reflect the size of the national population. The voters can vote only for national parties, which campaign with national platforms. The election gives voters no opportunity to express themselves about the politics of the EU. The result of the election is usually evaluated under a national perspective: did the national ruling parties or the national opposition parties win?

Yet, after the elections have taken place, the national political parties (presently more than 200) do not play a decisive role in the European Parliament. There, European factions, loose associations of ideologically related parties, are decisive. But these factions are neither rooted in society nor do they maintain contact with the voters. This affects the impact of European elections. The parties for which one may vote are not the actors in the European Parliament. The factions that are the actors on the European level do not stand for elections. The legitimacy chain running from the voters to the Parliament is thus interrupted. The main source of democratic legitimacy is throttled.

This could, of course, be changed. The Treaties already envisage a European election law and European political parties. An implementation of these Treaty provisions would certainly strengthen the representativeness of the European Parliament, but hardly suffice to solve the legitimacy problem. The success of parliamentary representation does not only, and not even primarily, depend on institutional guarantees. The capacity of Parliament to fulfil its function as a mediator between the citizenry and government has societal preconditions. In order to keep government in contact with the citizens, Parliament must be embedded in an ongoing process of opinion formation and interest articulation so that democracy does not exhaust itself but culminates in periodical elections.

In Europe, these preconditions are weakly developed or completely missing. The European public sphere and European public discourse is poor compared to the national situation (which, itself, is not always satisfactory). The societal institutions that mediate between the people and the political organs of the EU are either missing or underdeveloped. There are no European parties. Interest groups, popular movements, NGOs are quite weak on the European level and, most important, there are no European media. The absence of a sufficient societal substructure, which is needed for a vibrant democracy, makes it unlikely that full parliamentarisation would reach its goal, namely to close the gap between the citizenry and the institutions.

Furthermore, the power of the European Parliament cannot be enhanced without decreasing the power of the Council. As a matter of fact, many reform plans want to reduce the Council to a second chamber of the European Parliament. In turn, the Commission would be upgraded to a genuine European government

---

[21] See R Rose, *Representing Europeans* (Oxford, Oxford University Press, 2013).

dependent on parliamentary support. For many, a directly-elected European President is the apex of the reform. However, it seems doubtful that the weakening of the Council, and with it the democratic resources from the Member States, would be adequately compensated by strengthening the European Parliament as long as the socio-political substructure of European parliamentarianism is missing or underdeveloped.

On the contrary, one must fear that the legitimacy structure of the EU as a whole would suffer, rather than profit, from the reform. Originally, the democratic legitimacy of European politics emanated exclusively from the Member States. The Council, in which their democratically elected and accountable governments are represented, was the central organ of the EU and its exclusive legislator. A decision of the Council required unanimity. This meant that no Member State was subject to laws to which its democratically-legitimated organs had not consented. If the citizens disagreed with their governments, they could voice this in the national election.

The unanimity requirement was given up with the Single European Act of 1986. In certain matters, growing in number with every Treaty amendment, the Council now decides by a majority. As a consequence, it can happen that Member States are subject to laws and legal acts to which their democratically accountable representatives have not agreed. To the same extent, the legitimation chain which runs from national elections over the national parliament and government to the European organs is broken, at least for states that are outvoted in the Council.

This legitimation gap could no longer be bridged by national democracies. As compensation, the European Parliament got a share in European legislation which considerably increased over time. The monistic legitimation of the EU has since been replaced by a dualistic one. The reform project would return to a monistic legitimation, yet one that would not consist in hetero-legitimation but in auto-legitimation. Therefore, the question is whether the EU has sufficient legitimation resources to support itself. This is more than doubtful, given the weak societal substructure of the European democracy. Rather it is likely that a full parliamentarisation of the EU would minimise the external legitimation without being able to increase the internal legitimation.

Finally, and most importantly in this context, the parliamentarisation of the EU would leave the effects of over-constitutionalisation completely unaffected. In the area that is determined by constitutional law, elections do not matter and parliaments have no say. This source of the democratic deficit can only be repaired by a politicisation of the decision-making processes in the EU. If one wants to enhance the legitimacy of the EU the power to decide questions of high political salience must be shifted from the executive and judicial branches to the political organs, the Council and the European Parliament. The only way to achieve this goal is to scale back the Treaties to their truly constitutional elements and downgrade all Treaty provisions of a non-constitutional nature to the status of secondary law.

This should not be misunderstood as a reversal of the constitutionalisation of the Treaties and a rollback of the present state of integration. Rather, it draws out the consequences of precisely that constitutionalisation by giving the constitution-alised Treaties the outlook of a constitution. Not a single norm of the Treaties would be sacrificed. Neither would the function of the ECJ as guardian of the Treaties be undermined. This solution would merely open the door for a re-direction of the Court's jurisprudence by the politically legitimated and accountable organs of the EU, if they find it necessary. This seems to be a more appropriate way to deal with the European legitimacy problem than a resumption of the Constitutional Treaty.

4

The EU's Constitutional Moment: A View from the Ground Up

KALYPSO NICOLAIDIS

This chapter transcribes a conversation between one of the book's editors, Nick Barber, and me. We have kept it free-flowing to reflect this. It offers some reflections based on my role in the Constitutional Convention as a 'sherpa' to the Greek Presidency (Spring 2013). As the representative of the last Presidency of the Convention, the Greek Minister of Foreign Affairs, George Papandreou, was part of the Praesidium which met behind closed doors, with one sherpa each, under the alternate chairmanship of Valéry Giscard d'Estaing and Giuliano Amato. Praesidium members prepared and discussed the various amendments percolating up from the Convention and down from the secretariat and the President. Members of the Greek team, including myself, took turns in joining the minister in these meetings in addition, of course, to taking part in the Convention debates proper.

In a different space, the Greek team was especially attuned to one of the great power games played out on the Convention floor, that between big and small states – pardon me, smaller states – and chaired a group bringing together representatives of the latter group, self-styled as 'friends of the Community method'.

In anticipation of its privileged role in the Convention process, the Greek government entrusted me with creating and chairing an international group of experts which met at regular intervals in various European cities to provide advice and feedback. Members included Paul Magnette and Joseph Weiler, Stanley Hoffmann, Anand Menon, Helen Wallace, Haris Pamboukis, Nikos Kotzias and Jean Nestor.

The original plan before the launch was for the Greeks to foster a renewed democratic covenant through the Convention and our group was tasked with translating this commitment in constitutional terms. After all, said the Greeks, we invented democracy, didn't we?! I wrote a draft inaugural speech for George Papandreou that would have turned this narrative on its head:

> We Greeks started to invent democracy way back when, but failed to make it inclusive of women, slaves and strangers. Our modern era proceeded to reinvent democracy and, in the process, to make it genuinely inclusive. A never-ending task, in the making for the last two centuries. To the extent that modern Greeks can humbly claim a bit of historical

> legacy, we feel especially responsible for bringing this commitment to inclusiveness to the European level: A European democracy, for all. That should be our shared motto.

Would a Greek minister have said this? We will never know. For the day of the speech in January 2003, Papandreou had to choose whether to fly to New York instead of Brussels to talk about War in Iraq rather than Eternal Peace in Europe. Between these two agendas, guessing which came first is not, hum, rocket science.

NB: *Can you say more about how you see the origins of the Draft Constitution?*

When asked this question, many refer back to Joschka Fischer's 2001 speech at Humboldt University as the starting point for the story of the Draft Constitution. But of course, the roots of the Draft Constitution reach much deeper in time. You could even say that some dreamers after World War II hoped to create a new kind of European nation to replace the flawed nation states, and that they dreamed of a constitutional order for Europe at the time of The Hague Summit back in 1948. But we got instead a Union, not a state, and a Treaty not a Constitution. Why, some 50 years later, this urge to cross the Rubicon and give the EU something called a Constitution, albeit to start under the guise of a constitutional treaty? There were at least three possible motivations.

The first was a simple, almost mechanical, need to modify the Treaties in light of the enlargement of the Union to East and Central European states that was to come in 2004. The old decision-making rules found in the Treaties would have struggled to cope with these extra members. Member States were aware of the challenges that this new round of accessions would bring when discussing the reforms that eventually became the Amsterdam Treaty in 1997, but the Amsterdam modifications to Europe's structures were widely regarded as inadequate; a temporary solution at best. Enlargement would have required institutional adaptation in any event, but in power-political terms it raised worries in the larger Member States that they would lose power to their smaller, more numerous partners. To some extent the production of the Constitution was driven by the Gulliver syndrome that is, a fear by the large states of Europe that the inclusion of many more smaller states after enlargement might slow decision-making within the Union or, worse still, that the larger number of smaller states might be in a position to band together to tie them down. Did this concern really warrant a Constitution?

Second, as I wrote at the time with Andrew Moravcsik, the Draft Constitution also aspired to entrench and build upon the constitutional settlement that had been developed in the 1990s. So the Convention was not only part of the ongoing constitutionalisation process of the Union, but would take this process to a new level. For some, the broader question of the identity of the Union had been left unresolved in Amsterdam; the Draft Constitution was an opportunity for the Union to reflect on the settlement it had already reached and express it in a form that would bring into being a new European body politic. The Draft Constitutional Treaty provided an opportunity to manage, recognise and make visible the existing settlement.

But was this a 'constitutional moment', a moment when a fundamental shift in the nature of the Union should be formally recognised in a new type of Covenant?

Third, the Draft Constitution was a response to the legitimacy deficit debate that had been going on since Maastricht: resistance to the creeping competences of the Union; the feeling that this was a centralising project that lacked proper democratic controls; and the persistence of a wide gap between the people and the institutions of Europe at a time when the launch of the Euro required, on the contrary, that democratic anchoring be strengthened. People needed to be reassured that this construct served them. There was a hope that, perhaps, the structures of the Union could be clarified, simplified and presented in a more accessible form. This may be the context in which Joschka Fischer's speech should be placed: he was arguing that we needed to name the animal, to give a story to the project, to make the Union seem less remote and less alarming. Constitutions do two kinds of things. Most obviously, they allocate power within the system – creating and shaping institutions. But constitutions also tell a story about the polity, a story about what type of state it is, and what it aspires to be. Constitutions present the values and character of the common polity to its people, and some would argue that in doing so they actually constitute the people. The time and angst expended on the Preamble to the Draft Constitution shows the concern of the Convention with this, symbolic, side of the Constitution's nature. Some believed that by presenting the Union as a federation, at least through implicit analogy with the United States, a Constitution would make the Union more comprehensible to its people, as well as, somewhat in tension with the United States analogy, underline what the Union is not; that it is not some sort of super-state, and has no aspiration to become one. And, perhaps, along with a recognition of the Union as a federation would come the establishment of effective democratic structures. People are familiar with federations, and, it was hoped, would be more willing to engage with its constitutional structures.

The decision to label this document a 'constitutional Treaty' (a Treaty that would give birth to a Constitution) prompted widespread debate amongst academics and politicians. There was debate over whether the label was a wise one, but also over what it connoted. The supposed Constitution was not a constitution in classical political terms, yet perhaps it merited the title. This uncertainty over the nature of the document recurred throughout the story of the Draft Convention. Indeed, even with the Laeken Declaration, the Declaration that heralded the start of the process, it was not clear whether the final document would be presented as a constitution. There was broad consensus on the need for a treaty change, but little consensus over the form that this change should take. So paradoxically the very fact of 'constitutional moment' was itself contested throughout this Convention.

These three strands, three explanations of the origins of the project, could all be taken as implying arguments for or against a constitution. Regarding the first strand, it could be argued that the reunification of Europe after the fall of the Eastern Bloc was a moment that required a constitution; the territory of EU was now, in broad lines, determined. But, expansion need not have required a new constitutional form. And conversely, the United States adopted a constitution well before its borders were set. The relationship between constitutional settlement and territorial settlement is, then, ambiguous, at best. Even if it were to be argued that the expansion of EU, this 'big bang' should be celebrated and marked by the adoption of a constitution, others could, equally well, argue that the Union should continue to be defined as a fluid entity, one whose borders could still change. It could also be argued (second strand) that the Constitutional settlement was precisely about incremental treaty change not a big bang Constitution.

As to the third strand, I often draw the distinction between mimetic and transformative reasoning. There are two kinds of ways of thinking about the EU. One is mimetic: understanding the EU as more or less like the nation state – as like a more decentralised Germany, but borrowing a great deal from the USA. The second is transformative, inventing a new form of polity which involves transforming our understanding of both the nation state (into 'member states') and the older, Westphalian, European system of states itself. Through the classic mechanisms of international law a new type of entity has emerged, one which is not seeking to jump into a new form of state, but is rather something different, something new. I argued at the time that we should be referring to a federal union not a federal state. A deeper form of collaboration which involves, in addition to economic interdependence, democratic interdependence. What happens in the democratic game of one Member State impacts on other Member States, and there is the challenge of intermingling political legitimacies.

NB: *If these were the goals, did the Convention achieve them? What was the process like?*

Well in the end, the Convention did not contribute a Constitution as classically understood, but one more Treaty reform. Nevertheless, it provided a chance for what might be termed constitutional pedagogy; an opportunity for the people of Europe to formulate an account of the European project, which could then be formalised into a constitutional text. The process could have enabled people to learn from each other, and to produce a text that would stand as an articulation of the values and point of the Union.

And indeed, as I argued at the time with Paul Magnette, the process did involve much more Habermasian logic of persuasion than ever before in Treaty reform, although in the end and unsurprisingly the bargaining logic prevailed, both in the Convention and in the IGC that followed. But the fact that the process included people beyond the usual suspects of politics, especially legal scholars, did mean that we were able to generate text that encapsulated better than ever before what European democracy looks like. Articles 9 to 12 of the final Treaty summarise a great amount of non-mimetic thinking about European democracy. Indeed, these debates inspired my own concept of demoicracy, which I developed at the time to try to translate them in theoretical terms (defined as 'a union of peoples who govern together but not as one'). It was striking, above all, that European democracy was going to rely on a notion of European people or the primacy of the European

Parliament in expressing its 'will'. This meant that the Draft Constitution – and later the Lisbon Treaty – enshrined the European Council and clearly assigned to this club of executives a core representative function alongside the Council, which is not to the taste of traditional constitutionalists. Most importantly, if we have European peoples plural then the democratic focus is on citizenship, with all the rights, obligations, aspirations that it implies. Unfortunately, the text does not reflect an inclusive notion of citizenship all the way down, speaking instead in paternalistic terms of citizens 'who shall receive attention' from EU institutions. And while the European Citizen Initiative became the flagship of 'democratisation' when the Convention members tried to sell the Constitutional treaty in the latter phase, this was not something that at least the leadership of the Convention had embraced with enthusiasm, to say the least.

Perhaps this substantive lacuna is unsurprising, as many in the Convention were ill-placed to facilitate the learning process that underpins the logic of persuasion and the construct of a modern democratic ethos. Too many Convention members, crucially including the President of the Convention – Giscard d'Estaing, who thought not only in mimetic terms but who did not believe in what I would call 'the promise of democratic effervescence'. Delegates struggled to escape their statist biases. Perhaps worse still, supporters of the statist approach to the project thought of themselves as idealists, as defenders of the true calling, the true ambition for Europe. Those who had other visions of Europe were regarded as anti-EU, as objectors who needed to be overcome. The main drafters failed to fashion a constitution that reflected the truly novel nature of the Union.

The pedagogic potential of the Convention was further undermined by the failure to engage those outside of the Convention. During the Convention there was an aim, an intention, to engage, and there was some engagement in various forms. For example, NGOs were included in the process to a limited extent. They had tables set out in the corridors leading to the Convention floor which allowed them to engage with delegates. There was a one-day opportunity for some of the NGOs to speak to the Convention, with each given a short timeslot to make their case. But the utility of this contribution was limited. The NGOs that were present were a small microcosm of the broader political community. And their one-day opportunity to address the delegates turned into a shambles, as most of the speakers failed to focus on details and instead turned lyrical, treating their moment on the stand more as a chance to express their grand vision of Europe rather than as a chance to influence the delegates. The delegates were bored for a day, and then the process moved on.

Of course, the very diversity of delegates also made it harder for the Convention to engage with those outside of the room. There were delegates from the Member States, from national parliaments, from the European Institutions. And cross-cutting these categories were political groupings like the Christian Democrats or the Social Democrats, organisations which had regular meetings outside of the Convention. They found it difficult enough to engage with each other, let alone to talk to those outside the Convention. In contrast to a legislative assembly, the Convention lacked established political connections which would facilitate decision-making: it was a new-born political body, and struggled to find its voice, even if many delegates did try to do what they could, on the ground.

In some respects, the Convention now seems very dated. There was only very limited use of the internet, for instance. It is it possible to imagine a different form of Convention made full use of the early possibilities of e-democracy provided by new technologies. The Convention could have, should have, used the internet to publicise its debates and to enable people to comment and engage with proceedings in innovative ways.

In addition to this gloomy picture, the President of the Convention – Giscard d'Estaing – was not the best person to engineer democratic decision-making. While Giscard had a deep knowledge of European Institutions and had himself introduced the notion of the European Council in the 1970s, he had an autocratic manner that impaired his capacity to engage with people. There are many different ways of failing to be democratic – and d'Estaing suffered from many of them. He could not engage with people, and, moreover, demonstrated a contempt for small countries. As part of the Greek delegation, working with the Greek government, I helped coordinate a group (called 'the friends of the Community method') that sought to bring together the smaller countries and protect the interests of those smaller countries in the European project – by, for example, protecting the rotating Presidency. But being French as well, I often mingled with the French group. There is no question that the delegates from France, including Giscard, least appreciated the need for federal balancing, and the need to protect the smaller nations. Federal equality should have been central to the Draft Constitution, but the French delegates privileged the Franco-German axis as usual. Giscard's attitude bordered on the contemptuous in his comments on the smaller members, overheard asking his staff, 'who do they think they are,' or 'they are less than a third of the Union'.

Giscard was not, of course, the sole author of the Draft Constitution – and he did give way on various issues. He was an expert at recognising the points at which to expend political capital. But his position in the Praesidium allowed him to dominate that body and, through that body, the Convention itself (the Praesidium was the body that guided the Convention, formulating drafts and deciding what measures would be put to the floor). Only limited records were kept of discussions in the Praesidium in spite of the crucial role it played, so it might now be impossible to fully assess how it operated. For scholars today, the Praesidium is a 'black hole' within the drafting process. As a small example: who can recall today how much contestation occurred in the Praesidium around the drafting of the Preamble? We all believed that this would be a very important statement, a chance to spell out what the Constitution was all about. So with the Greek delegation, I spent time gathering inspiring Preambles from countries around the world, such as some from the Pacific like the Marshall Islands who tend to tell a story very directly, emphasising diversity. We produced drafting suggestions but the President was not interested. He retreated into his ivory tower, probably gazing at the horizon of his posterity late at night, and drafted it by himself. Who did he think he was?

In retrospect, it is a shame that Giuliano Amato was not in charge of the process. Amato was a far more ebullient character, winning people over with charm and humour. Because Greece was one of the three states that had the Presidency during the Convention, and because I was an advisor to the Greek Foreign Minister, I sat in the Praesidium a few times. The difference in style between Giscard and Amato was dramatic. Whereas the former sought to stifle debate, Amato sought to encourage it. Perhaps if he had been the President of the Convention things might have turned out differently. He would have been more open to discussion, and more willing to compromise. And, crucially, Amato knew, and could deploy, the power of humour (promising a recalcitrant Praesidium member that his stubborn resistance was duly noted and could be inscribed on these walls for posterity to acknowledge).

If there had been a President who had recognised the need to avoid federal mimetism, who had been able to engage with the public more broadly, who had been more consensual, and, perhaps, more open to using social media as a tool to build consensus around the Constitution, the fate of the Draft Constitution might have been very different.

NB: *To what extent does the constitutional process explain the results of the referendums?*

Throughout the Convention, some of us had been worried about the lack of buy-in from citizens, who after all were supposed to be the authors of this new constitutional treaty. One of my personal crusades was a proposal on behalf of the Greek team for holding an ambitious constitutional *agora*, an open space in which the merits of the Draft Constitution could be debated in a festive atmosphere. I referred to it as 'the Woodstock of European politics', a five-day festival that would happen in Athens, from the beaches to the parks, held between the end of the Convention of the European Council adopting the draft in June 2003 and its adoption by the Heads of State, a chance for people from all over Europe to debate the document, with the possibility of amending the text. I suggested this about a year before the end of the Convention. The Greek Presidency was supportive, and, I hoped, there would be a symbolic benefit in enabling the people to debate the Draft Constitution before it returned to the Heads of State. We presented this to Giscard in the Praesidium, arguing that it would change the ethos of this exercise, but he was not interested, and we made no headway. Needless to say, the failure to engineer popular ownership of the Draft Constitution had lasting consequences. Publics across Europe could have been engaged upstream in different ways of course but it was wrong to do so only at end when they were asked to rubber-stamp a process they had not been connected to. This is a point we tried to make during the IGC with a group of approximately 100 EU scholars from around the world in a document entitled *Making it Our Own*, where we suggested amendments to the text addressing citizens' concerns such as power, repatriation and the like. Again here, it proved impossible to burst the drafting bubble.

Which brings us to the loud French and Dutch 'Nos' in the spring of 2005 after the timid Spanish 'Yes'. Whilst there were many factors that led to the rejection of the Draft Constitution in France and the Netherlands, the opacity of that document did play a role. The Draft Constitution singularly failed to resonate with voters and it might be this lack of identification that allowed other issues to come forward in the campaign, such as the fear of the Polish plumber in France. That the campaigns were so strongly affected by issues not related to the Draft Constitution is, itself, evidence of its failure to engage with the people it was supposed to address. People did not care enough about the text to overlook the context. The lack of proper engagement entailed that, for many voters, the Draft Constitution fell from the sky; it was not a project people had invested in, even those who might, in other circumstances, have supported the substance of the proposals. People did not care, and had not even noticed the Convention.

I campaigned for 'Yes' in the French and Dutch referendums by arguing that the label of a constitution did not necessarily connote that the thing being constituted was a state. After all, we can adopt constitutions for clubs of all sorts. But for this message to come across clearly it should have been written in a different way. The Preamble, for example, should have emphasised the peoples of Europe – 'We the peoples of', and list every country. The Constitution needed to be clearly for a different kind of animal: it needed to be obvious that this was not a mimetic exercise. The primacy clause, in particular, created problems for the Yes campaign. As I campaigned in neighbourhood markets, in meetings or on TV, I constantly sought to explain that the Constitution only asserted primacy in circumscribed areas and context rather than a general assertion of primacy. Moreover, it depended on prior agreement by the states – states who had agreed to accept the outcome of any adjudicator of these disputes. This was targeted primacy, circumscribed primacy. But it was understood, wrongly, as all-encompassing, an assertion of power by the Union over national laws in general. To be sure, there was much to defend in the Draft Constitution including as mentioned the passage designed to lay out how the EU combines representative, direct and participatory democracy in novel ways. Nevertheless I was somewhat uncomfortable, defending something that was not what I thought it should have been.

The French campaign was dominated by debate over the dreaded 'country of origin' principle and the ability of workers in the accession states to travel to France – even if this was about the new Draft Directive on services by Commissioner Bolkenstein and had nothing to do with the Draft Constitution. Having long worked on mutual recognition in the single market, I believe that this principle was at the heart of the European construct even if it needed to be managed with care. But it became anathema to defend it and even counterproductive if you wanted to campaign in favour of the Constitution. Even politicians sympathetic to the European project used the debate over the Draft Constitution to air their concerns over these issues. We struggled to maintain public focus on the Draft Constitution itself, as opposed to the Polish Plumber controversy.

After the referendums rejected the Draft Constitution, I was very concerned by the suggestion that it should be put to another referendum – and concerned when much of the substance of the Draft Constitution was resurrected in the Lisbon Treaty. Something like the Lisbon Treaty was necessary; the pressures of accession were real. And thankfully, the Treaty did remove much of the statist paraphernalia. Nevertheless, the decision to press forward with the substance of the Draft Constitution after its rejection by the French and Dutch peoples did lasting harm to the European project. It may have been a necessary sin, but it was a sin all the same. Much water has flowed under the bridge since then. The constitutional settlement consolidated by the Lisbon Treaty has proven resilient even if the substance of EU policies have become deeply contested. But I believe that the EU has yet to undergo what I called at the time our 'democratic atonement'.

5

Treaty Amendment, the Draft Constitution and European Integration

PAUL CRAIG*

The significance of the Constitutional Treaty in the development of European integration is contestable, as attested to by the title of the project that gave rise to this book, framed in terms of the rise and fall of the European Constitution. Viewed in descriptive terms, it is a statement of the obvious, insofar as it signifies the fact that the Constitutional Treaty was never ratified. Viewed from a more normative perspective, the statement is implicitly tendentious, insofar as it might be taken to suggest that the failure to ratify the Constitutional Treaty has some deeper resonance for the limits of European integration, which is, as will be seen below, debatable to say the least. The argument in this chapter proceeds in four stages.

First, the decision to establish the Convention on the Future of Europe was not irrational or misguided when seen in the light of the circumstances that prevailed at the turn of the new millennium. We should be duly mindful of reasoning with the benefit of hindsight, and concluding that the failure to ratify the Constitutional Treaty attested to the error in the establishment of the Convention that led to its drafting. The contention that this failure is proof that the enterprise was misguided is, as will be argued below, a non-sequitur. The point being made here is, however, temporally prior, *viz* that the decision to engage in more far-reaching reflection on the nature of the EU was warranted when viewed from the time when the decision was taken.

Secondly, it was not preordained that the Convention would produce a formal Draft Constitutional Treaty. The fact that it did so was the result of a conscious decision made by the President of the Convention, and the members of the Praesidium. This choice was readily explicable, and rational when viewed from the circumstances that prevailed when the Convention deliberations began. There had, over the Community's history, been frequent recourse to high-level deliberations concerning its future direction, which commonly produced worthy

* Professor of English Law, St John's College, Oxford. I am grateful for comments on an earlier version of the chapter by Neil Walker and other participants at a workshop at Trinity College, Oxford.

recommendations that were well received and led to little change. The Chairman of the Convention, Valéry Giscard d'Estaing, was cognisant of this and had no wish to preside over yet another such enterprise. This explains the astute political move, early in the Convention deliberations, when it was revealed that the Convention would indeed seek to draft a new Constitutional Treaty. This duly concentrated the minds of the participants, who engaged with the process mindful that the real outcome would be concrete Treaty provisions.

Thirdly, it is mistaken to regard the failure to ratify the Constitutional Treaty as signifying some dramatic turning point in European integration, such that its rejection was a symbolic of loss of faith in the European ideal from which the EU never recovered. As an academic hypothesis, this has a nice ring to it, all the more so for being cast in duly apocalyptic terms. It does not, however, withstand serious examination, for two related reasons: the rationale for the French and Dutch rejection of the Constitutional Treaty in national referendums had scant connection to anything novel in the Constitutional Treaty; and 90 per cent of the changes contained in the Constitutional Treaty were accepted and incorporated in the Lisbon Treaty. The deliberations in the Convention on the Future of Europe were not, therefore, wasted rhetoric, nor was the drafting of the Constitutional Treaty a fruitless exercise. To the contrary, the regime that currently governs the EU is based on Treaty articles that were cut and pasted from the Constitutional Treaty into the Lisbon Treaty.

Fourthly, the legal and political reality is that European integration did not stop in 2004–05, with the demise of the Draft Constitutional Treaty. The EU has been beset by three very significant challenges in the last decade: the financial crisis, the migration crisis and the rule of law crisis. There is, moreover, the challenge posed by Brexit. These crises have tested the EU's resilience and continue to do so. There is, however, scant, if any, connection between these crises and the demise of the Constitutional Treaty. There is, by way of contrast, a connection between these crises and the development of EU integration. Thus while they posed severe challenges for the EU, they have also, in some instances, been the catalyst for increased integration, largely achieved within the framework of the Lisbon Treaty, as attested to by the enactment of a plethora of measures designed to increase centralised control over fiscal policy in the light of the financial crisis.

I. Constitutional Treaty: Rationale for the Convention

It is important to understand the rationale for the creation of the Convention on the Future of Europe, which was the institutional forum through which the Constitutional Treaty was produced.[1]

---

[1] P Craig, 'Constitutional Process and Reform in the EU: Nice, Laeken, the Convention and the IGC' (2004) 10 *European Public Law* 653.

The first 30 years of the Community's existence saw relatively little by way of Treaty amendment. There was the Merger Treaty, and Treaties securing the accession of new Member States, but subject to these changes, the original Rome Treaty provided the stable foundation for the legal and political ordering of the EEC. The period thereafter was markedly different, and the change dates from the Single European Act 1986 (SEA 1986). From the SEA 1986 until the end of the millennium there was the Maastricht Treaty 1992, the Treaty of Amsterdam 1997 and the Nice Treaty 2001. There was in addition the EU Charter of Rights 2000. Each Treaty revision was preceded by an Intergovernmental Conference (IGC), which would often last for 18 months. There was force in Bruno de Witte's observation that the EU was in a permanent state of Treaty revision.[2]

This was more especially so, given that the Nice Treaty identified future topics for Treaty reform, the expectation being that they would be dealt with via Treaty revision culminating in 2004, being preceded by an IGC, which would on normal reckoning begin work within 18 months of ratification of the Nice Treaty. The Declaration on the Future of the Union was formally appended to the Nice Treaty.[3] It called for a 'deeper and wider debate' about the future of the EU, which would 'encourage wide-ranging discussion with all interested parties'.[4] It set a timetable for this process to be continued through initiatives to be set out in a Declaration made at the Laeken European Council in December 2001. The Laeken Declaration should address, 'inter alia', the delimitation of competences, the status of the Charter of Fundamental Rights, simplification of the Treaties, and the role of national Parliaments in the European architecture.[5] It would then be for the IGC in 2004 to make the necessary Treaty changes 'after these preparatory steps'.[6] The calendar year 2001 between Nice and Laeken saw the emergence of consensus among the major institutional players about two crucial issues.

The first concerned the content of the reform agenda. It came to be accepted that the four issues left over from the Nice Treaty were not discrete. It came to be recognised that competences, and the status of the Charter, resonated with other issues concerning the institutional balance of power within the EU, and also with the vertical distribution of authority between the EU and the Member States. It became clear that the ideal of simplification of the Treaties could not realistically be accomplished without considering substantive modification of the existing Treaty provisions. The very fact that the Nice Declaration stated that future reform should address 'inter alia' the four issues adumbrated above lent further weight to the expansion of the topics for discussion that resulted in the Laeken Declaration.

---

[2] B de Witte, 'The Closest Thing to a Constitutional Conversation in Europe: The Semi-Permanent Treaty Revision Process' in P Beaumont, C Lyons and N Walker (eds), *Convergence and Divergence in European Public Law* (Oxford, Hart, 2002).
[3] Treaty of Nice, Declaration 23 [2001] OJ C80/1.
[4] Ibid, [3].
[5] Ibid, [5].
[6] Ibid, [7].

There was also growing consensus on the second issue, the reform process. If a broad range of issues was to be discussed, if the next round of Treaty reform was not simply to be a further episode in tinkering with the Treaties, then the idea that the result, whatsoever it might be, should be legitimated by input from a broader 'constituency' than hitherto assumed greater force. There was an element of 'traditional reform fatigue', leading to the desire for new institutional mechanisms that could consider matters central to the future of the EU.

This consensus was exemplified at the highest level by deliberations in the Council and European Council. The Goteborg European Council in June 2001 was influenced by a paper prepared by the Secretary-General,[7] which contributed to the growing realisation that the four issues identified in the Nice Declaration could not be considered in isolation and that debate about the future of Europe would necessarily address fundamental issues of institutional competence. This was acknowledged by the Goteborg European Council, which made reference to the Secretary-General's Report, and recognised that modernisation of Community institutions would be central to future reforms.[8]

The deliberations of the Goteborg European Council concerning the reform process were shaped by a paper prepared by the Swedish Presidency of the Council.[9] It canvassed a number of options as to how the debate about the future of Europe should be taken forward, such as classic IGC mode, and the establishment of a small group of 'wise men'. It also raised the possibility of 'creating a broad and open preparatory forum',[10] drawing on the process used for the Charter of Fundamental Rights. The Goteborg European Council was relatively brief about the specifics of the reform process, but the Presidency paper put the Convention model firmly on the agenda and the European Council noted that the debate about the future of Europe 'involving all parts of society' should be actively pursued.[11]

This growing consensus about the approach to content and process was affirmed by later meetings of the General Affairs Council.[12] Thus the GAC 'favoured an approach consisting of enlarging on the themes and objectives listed in the Nice Declaration, in the form of questions, with the dual aim of making the Union meet its citizens' expectations more successfully while functioning more effectively'.[13] The GAC also confirmed the broad convergence of views in favour of the Convention model, detailing matters such as the number and type of participants, the establishment of a Praesidium and support from a Secretariat.[14]

---

[7] Preparing the Council for Enlargement, POLGEN 12, 9518/01, Brussels, 7 June 2001.

[8] Goteborg European Council, 15–16 June 2001, [16]–[18].

[9] Report on the Debate on the Future of the European Union, POLGEN 14, 9520/01, Brussels, 8 June 2001.

[10] Ibid, [56].

[11] Goteborg European Council (n 8) [15].

[12] 2372nd Council Meeting, General Affairs, 12330/01, Brussels, 8–9 October 2001.

[13] Ibid, 18.

[14] Ibid, 18. See also, 2386th Council Meeting, General Affairs, Brussels, 19–20 November 2001, 11.

The GAC meetings paved the way for the Laeken European Council.[15] In terms of the reform agenda, the Laeken Declaration gave the formal imprimatur of the European Council for the broadening of the issues left open post-Nice. These issues may always have been the tip of the iceberg. The Laeken Declaration nonetheless made this explicit. The four issues post-Nice became the 'headings' within which a plethora of other questions were posed, which raised virtually every issue of importance for the future of Europe. In terms of the reform process, the Laeken Declaration formally embraced the Convention model with a composition designed to enhance the legitimacy of the results that it produced, whatsoever those might be.

The other principal institutional actors took the same view as the Council and the European Council. The Commission made clear its belief that the four questions identified in the Nice Declaration were not the only ones to be considered when reflecting on the future of the Union,[16] and the same theme was evident in Romano Prodi's speeches between April and December 2001, calling for the Laeken Declaration to establish 'an ambitious and comprehensive agenda',[17] which would be legitimated through a discursive forum open to a wide range of people, by way of contrast to the narrow IGC process.[18] The Commission reiterated these views on the eve of the Laeken Summit.[19]

The European Parliament pressed strenuously in the same direction as the other major institutional actors. This is apparent in its Resolution concerning the Future of the European Union in May 2001.[20] It expressed regret at the narrow compass of the Nice Treaty, and noted that a Union of 27 Member States required more thoroughgoing reform in order to guarantee democracy, effectiveness, transparency and governability.[21] The medium through which such reform should be pursued should be radically different from the IGC model, which the European Parliament argued had outlived its usefulness as a method for Treaty reform. The Convention model should be employed, thereby enabling a wider participation of affected interests.[22] Consensus between the European Parliament and national parliaments in favour of the Convention model was secured by July 2001.[23]

---

[15] Laeken European Council, 14–15 December 2001.

[16] Commission Communication, *On Certain Arrangements for the Debate about the Future of the European Union*, 25 April 2001, 4.

[17] 'On the Road to Laeken', Speech by Romano Prodi to the European Parliament, Speech/01/326, 4 July 2001, 4.

[18] Speech to the European Parliament's Committee on Constitutional Affairs, Romano Prodi, Speech/01/343, 10 July 2001, 3.

[19] *Communication from the Commission on the Future of European Union, Renewing the Community Method*, COM(2001) 727 final, 4.

[20] The Treaty of Nice and the Future of the European Union, A5-0168/2001.

[21] Ibid, [1]–[2].

[22] Ibid, [5]–[7].

[23] *Second Meeting with National Parliaments on Future of Europe Secures Consensus in favour of a Convention to Prepare for Treaty Reform*, 16 July 2001.

The European Parliament's aspirations were reiterated forcefully in the Report of the Committee on Constitutional Affairs for the Laeken European Council.[24]

The preceding history should not be forgotten when thinking about the subject matter of this chapter. There was good reason for setting up the Convention on the Future of Europe. The EC had been through 15 years of piecemeal Treaty reform, dating events from the SEA 1986, with the prospects of a further round of interstitial change in 2004. It was not surprising that the institutional players should think that it was time for more considered reflection on the nature of the EC, its powers and the integration process. This was more especially so, given that the four issues listed in the Declaration on the Future of the Union appended to the Nice Treaty, which were to be considered in the next Treaty reform, were not readily separable from broader matters concerning the future of the EU. To put the same point in a different way, resolution of those four issues would inevitably entail consideration of wider issues, explicitly or implicitly. It should, moreover, be emphasised that all the key institutional players, including the Member States, were agreed on the broadening of the substantive agenda, and the nature of the deliberative process, which should pertain in the Convention on the Future of Europe.

II.   Convention on the Future of Europe: Emergence of the Draft Constitutional Treaty

The Laeken European Council duly instituted the Convention on the Future of Europe, which began work in March 2002.[25] It was chaired by Giscard d'Estaing, with two Vice-Chairmen, Giuliano Amato and Jean-Luc Dehaene. There was one representative from each of the 15 Member States, 30 members of national parliaments, two from each Member State, 16 MEPs and two Commission representatives. There were also representatives from the accession candidate countries, who could take part in the proceedings without, however, being able to prevent any consensus that might emerge among the Member States. Observer status was accorded to the European Ombudsman and to members of the Economic and Social Committee, the European social partners and the Committee of Regions. The Presidents of the Court of Justice and of the Court of Auditors could be invited by the Praesidium to address the Convention.

The Praesidium of the Convention was composed of the Convention Chairman and Vice-Chairmen and nine members drawn from the Convention, these being the representatives of all the governments holding the Council Presidency during the Convention, two national parliament representatives, two European Parliament representatives and two Commission representatives.

---

[24] *Report on the Laeken European Council and the Future of the European Union*, A5-0368/2001.
[25] Laeken European Council, 14–15 December 2001, Annex 1, 24. The seminal work on the Convention on the Future of Europe is, P Norman, *The Accidental Constitution, The Making of Europe's Constitutional Treaty*, 2nd edn (Brussels, EuroComment, 2005).

The time limit within which the Convention had to consider the issues assigned to it by the Laeken Declaration was very tight. The Convention was instructed to finish its deliberations within a year, and to present its conclusions to the European Council meeting in the summer of 2003. The Convention decided to proceed via consensus, rather than formal voting, which thereby gave the Praesidium considerable power to determine whether the requisite consensus had been reached.[26] The Convention used a three-stage methodology. There was the listening stage from March till June 2002. This was followed by the examination stage, in which working groups considered particular topics, which occupied the latter half of 2002. There was then the proposal stage, in which the Convention discussed draft articles of the Constitution, normally on the basis of proposals from the working groups. The decision to establish such groups was made in May 2002,[27] with six groups being initially established, with a further five such groups created thereafter.[28] Working groups were not used for issues concerning the inter-institutional distribution of power, which were discussed in the plenary session because of their centrality and the controversial nature of the subject matter.

It was not preordained that the Convention would produce a formal Draft Treaty. The fact that it did so is to read a sense of historical inevitability into events with the benefit of hindsight. Talk of a constitutional text featured only at the very end of the Laeken Declaration in the context of Treaty simplification. The language of the Declaration was, moreover, cautious: 'the question ultimately arises as to whether this simplification and reorganisation might not lead in the long run to the adoption of a constitutional text in the Union.'[29] It is true that in the opening ceremony Giscard d'Estaing mentioned the possibility of a Constitutional Treaty emerging from the Convention,[30] but many Member States felt that the Convention might be nothing more than a high-level talking shop, which produced recommendations.[31] There was, therefore, nothing inevitable about the Convention producing a coherent constitutional document. It was not a foregone conclusion.

The reality was that the Convention developed its own institutional momentum and vision. The idea took hold that the Convention should produce a coherent document, and that this should take the form of a Constitutional Treaty.[32] The defining 'Convention moment' when the idea that a Constitutional Treaty should

---

[26] Ibid, 37–38.

[27] CONV 52/02, Working Groups, Brussels 17 May 2002.

[28] The initial 6 groups dealt with: subsidiarity, rights, legal personality of the EU, national parliaments, competences, and implications of a single currency for closer economic cooperation. The groups established later covered external action, defence, simplification of instruments, the area of freedom, security and justice, and social Europe.

[29] Laeken European Council, 14–15 December 2001.

[30] Norman, *Accidental Constitution* (n 25) 39.

[31] Ibid, 34–35; P Norman, *From the Convention to the IGC (Institutions)* (London, Federal Trust, September 2003) 2.

[32] There was considerable uncertainty as to whether the Convention should seek to produce a Constitution or a Constitutional Treaty, Norman (n 25) 63–64.

be drafted by the Convention took hold was September 2002.[33] A paper from the Secretariat, entitled *Simplification of the Treaty and Drawing up of a Constitutional Treaty*, was central to this process.[34] The Secretariat discussed options for making the Treaties more accessible, such as Treaty simplification, codification and merger, and pointed to difficulties or limitations with such options. It then raised the possibility of drawing up a Basic Treaty, which addressed matters such as the values of the Union, citizenship, institutions, decision-making procedures, competences and the like. It thus laid the initial foundations for what was to become Part I of the Constitutional Treaty.[35]

This was followed by a plenary session on 12–13 September 2002, two days after the Report from the Secretariat.[36] The Chairman of the Convention, Giscard d'Estaing, drew together the impending reports from the working groups, with the Secretariat paper, which was to provide the foundation for the new Treaty architecture. This made it possible for the Convention to 'reflect on the form of the end product, i.e. the draft Constitutional Treaty for Europe'.[37] The plenary session at the beginning of October 2002 carried forward these initiatives.[38] The debate revealed broad consensus for the idea that there should be a single legal personality, which would supplant the legal personalities of existing bodies. This would then 'pave the way for merger of the treaties into a single text', which would consist of two parts, 'the first, fundamental part, containing provisions of a constitutional nature, and the second mainly policies'.[39]

Giscard d'Estaing presented the Preliminary Draft Constitutional Treaty to the second plenary session in October 2002.[40] Its publication[41] was an astute political move, notwithstanding the fact that there was much that was unclear or ambiguous. The Draft represented an exercise in 'outline constitutional architecture'. It was premised on the idea of a single Treaty with three parts, the first containing the constitutional principles, the second dealing with Union policies and the third with general provisions concerning ratification and the like.

Publication of the Preliminary Draft Constitutional Treaty was important 'internally', sending a message to Convention members that progress was being made towards something concrete and providing a framework for conclusions of the working groups. It was equally important 'externally' for the relationship between the Convention and key state players. As Norman states, 'publication of

---

[33] Ibid, 54–55.

[34] CONV 250/02, *Simplification of the Treaties and Drawing up of a Constitutional Treaty*, Brussels 10 September 2002.

[35] Ibid, 11–15.

[36] CONV 284/02, *Summary Report on the Plenary Session – Brussels 12 and 13 September 2002*, Brussels 17 September 2002.

[37] Ibid.

[38] CONV 331/02, *Summary Report on the Plenary Session – Brussels 3 and 4 October 2002*, Brussels 11 October 2002.

[39] Ibid, 2, 4.

[40] CONV 378/02, *Summary Report of the Plenary Session – Brussels 28 and 29 October 2002*, Brussels 31 October 2002.

[41] CONV 369/02, *Preliminary Draft Constitutional Treaty*, Brussels 28 October 2002.

the skeleton gave a palpable boost to the Convention's proceedings and structured the subsequent discussions'.[42]

The difficulty of drafting detailed Treaty articles depended very much on the subject matter. In some instances, there was a relatively clear consensus on the way forward, more especially when the topic had been thoroughly discussed in a working group. In other instances, there was greater contestability, in particular surrounding key issues concerning the inter-institutional distribution of power. These included matters such as the method of choosing the Commission President, the composition of the Commission, the Council formations, the functions of the European Council, whether there should be a longer-term President of the European Council as opposed to the rotation system, the composition of the European Parliament and its role within the legislative process, which were only formally discussed at the beginning of 2003.[43] The views of the larger Member States necessarily impacted on the internal Convention discourse. There was much high drama during this period, none more so than when Giscard d'Estaing announced the initial provisions on the Presidency of the European Council in April 2003, which 'provoked shock and awe in about equal measure, particularly among the integrationist Convention members from the European Parliament and some of the smaller Member States'.[44]

The closing stages of the Convention[45] saw the increasing centralisation of initiative to the Praesidium and the Secretariat, in part at least because the European Council refused to extend the time for the Convention deliberations, and required the Convention to present its conclusions to the European Council meeting in Greece on 20 June 2003. The tight timescale increased the centralisation of initiative to the Praesidium and the Secretariat. The centralisation of initiative was enhanced by the very limited timescale within which amendments to the draft articles could be made, which was normally a week. It was for the Praesidium to decide which amendments should be taken seriously. The tightness of the timetable did not conform to some 'ideal-type' vision of the final stages of drafting a constitution or constitutional treaty. The Convention did not, however, exist in an ideal-type world. It conducted its task against the real-world conditions laid down by the European Council.

III. European Integration: The Significance of the Constitutional Treaty

The Draft Constitutional Treaty never became law, for reasons that will be explicated below. The discussion within this section considers the significance of the

---

[42] Norman (n 25) 59.

[43] CONV 473/02, *Summary Report on the Plenary Session – Brussels 20 December 2002*, Brussels 23 December 2002; CONV 477/03, *The Functioning of the Institutions*, Brussels 10 January 2003.

[44] Norman, *From the Convention* (n 31) 3.

[45] Norman (n 25) chs 15–17.

Treaty within the overall process of integration, notwithstanding the fact that it never took legal effect.

A. The Myths

There are two myths concerning the Constitutional Treaty, the first is procedural, the second is substantive. We need to dispel both before moving forward.

i. The Procedural Myth

The procedural myth takes the following form: the Draft Constitutional Treaty was created primarily by the leading EU institutional players in Brussels and foisted on unwilling Member States, who nonetheless at the end of the day showed sufficient resolve to reject it. This story may appeal to those of Eurosceptic persuasion, but it bears no relation to reality. The Member States were central to the process that generated the Draft Constitutional Treaty. Their influence in this respect was evident in the decision to establish the Convention; in its deliberations; and in the determination as to what should happen to the Draft Treaty when it had been concluded. These will be considered in turn.

Member State influence concerning the decision to establish the Convention on the Future of Europe can be traced to the Nice Treaty. The Member States were the principal players in this round of Treaty amendment, just as they have been in other such revisions. They framed the Declaration on the Future of the European Union that was appended to the Nice Treaty, which, as we have seen, was the catalyst for the Laeken Declaration. The Member States were central to the decision to expand the remit for future Treaty deliberation from the four issues listed in the Nice Declaration, to the more ambitious agenda contained in the Laeken Declaration. This approach was promoted by Sweden and Belgium who successively held the Presidency of the European Council during 2001, and it was accepted by the Member States in the European Council. The Commission and the European Parliament were also, as we have seen, in favour of this shift. It does not, however, alter the salient fact for present purposes, which is that the Member States were central to the deliberations that led to the creation of the Convention.

The Member States were also the prime players within the Convention when the Constitutional Treaty was being drafted. The membership of the Convention was designed to enhance participation as compared to the traditional IGC, and it did so. The principal influence on the big issues was, however, that of the Member States and their representatives within the Convention. It was not fortuitous that the representatives from Member States were 'upgraded' when it became clear that the Convention really meant business, and that it would draft a real Treaty. The most potent manifestation of this was what Norman dubbed the invasion of the foreign ministers,[46] when Dominique de Villepin and Joschka Fischer joined the Convention to represent France and Germany respectively, as did the foreign ministers from some other states. It is, by way of contrast, generally accepted that the Commission punched below its weight during the Convention deliberations, and that, as will be seen below, it lost out on a number of the key battles concerning institutional issues.

The Member States within the European Council were, in addition, central to the determination as to what should happen thereafter. Giscard d'Estaing duly delivered the Draft Constitutional Treaty to the European Council in June 2003.[47] The IGC deliberations did not, however, begin in earnest until the autumn under the Italian Presidency. The Laeken Declaration provided that the Convention deliberations would be no more than the 'starting point for the discussions in the Intergovernmental Conference, which will take the ultimate decisions'.[48] This was in line with the view that the Member States hold the reins of power in grand constitutional moments. It was, nonetheless, unclear when the IGC initially convened whether it would seek to re-open the Convention's text. There were some Member States who favoured acceptance of the text as it stood, mindful of the dangers of opening Pandora's Box. However, they made it clear that if the text were re-opened then there were issues that they would place on the table for reconsideration. Other Member States were less reticent, and pressed for reconsideration of certain provisions. The latter view won the day, and the IGC proceeded to 'pick its way' through the Constitution, albeit not in any systematic manner. Institutional issues predominated, not surprisingly. The IGC made some important changes concerning the Commission, Council formations and the Council Presidency. There were in addition real difficulties concerning qualified majority voting. The Member States failed to agree on the Constitutional Treaty in the December 2003 meeting of the European Council. Ireland took over the Presidency of the European Council for the first half of 2004, and agreement on the Constitutional Treaty was secured at the Brussels European Council in June 2004.[49]

ii. The Substantive Myth

The substantive myth is somewhat more complex than its procedural kin, but it is also unfounded. The core of the substantive myth is as follows: the Draft

[46] Norman (n 31) 2; Norman (n 25) 129–33.
[47] CONV 820/03, *Draft Treaty Establishing a Constitution for Europe,* Brussels 20 June 2003; CONV 850/03, *Draft Treaty Establishing a Constitution for Europe,* Brussels 18 July 2003; this is the final version of the Convention's work, submitted in July 2003, in which some changes were made from the version submitted in June 2003.
[48] Laeken European Council, 14–15 December 2001, 5.
[49] Council of the European Union, Brussels European Council, Presidency Conclusions 10679/04, ADD 1, CONCL 2, Brussels 18 June 2004.

Constitutional Treaty was a significant step towards a more federal EU; it embodied statist ambitions for the EU, grounded in expanded EU authority over and beyond what had gone before; and this was reflected in the nomenclature of the term 'constitutional' within the Treaty. The failure of the Treaty should, on this view, be seen as indicating rejection of the preceding aspirations; its demise, therefore, signalled a turning point, such that the integration process slowed considerably thereafter. The preceding hypothesis does not withstand examination, but we need to tread carefully to understand why this is so. It is important in this respect to disaggregate two points, which are related but distinct.

The first concerns the signification of the term 'constitutional' in the nomenclature of the Draft Treaty. It can be accepted, with the benefit of hindsight, that this was not a wise move, because it raised fears in some quarters that the EU might harbour such federal-statist ambitions. It was, therefore, unsurprising that the term was dropped from the Lisbon Treaty. That having been said, there is, however, no a priori reason why the language of 'constitution' should necessarily have such a connotation. This is, in part, because organisations and institutions other than states can have a constitution as the foundational document. It is, in part, because there is nothing in the terminology of constitution that determines the division of power within a polity between the centre and its constituent parts.

The terminology of constitution is neutral between a highly federalised entity, in which power is predominantly accorded to the centre, and an entity in which states' rights are afforded prominence, with substantive and procedural checks on incursion by the federal arm of government. To put the same point in another way, an international Treaty shorn of any constitutional appellation may well accord more power to central decision-makers than a Treaty that embodies the adjectival language 'constitutional' in its title. The Constitutional Treaty did not, as will be seen below, attempt to construct a federal-statist EU. There is, moreover, nothing a priori in the language of constitution that tells one anything as to the mode of constitutional amendment. This language carries no suggestion that the power over such amendment should lie principally with the federal arm of government, to the exclusion of the states. This is attested to by the fact that the existing mode of Treaty amendment in Articles 48–49 TEU was taken over directly from Articles IV-443–444 CT, and embodies a procedure in which Member States exercise control at various stages of the process.

The second reason why the preceding hypothesis is mistaken is that it is not borne out by the provisions of the Constitutional Treaty. It did not contain far-reaching new powers of a kind designed to transform the EU into some kind of super-state. To the contrary, there was relatively little new in terms of substantive heads of competence accorded to the EU by the Constitutional Treaty. The SEA 1986 and the Maastricht Treaty were both far more significant in this respect. Moreover, many institutional provisions of the Constitutional Treaty bolstered state rights, or were designed to do so, such as the revised provisions on subsidiarity.

This is further exemplified by the Convention debates and outcome concerning the locus of EU executive power.[50] A prominent version of the 'single hat' view was that there should be one President for the Union as a whole; the office of President should be connected formally and substantively with the locus of executive power within the Union; and the President of the Commission should hold this office. The Presidency of the European Council should continue to rotate on a six-monthly basis. The real 'head' of the Union would be the President of the Commission, whose legitimacy, it was hoped, would be increased by election. A prominent version of the 'separate hats' view was that there should be a President of the Commission and a President of the European Council, and that executive power would be exercised by both. It was central to this view that the Presidency of the European Council would be strengthened. It would no longer rotate between states on a six-monthly basis. It was felt that this would not work in an enlarged Union, and that greater continuity of policy would be required. This view was advocated by a number of the larger states, but was opposed by some of the smaller states, which felt that the Presidency of the European Council would be dominated by the larger Member States. The 'separate hats' view won out, as reflected in the creation of the long-term Presidency of the European Council, held successively by Herbert van Rompuy and Donald Tusk.

The preservation of state power was evident once again in the debates and outcome concerning choice of the Commission President. The Commission proposed that its President should be elected by the European Parliament, subject to approval by the European Council.[51] It also recommended that other members of the Commission should be designated by the Council, acting by qualified majority in agreement with the Commission President, subject to approval of the full College of Commissioners by the European Parliament. The Member States were, unsurprisingly, not willing to surrender power over these issues. They were not willing for just any candidate to be considered for the post, and desired greater control over appointment of the Commission President than the mere approval that was embodied in the Commission proposal. The 'solution' in the Constitutional Treaty[52] was carried over directly into the Lisbon Treaty. Thus Article 14(1) TEU duly states that the European Parliament shall elect the President of the Commission. The retention of state power is, however, apparent in Article 17(7) TEU. The European Council, acting by qualified majority, after appropriate consultation,[53] and taking account of the elections to the European

---

[50] P Craig, *The Lisbon Treaty, Law, Politics and Treaty Reform* (Oxford, Oxford University Press, 2010) ch 3.

[51] CONV 448/02, For the European Union Peace, Freedom, Solidarity – Communication from the Commission on the Institutional Architecture, 5 December 2002, [2.3]; Peace, Freedom and Solidarity, COM(2002) 728 final.

[52] Arts I-20(1), 27(1) CT.

[53] Declaration 11 LT emphasises consultation between the European Council and European Parliament preceding choice of the candidate for Commission President.

Parliament, puts forward to the European Parliament the European Council's candidate for Presidency of the Commission. This candidate is then elected by the European Parliament by a majority of its members. If the candidate does not get the requisite majority support, then the European Council puts forward a new candidate within one month, following the same procedure. The result was, therefore, that the Commission President was indirectly-indirectly elected.[54]

The final version of the Constitutional Treaty also saw the ratcheting up of state control over appointment of the other Commissioners. The Convention proposed that the President-elect of the Commission would choose Commissioners from a list of three names put forward by each Member State, and that these would be approved by the European Parliament.[55] The President of the Commission would, therefore, be in the driving seat as to choice of other Commissioners, subject to approval by the European Parliament. This was modified by the IGC in December 2003, and the modified version of the CT was incorporated into the Lisbon Treaty. Member States make suggestions for Commissioners, but it is now the Council, by common accord with the President-elect of the Commission, that adopts the list of those who are to be Commissioners. The body of Commissioners is then subject to a vote of approval by the European Parliament. However, the formal appointment of the Commission is made by the European Council, acting by qualified majority, albeit on the basis of the approval given by the European Parliament.[56]

The provisions on competence in the Constitutional Treaty, which have been taken into the Lisbon Treaty, were also designed, inter alia, to provide a clearer delineation of the boundary of EU power than hitherto. The Laeken Declaration[57] specified in greater detail the nature of the inquiry into competence that had been left open after the Nice Treaty 2000. There were four more particular issues addressed under the heading of 'a better of division and definition of competence in the European Union'. These were the need to make the division of competence clearer and more transparent; the need to ensure that the Union had the powers required to perform the tasks conferred on it by the Member States; the need to ensure that there was not a 'creeping expansion' of EU competence, or its encroachment on areas left exclusively to the Member States; and the desirability of considering whether there should be some re-organisation of competence between the EU and the Member States. There were then four principal forces driving the reform process: clarity, conferral, containment and consideration. There was, however, little systematic rethinking of the areas in which the EU should be

---

[54] The reality after the last round of EP elections is that the European Council accepted that the candidate supported by the political grouping that secures the majority of seats in the EP will be accepted as the President of the Commission. This does not, however, alter the point made in the text, which is that the provisions in the Constitutional Treaty were framed so as to preserve state power over this issue.

[55] Art I-26(2) Draft CT.

[56] Art 17(7) TEU.

[57] European Council, 14–15 December 2001, 21–22.

able to act. The Convention on the Future of Europe did not conduct any root and branch reconsideration of all heads of EU competence.[58] Nor would this realistically have been possible within the time available. The emphasis was on clarity, conferral and containment. There is room for difference of opinion as to how far these objectives were achieved, and there are still concerns as to over-liberal use of Article 114 TFEU. This is not the place to engage with such debates. Suffice it to say for present purposes that the categorisation of competence, coupled with articulation of the legal consequences that flowed from each head of competence, did constitute improvement in terms of clarity, conferral and containment from the Treaty regime hitherto.

B. The Reality

i. *Legal Integration: Failure and Response*

The final version of the Constitutional Treaty[59] had to be ratified in accordance with the constitutional requirements or choices of each Member State. It was generally thought that problems with ratification would be most pronounced in the UK, but this was never tested because progress with ratification came to an abrupt halt when France and the Netherlands rejected the Constitutional Treaty in their referendums in 2005. A number of Member States therefore postponed the ratification process. The European Council in 2005 decided that discretion was the better part of valour, and that it was best for there to be a time for 'reflection', during which Member States were encouraged to engage in debate about the EU with their own citizens.

The negative referendums in France and the Netherlands, coupled with the period of reflection, generated discourse as to whether it was wise for the EU ever to have embarked on this ambitious constitutional project. This was reflected in the jibe 'if it ain't broke, why fix it?'[60] It was argued that grand constitutional schemes of the kind embodied in the Constitutional Treaty were unnecessary, because the EU could function perfectly well on the basis of the Nice Treaty, and dangerous, because the very construction of such a constitutional document would bring to the fore contentious issues concerning matters such as the range of EU competences,

---

[58] Economic governance was one of the limited substantive areas where the Convention did take stock of the limits of existing EU powers, and the desirability of reinforcing them so as to enable the EU to be able to perform its tasks properly within this area, CONV 357/02, Brussels 21 October 2002.

[59] Treaty Establishing a Constitution for Europe [2004] OJ C316/1; J Ziller, *La nouvelle Constitution europeene* (Paris, La Découverte, 2005); J-C Piris, *The Constitution for Europe: A Legal Analysis* (Cambridge, Cambridge University Press, 2006); O de Schutter and P Nihoul, *Une Constitution pour l'Europe: reflexions sur les transformations du droit de l'Union europeene* (Brussels, Larcier, 2004).

[60] A Moravcsik, 'Europe without Illusions: A Category Error' (2005) 112 *Prospect*; L Siedentop, 'A Crisis of Legitimacy' (2005) 112 *Prospect*.

the supremacy of EU law over national law and the inter-institutional division of power, which were best resolved through less formal mechanisms, as opposed to hard-edged constitutional provisions that invited high-profile constitutional controversy. There is force in this view. There is, nonetheless, a different interpretation of what had transpired. There are four salient factors to be borne in mind in this regard.

First, the reasons for rejection of the Constitutional Treaty in France and the Netherlands were eclectic and different, but they shared a common feature, which was that they had scant, if anything, to do with any novelty introduced by the Constitutional Treaty, nor were they principally motivated by the constitutional appellation attached to the Treaty.[61] We can never know what the outcome would have been if referendums had been held on a Treaty amendment in 2004 that was limited to the four issues left over from the Nice Treaty. We can also never know what the outcome would have been if the referendums had been held on a Treaty amendment that did not contain the word 'constitutional' in the title, but there is scant evidence to suggest that it would have been different. There is, thus, no reason to think that the discontent that drove the negative response to the Constitutional Treaty would have been markedly different if the title thereof had been different.

Secondly, it should, moreover, be recognised that the four issues left over from the Nice Treaty were not discrete. They raised, both directly and indirectly, broader issues concerning the nature of the EU, its powers, mode of decision-making and relationship with the Member States and their parliaments. The dissatisfaction with piecemeal IGC Treaty reform, monopolised by the Member States, should not be forgotten. If this traditional process had been adhered to in relation to the broadened reform agenda there would have been a raft of criticism about the 'legitimacy and representativeness deficit' inherent in the classic IGC model.

Thirdly, the Community had existed for more than 40 years, and expanded from six to 15 Member States, with impending accession of a further 10 states in 2004. Its competence had grown piecemeal through successive Treaty amendments. Those very Treaty changes occurred with increasing frequency, the normal result being interstitial modification of the status quo ante. Viewed from this perspective, the idea that took hold in 2001, and which came to fruition in the Laeken Declaration, that there should be more considered reflection of the nature of the Community project, the powers of its institutions, and the relationship between the Community and its Member States, was readily explicable politically and warranted in more normative terms, more especially because of the preceding point, *viz* that the four issues delineated in the Nice Treaty for future elaboration were not really discrete.

---

[61] R Dehousse, 'The Unmaking of a Constitution: Lessons from the European Referenda' (2006) 13 *Constellations* 151; G de Burca, 'The European Constitution Project after the Referenda' (2006) 13 *Constellations* 205.

Fourthly, critique as to the way in which the Convention operated should be kept in perspective. Thus some cast doubt on its participatory credentials, pointing to the increasing centralisation of initiative in the Praesidium, especially in the latter stages of the Convention, which left scant time for deliberation of amendments. This was problematic and did not conform to some 'ideal-type' vision of drafting a constitution. The Convention did not, however, exist in an ideal-type world. It conducted its task against the real-world conditions laid down by the European Council. When the European Council reaffirmed the deadline, the Praesidium had little choice but to take a more proactive role, since otherwise the Constitutional Treaty would not have been presented to the European Council in June 2003. The absence of the strict deadline would, moreover, still have required 'someone' to have been proactive in deciding which amendments should be pursued.

ii. Legal Integration: Status and Substance

The Constitutional Treaty was never ratified, for the reasons considered in the previous section. It would, nonetheless, be wrong to dismiss it as being of scant importance in the development of EU integration. The reason is readily apparent: the Constitutional Treaty never attained legally binding status, but its substance lives on through the Lisbon Treaty.

In 2006, the European Council commissioned Germany, which held the Presidency of the European Council in the first half of 2007, to assess and report on the current state of discussion concerning the Constitutional Treaty. The German Presidency sought agreement in the European Council in June 2007[62] on the outlines for a revised version of the Constitutional Treaty, which led to the birth of the Reform Treaty. An IGC was convened. It was agreed to excise the 'C' word, constitution, from the Reform Treaty. This was also the approach taken for other problematic terms, such as 'Union Minister for Foreign Affairs', and 'law' and 'framework law'. There were some detailed modifications of provisions concerning competences, the Common Foreign and Security Policy, the enhanced role of national parliaments, the Charter of Fundamental Rights and the area of freedom, security and justice.

This did not, however, mask the fact that the great majority of the changes introduced by the Constitutional Treaty looked set to remain within the Reform Treaty, renamed as the Lisbon Treaty. The issues had been debated in detail in the Convention on the Future of Europe after a relatively open discourse, and were considered once again in the IGC in 2004. There was, therefore, little appetite for those engaged in the 2007 IGC to re-open Pandora's Box. The Lisbon Treaty was

---

[62] Brussels European Council, 21–22 June 2007.

signed by the Member States on 13 December 2007,[63] and duly came into effect after ratification by all Member States. The legal reality is that almost everything novel in the Lisbon Treaty was taken over from the Constitutional Treaty, in most instances with little, if any, change from the 2004 provisions.

There was, however, some difference in the structuring of the material. The Lisbon Treaty is predicated on the divide between the TEU and the TFEU, with the Charter of Rights accorded the same status as the two constituent Treaties. The Constitutional Treaty had, however, a more elegant architecture. Part I of the Constitutional Treaty contained the key principles governing the EU, whereas these are now divided between the TEU and TFEU in the Lisbon Treaty. Part II of the Constitutional Treaty was the Charter of Rights, which was a clear and simple way of including it within the overall Treaty, as compared to the method chosen in the Lisbon Treaty.

IV. European Integration: Present Challenges

The legal and political reality is that European integration did not stop in 2004–05, with the demise of the Draft Constitutional Treaty, nor did it end with the Lisbon Treaty, which was constructed using building blocks taken from the Constitutional Treaty. The EU has, however, faced significant challenges in the last decade: the financial crisis, the migration crisis and the rule of law crisis. There is, moreover, the challenge posed by Brexit. These crises have tested the EU's resilience and continue to do so. There is no connection between these crises and the demise of the Constitutional Treaty. There is, by way of contrast, a connection between these crises and the development of EU integration.

This is not the place to investigate in detail the preceding crises, or the challenge posed by Brexit. These are complex topics, which warrant article or book-length treatment in their own right. Suffice it to say the following. The impact of each challenge on the overall process of EU integration needs to be carefully assessed. The fact there are three crises does not mean that the short-, medium- or long-term effects on European integration will be the same in each instance. This can be briefly exemplified in the following manner.

The immediate impact of the financial crisis was very destabilising for the EU, with doubts as to whether the Euro would survive, and doubts also as to the stability of the EU as a consequence of the economic fallout if the Euro failed. The EU weathered this storm, for the present at least, and it has in certain respects increased integration, largely achieved within the framework of the Lisbon Treaty, as attested to by the enactment of a plethora of measures designed to increase

---

[63] Conference of the Representatives of the Governments of the Member States, Treaty of Lisbon Amending the Treaty on European Union and the Treaty Establishing the European Community, CIG 14/07, Brussels 3 December 2007, [2007] OJ C306/1.

centralised control over fiscal policy. The six-pack[64] and the two-pack,[65] rather than the Fiscal Compact, provide the legal framework for enhanced EU supervision over national budgetary and fiscal policy. There are significant political, legal and economic issues flowing from this legislation, as attested to by the large body of literature devoted to the topic. There are, however, two salient points for present purposes. In process terms, the EU managed to enact this complex body of legislation expeditiously; there was no legislative sclerosis in the face of the economic storm. In substantive terms, there was general consensus that the Maastricht blueprint for economic and monetary union was flawed, and that if monetary union was to survive there would have to be greater EU controls over national fiscal policy than hitherto; in this sense the financial crisis has been the catalyst for increased EU integration.

This can be contrasted with the impact of the rule of law crisis.[66] The concerns raised by governmental behaviour in Hungary, Romania and Poland have not threatened the EU's survival in the immediate way that did the financial crisis. The medium- and long-term effects on European integration may, however, be greater, and are negative, not positive. Governmental behaviour in these countries cast into sharp relief the perceived need for the EU to be seen to be doing something about the problem. There were, however, concerns about using the

---

[64] Regulation (EU) No 1175/2011 of the European Parliament and of the Council of 16 November 2011 amending Regulation (EC) No 1466/97 on the strengthening of the surveillance of budgetary positions and the surveillance and coordination of economic policies [2011] OJ L306/12; Council Regulation (EU) No 1177/2011 of 8 November 2011 amending Regulation (EC) No 1467/97 on speeding up and clarifying the implementation of the excessive deficit procedure [2011] OJ L306/33; Regulation (EU) No 1173/2011 of the European Parliament and of the Council of 16 November 2011 on the effective enforcement of budgetary surveillance in the euro area [2011] OJ L306/1; Council Directive 2011/85/EU of 8 November 2011 on requirements for budgetary frameworks of the Member States [2011] OJ L306/41; Regulation (EU) No 1176/2011 of the European Parliament and of the Council of 16 November 2011 on the prevention and correction of macroeconomic imbalances [2011] OJ L306/25; Regulation (EU) No 1174/2011 of the European Parliament and of the Council of 16 November 2011 on enforcement measures to correct macroeconomic imbalances in the euro area [2011] OJ L306/8; Results of in-depth reviews under Regulation (EU) No 1176/2011 on the prevention and correction of macroeconomic imbalances, COM(2013) 199 final.

[65] Regulation (EU) 472/2013 of the European Parliament and of the Council of 21 May 2013 on the strengthening of economic and budgetary surveillance of Member States experiencing or threatened with serious difficulties with respect to their financial stability in the euro area [2013] OJ L140/1; Regulation (EU) 473/2013 of the European Parliament and of the Council of 21 May 2013 on common provisions for monitoring and assessing draft budgetary plans and ensuring the correction of excessive deficit of the Member States in the euro area [2013] OJ L140/11.

[66] A von Bogdandy, M Kottmann, C Antpöhler, J Dickschen, S Hentrei, M Smrkolj, 'Reverse Solange–Protecting the essence of fundamental rights against EU Member States' (2012) 49 *Common Market Law Review* 489; I Canor, 'My Brother's Keeper? Horizontal *Solange*: "An Ever Closer *Distrust* among the Peoples of Europe"' (2013) 50 *Common Market Law Review* 383; A von Bogdandy and P Sonnevend (eds), *Constitutional Crisis in the European Constitutional Area: Theory, Law and Politics in Hungary and Romania* (Oxford, Hart, 2015); D Kochenov and L Pech, 'Monitoring and Enforcement of the Rule of Law in the EU: Rhetoric and Reality' (2015) 11 *European Constitutional Law Review* 512; J.-W. Müller, 'Should the European Union Protect Democracy and the Rule of Law in Its Member States' (2015) 21 *European Law Journal* 141; D Kochenov, 'EU Law without the Rule of Law: Is the Veneration of Autonomy Worth It?' (2015) *Yearbook of European Law*; A Jakab and D Kochenov (eds),

nuclear strike weapon in Article 7 TEU, and concerns also about whether the requisite votes could be mustered to do so, given that the article was drafted on the implicit assumption that there would only be one 'bad guy' at any one point in time, an assumption that was belied by the facts. This was the rationale, in part, for the Commission's 2014 paper, which set out a new framework to strengthen the rule of law.[67] It was central to Commission strategy that compliance with the rule of law was a prerequisite for the protection of all fundamental values listed in Article 2 TEU; that such compliance was also a precondition more generally for upholding all rights and obligations derived from the Treaties and from international law; and that it was, more specifically, required to ensure the mutual trust on which the area of freedom, security and justice was grounded. The most efficacious method to deal with the problems continues to divide commentators. The apposite point for present purposes is that the longer that such problems persist, the more do they sap the energy of the EU, and the process of EU integration. This problem is, moreover, exacerbated by the fact that the particular problems in Hungary and Poland are symptomatic of a more general current of thought by the governing party in those countries, which is antithetical to many of the values on which the EU is based.

The challenge posed by Brexit and its impact on the process of European integration is different yet again. The true nature of that impact may not be known for some time. It is, from one perspective, clearly harmful to the integration process. The very realisation that a state might choose to leave, because dissatisfied with life in the EU, necessarily carries serious negative implications, including, although not restricted to, the possibility that it might generate similar demands in other countries. To be balanced against this is the fact that the immediate impact of the Brexit vote was to increase pro-European sentiment in other Member States, and to enhance the unity among the other 27 states when engaging in the Brexit negotiations. How long these sentiments persist post-Brexit remains to be seen. The effect of Brexit on EU integration will, in addition, be affected by the content of the withdrawal agreement, and the subsequent trade deal, which will serve as stark signals for any other state minded to emulate the UK.

The Enforcement of EU Law and Values: Methods against Defiance (Oxford, Oxford University Press, 2016); S Carrera, E Guild and N Hernanz, *The Triangular Relationship between Fundamental Rights, Democracy and the Rule of Law in the EU, Towards an EU Copenhagen Mechanism*, CEPS 2013, available at www.ceps.eu/system/files/Fundamental%20Rights%20DemocracyandRoL.pdf, www.europarl.europa.eu/RegData/etudes/etudes/join/2013/493031/IPOL-LIBE_ET%282013%29493031_EN.pdf, 4–15; C Closa and D Kochenov (eds), *Reinforcing the Rule of Law Oversight in the European Union* (Cambridge, Cambridge University Press, 2016).

[67] Commission Communication on Article 7 of the Treaty on European Union – Respect for and promotion of the values on which the Union is based, COM(2003) 606 final, 4–5.

V. Conclusion

There will be no attempt to summarise the entirety of the preceding argument. Suffice it to say the following. The Constitutional Treaty was but one staging post in the EU's history. It failed to secure ratification in some Member States, providing potent evidence that if you decide to let this reside with the people, then you have to accept that the decision may be motivated by considerations other than those felt to be central by the framers of the Treaty. The lesson from Chirac's failure to secure assent to the Constitutional Treaty was not lost on Sarkozy, who secured French ratification of the Lisbon Treaty without a further referendum. The decade of Treaty revision that began after the Nice Treaty was then concluded with the Lisbon Treaty, in which almost everything new came from the Constitutional Treaty. The hope that the EU, and the integration process, could proceed relatively smoothly on the basis of the new Treaty provisions proved, however, to be short-lived. The real world has the knack of generating exogenous or endogenous shocks that can profoundly shake the system, as transpired with the financial, migration and rule of law crises, and with Brexit.

6

The European Constitution and Europe's Dialectical Federalism

ERIN F DELANEY*

I. Introduction

The European integration project has been an engine of neologisms and a destroyer of definitions. Is Europe's mode of integration federalist? Functionalist? Neofunctionalist? Intergovernmental? Liberal-intergovernmental? Institutionalist? Is the integrative result a system of governance, a regime, a polity, an entity? Is it federal, confederal, federalist, supranational, international, *sui generis*? Integration theory asks these questions and more, seeking to explain, to analyse, and even to prescribe.[1] This chapter focuses on one particular theory of integration – federalism – and asks how the experience of the European Constitution has complicated our understanding of federalism as integration theory.

To take on this challenge, it is necessary to begin with some caveats and definitions. 'Federalism' as a theory of integration is contested on both descriptive and normative grounds. I do not aim in this chapter to defend federalism as either the best or the preferred way of understanding European integration. But it is undeniable that the federal idea has had tremendous relevance to the evolution of the European experiment.[2] And, given that the call for a 'United States of Europe' re-emerged in late 2017 as a political talking point in Germany,[3] the rhetoric of federalism remains an important strand in European discourse. Thus, for purposes

* In addition to the editors of this book and the participants at the conference from which it derived, I would also like to thank Mathilde Cohen, Peter DiCola and Peter Lindseth for their helpful comments. Mike Gajewsky and Kirsten Lee provided excellent research assistance. In 2003 and 2004, I was employed as a Research Officer on The European Constitution Project at The Federal Trust.

[1] For a brief overview, see T Diez and A Wiener, 'Introducing the Mosaic of Integration Theory' in A Wiener and T Diez (eds), *European Integration Theory* (Oxford, Oxford University Press, 2004).

[2] See generally D Sidjanski, *L'avenir fédéraliste de L'Europe* (Paris, Presses Universitaries de France, 1992); M Burgess, *Federalism and European Union: The Building of Europe, 1950–2000* (London, Routledge, 2000); M Burgess, 'Federalism' in Diez and Wiener, *European Integration Theory* (n 1) 2–43.

[3] Martin Schulz, Leader of the German Social Democratic Party (Party Conference Speech, 7 December 2017).

of this chapter, I accept *arguendo* the viability of federalism as integration theory, and ask how the European Convention and the resulting Constitution have challenged or shifted the theory and mechanisms of federal integration.

Even for those normatively committed to federalism as the method of organising Europe, the term contains a multiplicity of meanings. Scholars have described federalism as an ideology and a process: a 'philosophy of political life'[4] that supports the evoluative integration of 'territorial communities that previously had not been directly joined'.[5] Others see federalism as a theory with a destination – *federation*: 'a constitutional federal system and its institutions',[6] or a 'descriptive, institutional arrangement of fact'.[7] Michael Burgess has helpfully synthesised these viewpoints, arguing that federalism is in 'essentially a symbiotic relationship' with federation.[8] As a process, federalism is 'an organising concept' that encompasses 'the recommendation and (sometimes) the active promotion of support for federations'.[9] When put into the context of the European Union, Burgess' view is contested: the idea that federation should be the ultimate end-point of European integration is certainly not shared by all federalists.[10] In this chapter, however, I restrict my analysis to that strain of federal theory that comports with Burgess' definition: federalism that seeks federation.

And what does European *federation* itself mean, in this construct? Facing yet another word with its own phalanx of definitions and infinite variety of forms,[11] I propose some minimum elements based on general federal theory. This aspirational federation would presuppose a European *demos*, with democratically elected institutions and the robust protection of individual rights.[12] In addition, and at a

---

[4] PJ Proudhon, *The Principle of Federation* (1863), R Vernon trans (Toronto, University of Toronto Press, 1979) xii.

[5] I Duchacek, *Comparative Federalism: The Territorial Dimension of Politics* (New York, Holt, Reinhart and Winston, Inc, 1970) 189; see generally K Lenaerts, 'Constitutionalism and the Many Faces of Federalism' (1990) 38 *American Journal of Comparative Law* 206.

[6] Duchacek, *Comparative Federalism* (n 5) 189.

[7] P King, *Federalism and Federation* (London, Croom Helm, 1982) 21 (advocating the distinction between federation and federalism).

[8] Burgess, *Federalism and European Union* (n 2) 26.

[9] Ibid, 27. See S Mogi, *The Problem of Federalism* (London, George Allen & Unwin, Ltd., 1931) (describing federalism as both a political theory and a political technique).

[10] Kalypso Nicolaïdis has eloquently called for federalism beyond the state (or beyond 'federation'): a federal vision that dispenses with such 'ideal types' and encompasses a system of nation states and the multiple *demoi* that make up Europe. See, eg, K Nicolaïdis, 'Conclusion: The Federal Vision Beyond the Federal State' in K Nicolaïdis and R Howse (eds), *The Federal Vision* (Oxford, Oxford University Press, 2001) 443–84.

[11] TO Hueglin, 'Comparing Federalism: Variations or Distinct Models?' in A Benz and J Broschek (eds), *Federal Dynamics: Continuity, Change, and the Varieties of Federalism* (Oxford, Oxford University Press, 2013) 27–47.

[12] Some scholars argue that the difficulty of constructing a cohesive European *demos* would (and should) prevent a federation from emerging; they advocate instead for other institutional constructs that would recognise and privilege Europe's many *demoi*. See generally K Nicolaïdis, 'Our European Demoi-cracy' in K Nicolaïdis and S Weatherill (eds), *Whose Europe? National Models and the Constitution of the European Union* (Oxford, Oxford University Press, 2003) 137–52; R Bellamy, '"An Ever Closer Union Among the Peoples of Europe": Republican Intergovernmentalism and *Demoi*cratic Representation within the EU' (2013) 35 *Journal of European Integration* 499.

high level of generality, a European federation would have legal primacy and the authority to legislate in substantive policy areas with direct impact (and legislative effect) on individuals.[13] Ultimately, it would have to have the 'autonomous capacity to mobilise fiscal and human resources' in a legitimate and compulsory fashion.[14] And thus, federation is intertwined with constitutionalism: the goals of federal institutional development and rights protection, as well as limitations on the delineations of centralised power to ensure some authority remains with the Member States, require codified agreement and enforcement.[15]

Those committed to realising this robust version of a federal *finalité politique* of Europe have been long divided on the appropriate means for achieving the goal. The politics of federal integration have oscillated between competing logics of federalisation, reflecting some of the underlying tensions within the theory of federalism itself. Federalisation as a *process* privileges incremental integrative steps to achieve a functional weaving together of disparate territories; the ultimate federation (and concomitant constitutionalism) are byproducts. By contrast, federalisation as *compact* promotes immediate federation through formal constitutional negotiations, conducted in a constitutional convention and agreed upon by the *pouvoir constituant*.

Against this backdrop, and as a theory of integration, federalism can be understood as an unresolved dialectic between step-by-step incremental federalism and convention-based compact federalism. And the Convention on the Future of Europe and the proposed European Constitution highlight both the mutually reinforcing and destabilising elements of this dialectic. The Convention on the Future of Europe was both a fulfilment of and a rupture with federal European integration history – it exemplified the expression of formal federalisation through a constitution-drafting process even as it denied the continued relevance of incrementalism.

I argue below that despite early claims (or hopes) to the contrary, incremental federalism alone cannot achieve its federalising goals, which eventually must be realised through a convention-based 'Big C'-constitutional end game.[16] And thus, although its particular timing might not have been predicted, the calling for

---

[13] See NW Barber, 'The Two Europes' in this volume; G Sawer, *Modern Federalism* (London, C.A. Watts & Co, Ltd, 1969), 1–2. *cf* A Hamilton and J Madison, 'Federalist Paper No 20' *The New York Packet* (New York, 11 December 1787).

[14] P Lindseth, 'The Metabolic Constitution: Legitimate Compulsory Mobilisation and the Limits of EU Legal Pluralism' in G Davis and M Avbelj (eds), *Research Handbook in Legal Pluralism in EU Law* (Elgar, forthcoming). *cf* D Halberstam, 'Joseph Weiler, Eric Stein, and the Transformation of Constitutional Law' in MP Maduro and M Wind (eds), *The Transformation of Europe* (Cambridge, Cambridge University Press, 2017) 223–24 (defining a 'constitutional' vision of Europe as encompassing a 'generative space' ... 'that political and legal decisions can be generated at the European level in the first instance').

[15] *cf* AV Dicey, *Introduction to the Study of the Law of the Constitution*, 7th edn (London, Macmillan & Co, 1908); AV Dicey, *England's Case Against Home Rule* viii, 3rd edn (London, John Murray, 1887).

[16] See N Walker, 'Big "C" or Small "c"?' (2006) 12 *European Law Journal* 12, 12–14 (reconsidering whether a formal, convention-based constitutional process (big 'C' constitutionalism) is preferable to incremental structural change (small 'c' constitutionalism) for the EU).

a Convention on the Future of Europe should be viewed as the inevitable result of step-by-step federalisation. At the same time, however, the formal federalising aspirations of *conventionnels* were in many ways thwarted by the work that incremental federalism had accomplished. Constitution-writing could not occur on a blank slate, necessarily limiting the federal scope of the finished product. The inclusion of a formal exit right in a withdrawal clause serves as an example of the Convention's inability to transcend history and reconcile embedded and divergent views. Notwithstanding the Constitution's failure, step-by-step federalism might well re-emerge as a method of integration – perhaps, and ironically, facilitated by the withdrawal clause itself (now incorporated as Article 50 in the Lisbon Treaty). If this happens, given incrementalism's limitations, there may be another constitutional convention in Europe's future.

II. The Dialectical Tension

It is possible to identify and trace both the formal compact-based and incrementalist approaches to federalisation, though their histories have not been linear. Albeit brief, the following schematic approach to European integration history highlights the areas of overlap and tension in these competing federalising mechanisms.

The formal approach to federalisation – the writing of a 'Big-C'-constitution delineating the institutions and divided powers of a federation – has the older provenance in the European story. In an exhaustive survey, Walter Lipgens documented the pre-war, wartime, and post-war history of the federalist movement, producing four volumes of evidence of the great surge of federalist feeling inspired by World War II.[17] The majority of this extensive documentation details the efforts of the early federalists to produce a constitution or 'grand bargain' solution to ensure ongoing European peace.[18] As Jürgen Habermas has written, these 'first-generation advocates … did not hesitate to speak of the project they had in mind as a "United States of Europe".[19]

As early as 1941, Altiero Spinelli wrote the Ventotene Manifesto, advocating for the federal reorganisation of Europe.[20] And in 1944, a diverse group of resistance

---

[17] The actual influence of these early federalists on European integration has been hotly contested, most famously by Alan Milward. For a discussion of the Lipgens-Milward dynamic, see W Loth, 'Integrating Paradigms: Walter Lipgens and Alan Milward as Pioneers of European Integration History' in F Guiral, FMB Lynch and SM Ramírez Pérez (eds), *Alan S Milward and a Century of European Change* (New York, Routledge, 2012) 255–67.

[18] See generally W Lipgens, *Documents on the History of European Integration* 4 vols (Berlin, Walter de Gruyter, 1985).

[19] J Habermas, 'Why Europe Needs a Constitution' (2001) 11 *New Left Review* 5, 5. As just one example, Paul-Henri Spaak, writing in 1951, remarked: 'Let us have the courage and the audacity to do, today, in Europe, what the Americans had the audacity and the courage to do in the second half of the eighteenth century, and our problems are solved.' As quoted in PF Smets, *La Pensée Européenne et Atlantique de Paul-Henri Spaak (1942–1972)* (Brussels, Goemaere, 1982) 261.

[20] P Stirk and D Weigall, *The Origins and Development of European Integration* (London, Pinter, 1999) Document 1.11.

fighters met near Geneva and issued a declaration calling for fellow Europeans 'to surrender full national sovereignty in favour of a single federal union'.[21] By 1948, in the final resolution of the Hague Conference creating the Council of Europe, delegates recommended 'the setting of a "Union or Federation," … "to transfer some of their sovereign rights in order henceforth to exercise them jointly"'.[22] This 'tide against nationalism' demanded a fundamental rethinking of sovereignty, prioritising grand bargain constitutionalism and a formal compact.[23] But the failure to launch a Federal Pact in the 1949–50 meeting of the Council of Europe dispelled any momentum these federalists had gained.[24]

Rather than approaching federalisation through all-encompassing grand bargain constitutionalism, the founders of what would become the European Union chose to address the issue incrementally. Incrementalism held out the possibility of putting the formal elements of federation into place over time. In his memoirs, Jean Monnet includes excerpts from the first draft of the Schuman Declaration, which he claims demonstrated most clearly what he wished to accomplish.[25] In his account, the draft began with the assertion that 'Europe must be organised on a federal basis', and ended with the clear summation of the proposal's aim: 'To make a breach in the ramparts of national sovereignty which will be narrow enough to secure consent, but deep enough to open the way towards the unity that is essential to peace.'[26] And although the final wording and tone of the Declaration was moderated, the European Coal and Steel Community (ECSC) was still presented 'as the first echelon of a European federation',[27] embodying an 'almost mystical immanent federalism'.[28]

What became known as the 'Monnet method' was 'a "series of transitional steps"'.[29] It was an approach to federalisation that prioritised 'a piecemeal,

---

[21] M Guibernau, 'The Birth of a United Europe: On Why the EU has Generated a "Non-Emotional" Identity' (2011) 17 *Nations and Nationalism* 302, 304.

[22] P Gerbet, 'The Origins: Early Attempts and the Emergence of the Six (1945–1952)' in R Pryce (ed), *The Dynamics of European Union* (London, Routledge, 1987) 40.

[23] Guibernau, 'Birth of a United Europe' (n 21) 304.

[24] See generally J Pinder, 'The Influence of European Federalists in the 1950s' in TB Olesen (ed), *Interdependence Versus Integration: Denmark, Scandinavia and Western Europe 1945–1960* (Odense, Odense University Press, 1995); Gerbet, 'The Origins' (n 22).

[25] The federalist influence of Jean Monnet has been detailed by numerous authors, not least by Monnet himself. See generally J Monnet, *Mémoires* (Paris, Fayard, 1976); R Mayne, J Pinder and JCdeV Roberts, *Federal Union: The Pioneers* (London, Macmillan for the Federal Trust, 1990); F Dûchene, *Jean Monnet* (New York, W. W. Norton & Co, 1994).

[26] J Monnet, *Memoirs*, R Mayne trans (New York, Doubleday, 1978) 295–96.

[27] HL Mason, *The European Coal and Steel Community: Experiment in Supranationalism* (The Hague, Martinus Nijhoff, 1955) 123. Note there was still hope for the constitutionalist movement with the development of the European Political Community. When that effort failed in 1954, the movement was effectively stifled for the next 30 years.

[28] W Diebold Jr, *The Schuman Plan: A Study in Economic Cooperation 1950–1959* (New York, Frederick A Praeger, 1959) 598 fn 5. Walter Hallstein described the ECSC as a first stage which, 'in its constitution-type structures, already intentionally anticipates the structure of the future, complete European federation'. W Hallstein, Lecture, (Georgetown University, 13 March 1953), as quoted in Pinder, 'European Federalists' (n 24) 233. See also W Hallstein, *Europe in the Making*, C Roetter trans (London, George Allen & Unwin, 1972).

[29] Pinder (n 24) 213.

incremental construction ... [and] at some undefined point in the future, the door to federation would open. There was neither deadline nor specific timetable for this shift from functionalism to constitutionalism (the building of political Europe)'.[30] As Monnet himself explained, '[w]e believed in starting with limited achievements, establishing de facto solidarity, from which a federation would gradually emerge'.[31] Or, as German jurist Hermann Mosler elaborated, when integration reached

> such a degree that breaking it up would be as difficult as dismembering a state, at that moment the transition to a ... European [federal] constitution would have taken place, even if the organisation were to exercise only a part of governmental functions.[32]

Thus, as Michael Burgess has written, Monnet's 'federal Europe would not be the launching pad – the point of departure – for European integration. Rather, it would be something that constituted the *finalité politique*'.[33]

Whether the Monnet method could deliver a fully formed federation was unclear.[34] Incrementalism made this aspirational goal 'contingent upon the cumulative effect of functional achievements'.[35] And many of these results were detached from the core goals of federalisation. The Monnet method was co-opted by a more technocratic approach to integration that disassociated the step-by-step integrative process from its federalist origins and asserted agnosticism for Europe's *finalité politique*.[36] Neofunctionalism and the logic of policy spillovers did not require federalism – let alone federation, with its concomitant normative commitments to an identifiable European *demos*, democratic accountability and individual rights.

Spinelli, for example, questioned whether federation – and political integration more specifically – would (or could) actually follow from incrementalism.[37] When functionalist integration began to stall in the early 1980s, the possibility for formal compact-based constitutionalism to reinvigorate European *federal*

---

[30] M Burgess, *Comparative Federalism* (London, Routledge, 2006) 239.

[31] As quoted in Burgess, ibid, 228.

[32] Mason, *European Coal and Steel Community* (n 27) 124.

[33] Burgess, *Comparative Federalism* (n 30) 229.

[34] *cf* K Nicolaïdis, 'Perils of Unity, Promise of Union' in Maduro and Wind, *Transformation of Europe* (n 14) 234–48, 241 ('The EC third way was born from the belief held by moderate federalists that power politics could be *transformed* in Europe without *transcending* the state system itself – in contrast with federalist schemes like EDC and even ECSC'). But see E Haas, *The Uniting of Europe: Political, Social, and Economic Forces, 1950–1957* (Stanford, Stanford University Press, 1958) (arguing that incremental integration in one sector would lead to integration in other sectors and culminate in the end-goal of a formal European federation).

[35] Burgess (n 30) 231.

[36] P Schmitter, 'A Revised Theory of Integration' (1970) 24 *International Organization* 836, 844 (presenting a neofunctional model which describes European integration but does not 'involve any assumptions about cumulative and irreversible progress toward a single goal'); see also W Sandholtz and A Stone Sweet, 'European Integration and Supranational Governance' (1997) 4 *Journal of European Public Policy* 297 (drawing on neofunctionalism in proposing a descriptive theory of European integration which explains how a given policy sector transitions from national to intergovernmental to supranational governance, but which does not take a normative stance on a specific outcome).

[37] Burgess (n 30) 231.

integration re-emerged. Spinelli, then a member of the European Parliament (EP), put together a Draft Treaty for European Union in 1984, seeking to short-circuit the step-by-step process. His efforts, though not successful as a formalist re-imagining of federal union, nevertheless led to renewed efforts by the Member States themselves to move integration forward.

The engine of European integration shifted to the Member States in a series of critical intergovernmental conferences in the mid-1980s. The result, the Single European Act, was the first major Treaty revision since the 1957 Treaty of Rome. Ongoing intergovernmental conferences produced Treaty revisions that were grand in their aspirations and more comprehensive than what the supranational institutions could accomplish internally. But the intergovernmental approach fell far shy of a federal 'Big-C'-constitution rooted in political union (and an identifiable European *demos*).[38] Nevertheless, the revisions and changes to the Treaties expanded the space for the internal, European-institution-based Monnet-method to continue to foster integration and some aspects of federation.[39]

By allowing certain institutions to capitalise on their 'power of autonomous organisation' (such as the Commission's power of initiative or the European Court of Justice's teleological approach to interpreting the Treaties),[40] functional incre-mentalism facilitated 'substantial jurisdictional changes ... in the operation of the system' itself.[41] These changes reflected a growing constitutionalism,[42] incorpo-rating elements of federalisation,[43] including functional limitations on national power,[44] the creation of proto-citizenship (the market citizen),[45] the expansion of policy tasks to new areas[46] and the introduction of initiatives to begin the construc-tion of a European *demos*.[47]

---

[38] M Télo, 'Pertinence et limites des theses fédéralistes: vers une constitution mixte?' in F Esposito and N Levrat (eds), *Europe: de L'Intégration à la Fédération* (Louvain-la-Neuve, Academia Bruylant, 2010) 163, 167.

[39] *cf* Halberstam, 'Transformation of Constitutional Law' (n 14) 227–28.

[40] A Vergés Bausili, 'Rethinking the Methods of Dividing and Exercising Powers in the EU' in J Shaw, P Magnette, L Hoffmann and A Vergés Bausili, *The Convention on the Future of Europe* (London, The Federal Trust, 2003) 99.

[41] Ibid, 98.

[42] JHH Weiler, *The Constitution of Europe* (Cambridge, Cambridge University Press, 1999).

[43] EF Delaney, *Promoting Federation: The Role Of A Constitutional Court In Federalist States* (PhD Dissertation, 2003).

[44] AM Burley and W Mattli, 'Europe before the Court: A Political Theory of Legal Integration' (1993) 47 *International Organization* 41; W Mattli and AM Slaughter, 'Revisiting the European Court of Justice' (1998) 52 *International Organization* 177.

[45] M Everson, 'The Legacy of the Market Citizen' in J Shaw and G More (eds), *New Legal Dynamics of European Union* (Oxford, Oxford University Press, 1995) 73–89.

[46] On the expanding policy competence at the European level, see M Pollack, 'Creeping Competence: The Expanding Agenda of the European Community' (1994) 14 *Journal of Public Policy* 95; M Pollack, 'The End of Creeping Competence? E.U. Policy-Making since Maastricht' (2000) 38 *Journal of Common Market Studies* 519.

[47] PA Kraus, 'A Union of Peoples?' in L Dobson and A Føllesdal (eds), *Political Theory and the European Constitution* (London, Routledge, 2004) 49. (A wide range of efforts to give content to European iden-tity included 'the introduction of Union citizenship, the proliferation of official European symbols in all realms of social life and the [adoption] of several important European programmes devoted to educa-tion and culture').

Whether recognised as proto-federal or viewed as *sui generis* and supranational, the political transformations drew attention to the institutional and democratic lacunae in the system. European developments 'imposed a burden on the political, economic, administrative and legislative fabric of the Member States', leading to renewed focus on 'questions of constitutional design and institutional balance',[48] and highlighting concerns, in particular, about identifying limits to supranational power.[49] The shift in perceived power to Europe raised questions about its democratic justification: neither the supranational institution-driven expansion of European-level competences nor the national elite-driven and opaque method of intergovernmental treaty reform was seen as sufficiently democratic to legitimise the increased scope of authority.[50]

Institutional redesign would be required to address the democratic deficit and the relation between national and supranational interests. The Union's institutions were 'overwhelmed' by the inherent challenges in the emerging federalist system, such as 'finding a balance between the protection of diversity and the development of a common political framework for Europeans'.[51] The logic of incrementalism is powerful in policy expansion or judicialisation, but institutions are more difficult to construct – and reconstruct – in a piecemeal fashion. Institutional re-design does not lend itself to incrementalism, due to the challenges of path dependency and institutional socialisation.[52] And thus scholars began to argue that the Monnet method 'must be transcended if the democratic deficit is to be overcome and a new phase of integration is to gain political legitimacy'.[53] In addition, the limitations of the intergovernmental model of treaty negotiation were becoming apparent: the foundational issues of democratic legitimacy and the development of a shared political culture or 'the legitimation of shared values' were not easily addressed by the elite political bargaining that marked intergovernmental conferences.[54]

---

[48] B Laffan, 'Introduction' in B Laffan (ed), *Constitution-Building in the European Union* (Dublin, Institute of European Affairs, 1996) 1–2.

[49] The Maastricht Treaty, signed in early 1992, first introduced the concept of subsidiarity as a general principle of EU law – and with it, the idea of limiting supranational action to those issues that cannot be resolved appropriately at the Member State level. Treaty on European Union, Feb. 7, 1992, [1992] OJ C224 art. 3(b), at 8. See also R Schütze, *From Dual to Cooperative Federalism* (Oxford, Oxford University Press, 2009) 247–49.

[50] GF Mancini, 'Europe: The Case for Statehood' (1998) 4 *European Law Journal* 29.

[51] Kraus, 'Union of Peoples?' (n 47) 52.

[52] See DL Horowitz, 'Constitutional Design: An Oxymoron?' in I Schapiro and S Macedo, *Designing Democratic Institutions*, Nomos XLII (New York, NYU Press, 2000). Note that certain institutions, such as a court, might be able to sustain incremental change (adding another Justice does not challenge the core purpose of the institution), while incremental change to others (such as a legislature) might be nearly impossible (slowly shifting between electoral regimes, adding a second chamber later in the life of the institution, etc). In addition, there may also be a distinction between institutions as organisations, and institutions as decision-making processes. Even within the latter group, distinctions can be made: incremental changes as to what *receives* qualified majority voting, for example, might be possible, but changing the baseline for what *qualifies* as a qualified majority is likely more difficult.

[53] P Gillespie 'Models of Integration' in Laffan, *Constitution-Building* (n 48) 142.

[54] Habermas, 'Why Europe Needs a Constitution' (n 19) 8; L Hoffmann, 'The Convention on the Future of Europe: Thoughts on the Convention-Model' in Shaw, Magnette, Hoffmann and Vergés Bausili, *The Convention on the Future of Europe* (n 40).

Because 'intergovernmental bargaining is, by its very nature, unable to go beyond a *modus vivendi* – or an imperfect constitutional contract', there was pressure to create a 'deeper, larger and more precise agreement'.[55]

The pressure to delineate and democratise resonated with federalising goals. And politicians made these implications clear: in his speech at Humboldt University in 2000, Joschka Fischer designated Europe's *finalité politique* as a federation. He argued that the 'crisis of the Monnet method can no longer be overlooked, a crisis that cannot be solved according to the method's own logic'.[56] The Monnet method failed to resolve the foundational questions that would allow for meaningful political integration. And, in the absence of formal compact-based federation, there could only be weak integration, an elitist intergovernmentalism produced by national politicians, disassociated from a true European *demos*.

The challenge of institutional revision in the context of a democratic deficit thus revitalised the theory of federal legitimacy, or the argument that 'the Union can only be democratic if it follows the traditional devices of federalism'.[57] These 'traditional devices', including resolving questions of sovereignty and the separation of powers as well as identifying and empowering the federal *demos*, require constitutional clarity and widespread commitment and are at the heart of formal federal constitutionalism. In 2003, Paul Magnette suggested this view of federal legitimacy was widespread, resonating with and defended by 'the Commission, by the majority of the EP since its direct election in 1979, as well as by Germany and the Benelux countries, and recently advocated by Jürgen Habermas'.[58] The federal focus was further reflected in the 'currency that federalist terminology found in the 1990s in scholarly literature on European integration',[59] and indeed in the flurry of literature at the turn of the century that focused on federalising the Union and on comparative insights from national federations.[60]

Contemporaneous commentary identified the inherent dangers in forcing a resolution of these issues through a formal federal constitution. As Joseph Weiler pointed out, key European actors accepted the incrementally developed *acquis communitaire* 'as an autonomous voluntary act, endlessly renewed on each

---

[55] P Magnette, 'Will the EU Be More Legitimate After the Convention?' in Shaw, Magnette, Hoffmann and Vergés Bausili (n 40) 28.

[56] J Fischer, 'From Confederacy to Federation – Thoughts on the Finality of European Integration' (Speech at Humboldt University, Berlin, 12 May 2000).

[57] Magnette, 'Will the EU Be More Legitimate After the Convention?' (n 55) 23.

[58] Ibid.

[59] A Lev, 'Federalism and the Ends of Europe' in A Lev (ed), *The Federal Idea* (Oxford, Hart Publishing, 2017) 189–210. See, eg, the Introduction to the fourth edition of Trevor Hartley's book, *The Foundations of European Community Law*, in which he writes: 'In the past, the word supranational was used to describe [features of the EU]; today this term seems a little passé: they are simply referred to as being "federal".' T Hartley, *The Foundations of European Community Law*, 4th edn (Oxford, Oxford University Press, 1998) 10.

[60] See, eg, Burgess, *Federalism and European Union* (n 2); D McKay 'Policy Legitimacy and Institutional Design: Comparative Lessons for the European Union' (2000) 38 *Journal of Common Market Studies* 25; E Delaney and J Smith, 'Introduction: Europe's Constitutional Future: Federal Lessons for the European Union' (2005) 15 *Regional and Federal Studies* 131.

occasion, of subordination, in the discrete areas governed by Europe.[61] By failing to identify the sources of authority, by leaving open core questions of sovereignty (or in the legal setting, *Kompetenz-Kompetenz*), the Monnet-method allowed for flexibility and constitutional 'tolerance'.[62] A formal constitution could 'upset this delicate balance'.[63]

Notwithstanding these warnings, by the turn of the twenty-first century, 'the reigning assumption seems to have been that anything as important as federalising and democratising the European Union must be treated as a momentous and concentrated *event* – not a gradual and fitful *process*'.[64] In short, the result of the Monnet-method itself was the need 'to shift from Monnet's Europe of "functionalism" to Spinelli's Europe of "constitutionalism"'.[65] This resulting pressure for formal constitutionalisation led to the Convention on the Future of Europe.[66] (This call for a Convention stripped away the agnostic veneer of functionalism; incrementalism may no longer be able to claim a neutral valence.)

When the European Union's Heads of State and Government agreed in the Laeken Declaration to create a new form of treaty revision process by authorising a 'Convention on the Future of Europe', they introduced the possibility of formal constitutionalisation. For the 'first time ever in a document endorsed by all', there was a 'specific reference to the "C" word, in a passage contemplating a trajectory "Towards a Constitution for European citizens"'.[67] That said, it is not clear that the Convention's work product was itself intended to be a 'constitution'. The Convention was asked to 'draw up a final document, which may comprise either different options, indicating the degree of support which they received, or recommendations if consensus is achieved'.[68]

The Convention, under the leadership of Valéry Giscard D'Estaing, took the full scope of potential authorisation and portrayed itself as a 'collective opportunity' to construct a Constitution for Europe, an approach which 'spoke eloquently to the federalist majority amongst the Convention members'.[69] To the extent that some *conventionnels* hoped for a federal constitutional solution to the delineation and democratisation challenges inherent in the existing supranational system, the

---

[61] J Weiler, 'A Constitution for Europe? Some Hard Choices' (2002) 40 *Journal of Common Market Studies* 563, 568.

[62] Ibid.

[63] J Shaw, 'What's in a Convention? Process and Substance in the Project of European Constitution-Building' in Shaw, Magnette, Hoffmann and Vergés Bausili (n 40) 50.

[64] P Schmitter, 'Is Euro-Federalism a Solution or a Problem?' in Dobson and Føllesdal, *Political Theory and the European Constitution* (n 47) 21.

[65] Burgess, *Federalism and European Union* (n 2) 265.

[66] *cf* L Hoffmann and J Shaw, 'Constitutionalism and Federalism in the "Future of Europe" Debate: The German Dimension' (2004) 13 *German Politics* 625, 627. The success of the Convention on Fundamental Rights and Freedoms also influenced the push for a convention. Shaw, Magnette, Hoffmann and Vergés Bausili (n 40).

[67] Shaw, 'What's in a Convention?' (n 63) 44.

[68] Point 6, Draft Minutes, General Affairs Council, 8 Oct. 2001 (Document 12551/01).

[69] Shaw (n 63) 51–52.

resulting Constitution fell short of that aim. In some ways, the finished product was a betrayal of the formal federal constitutional aspiration, but those limitations were a function of the thick institutional developments and legacy decisions made through incrementalism. Federalist *conventionnels* were not writing on a clean slate, and the opportunities for transformative change were circumscribed.

III. A Federation Out of Reach: The European Constitution

It was clear from the outset of the Convention that a formal federal constitutional construct was in the minds of key leaders – the Praesidium's preliminary draft even included the word 'federal'. But the *conventionnels* were operating against a complicated political backdrop of 50 years of European integration efforts. Many aspects of the final proposed Constitutional Treaty showcase the difficulty of turning to convention-based federal constitutionalism after decades of process-based federalism; this section will focus in particular on the inclusion of a withdrawal clause. The addition of a withdrawal clause to the draft European Constitution fundamentally challenges any attempt to categorise the ultimate product as a federal constitution. And the clause reflects the variation in attitudes of Member State delegations to the constitutional project itself – contradictory views that had heretofore peacefully co-existed by privileging the technocratic Monnet-method.

Formal exit of a member state from a federation – secession – is an unusual provision in a federal constitution. The (aspirational) enduring nature of federations is rooted in the concept of loyalty and the privileging of voice in the ongoing constitutional arrangements: the combination of an expectation that 'over a period of time, the right turns will more than balance the wrong ones',[70] and the protected influence for the member state at the federal level (usually through state representation in a federal legislature).[71] Secession is the 'discontinuation of a constitutional association',[72] and as such, a textual provision for constitutional dissolution is a rarity.[73] Further, in looking at those few constitutions with secession clauses, the

---

[70] A Hirschman, *Exit, Voice and Loyalty* (Cambridge, Harvard University Press, 1970) 78.

[71] JA Schmidt, 'Representation of Component Federal Units in Federal Systems', *Max Planck Encyclopedia of Comparative Constitutional Law* (2016); W Swenden, *Federalism and Second Chambers* (New York, Peter Lang, 2004) 25.

[72] Burgess (n 30) 281.

[73] The Constitutions of Ethiopia, St. Kitts and Nevis, and Serbia and Montenegro include secession provisions. A Kreptul, 'The Constitutional Right of Secession in Political Theory and History' (2003) 17 *Journal of Libertarian Studies* 30. Historical examples of explicit constitutional guarantees of secession include: the 1921 Liechtenstein Constitution, the 1931 Chinese Constitution, the 1947 Constitution of the Union of Burma, the 1968 Constitutional of the Czechoslovak Socialist Republic, the 1974 Constitution of the Socialist Federal Republic of Yugoslavia and the 1977 Constitution of the Soviet Union. G Anderson, 'Secession in International Law and Relations: What Are We Talking About?' (2013) 35 *Loyola LA. International & Comparative Law Review* 343, 351–52. In the Soviet case, in particular, viewing the secession clause as providing a meaningful 'right' of secession is of questionable

clauses do not provide a right for *unilateral* secession.[74] Unilateral withdrawal is considered to be an indicium of a treaty arrangement, and its absence in the federal context is one 'reason why federal governments are generally not regarded as treaty arrangements'.[75]

The withdrawal clause was introduced early in the negotiations as an effort 'to underline the continued autonomy of the member states',[76] in the face of a number of provisions that suggested the contrary. The preliminary draft issued by the Praesidium in October 2002 reflected core federal aspirations: renaming the EU as 'United Europe' and creating a bicameral body called the 'Congress of the People' that would incorporate the existing European Parliament and a new house representing national parliaments.[77] The draft designated the Union's constitutional structure as having a single legal personality and incorporated the Charter of Fundamental Rights.[78] Critically, the draft gave some participants the 'impression that the states were no longer sovereign and that the Union Constitution gave powers to the Member States'.[79] The withdrawal clause was introduced as a reassurance that the Member States would remain the 'masters of the treaties'. And, even when some of the more overtly federalist aspects of the draft were rethought or removed in negotiations and deliberations, the withdrawal quid pro quo remained.[80]

The withdrawal clause is most obviously about ensuring reluctant European Member States a measure of protection from the threat of European federation – a statement which on its own demonstrates the inability of the Convention to usher in a federal state through formal constitutional measures. But the debates within the Convention over the withdrawal clause also showcase the co-existence of irreconcilable notions of European integration – from its legal nature, to its permanence as a political matter, to its pervasiveness within Member States themselves.

Although the 'innovative' withdrawal clause received little scholarly attention at the time and was not a major point of broader political debate,[81] the Praesidium's

---

validity or use. C Sunstein, 'Constitutionalism and Secession' (1991) 58 *University of Chicago Law Review* 633.

[74] Kreptul, 'The Constitutional Right of Secession in Political Theory and History' (n 73) 80; M Gatti 'The Article 50 Procedure for Withdrawal from the EU: A Well-Designed Secession Clause' (2017) (EU Studies Association Conference, Miami, 4–6 May).

[75] King, *Federalism and Federation* (n 7) 117.

[76] TV Olsen, 'Europe: United Under God? Or Not?' in Dobson and Føllesdal (n 47) 82.

[77] J Shaw, 'Notes on the Praesidium's Preliminary Draft Constitutional Treaty' (2002) *Federal Trust Online Paper 09/02* 3.

[78] A pragmatic and holistic view of the draft would suggest that once the Member States 'irreversibly vested third parties, namely the nationals of the Member States, with a legal heritage of rights', J Herbst, 'Observations on the Right to Withdraw from the European Union: Who Are the "Masters of the Treaties"?' (2005) 6 *German Law Journal* 1755, 1759, they had passed the 'point of no return', permitting a relationship between the individual and the Union-level, unmediated by the nation state.

[79] Olsen, 'Europe: United Under God?' (n 76) 82.

[80] C Hillion 'Leaving the European Union, the Union Way' (2016) 8 *SIEPS European Policy Analysis* 1, 9.

[81] See Shaw, 'Notes on the Praesidium's Preliminary Draft Constitutional Treaty' (n 77).

choice was criticised by Convention delegates. From the perspective of European federalists, including a withdrawal clause undermined the core goals of solidarity and 'ever closer union'.[82] As Jean Monnet himself said during negotiations over the Coal and Steel Community in 1950: 'In a federation, no State can secede by its own unilateral decision. Similarly, there can be no Community except among nations which commit themselves to it with no limit in time and no looking back.'[83] Those *conventionnels* objecting to the inclusion of the clause highlighted it as a sell-out of these foundational principles,[84] particularly the longstanding commitment to 'creating an ever closer union among the peoples of Europe'.[85] As the European People's Party Convention Group argued in its proposal for striking the clause from the draft, '[s]uch an explicit exit clause could allow Member States to blackmail the Union, paralyse its decision-making processes and even endanger the stability of the Union'.[86]

In contrast, others criticised the withdrawal clause as a meaningless gesture. A first group rooted their claims in international law and the *realpolitik* of powerful Member States, arguing that withdrawal from the European Treaties had always been available under the Vienna Convention on the Law of Treaties (notwithstanding the commitment to ever closer union and dictum from the European Court of Justice). And, in any event, the omission of a withdrawal clause 'would hardly prevent a member state's leaving'.[87] In fact, 'insisting on the impossibility of withdrawal might be counterproductive',[88] by incentivising Member States to attempt other methods of avoiding responsibilities or obligations.[89] A second group saw little reason for concern on alternative grounds: no Member State would want to (or could) ever leave. It was implausible that a Member State would 'reject[] all aspects of EU membership'.[90] Years earlier, scholars had opined that 'the point of no return has been passed and Member States will find it politically impossible to defect from the Community as a whole',[91] and nothing in the intervening time gave any indication of a change.

---

[82] Hillion, 'Leaving the European Union' (n 80) 8.

[83] Mayne (trans), Monnet, *Memoirs* (n 26) 326.

[84] See, eg, Brok, Santer, Stylianidis, Szajer, Van Der Linden, Alonso, Basile, Cisneros, Cushnahan, Demetriou, Dolores, Frendo, Giannakou, Korhonen, Kroupa, Maij-Weggen, Mladenov, Piks, Rack, Van Dijk, Zieleniec, and Zile, *Suggestion for Amendment of: Subject: Title X: Union Membership.*

[85] See, eg, J Meyer, *Vorschlag für die Änderung von: Art. 46, Teil I, Titel X des Verfassungsentwurfs (CONV 648/03)*; GM de Vries and TJAM de Bruijn, *Suggestion for Amendment of Article: 46.*

[86] EPP Convention Group, *Suggestion for Amendment of Article 1–59.*

[87] L Dobson, 'Conceptions of Freedom and the European Constitution' in Dobson and Føllesdal (n 47) 118.

[88] Herbst (n 78) 1760.

[89] *cf* J Weiler, 'Alternatives to Withdrawal from an International Organisation: The Case of the European Economic Community' (1985) 20 *Israel Law Review* 282, 287.

[90] D McKay, 'The EU as a Self-Sustaining Federation: Specifying the Constitutional Conditions' in Dobson and Føllesdal (n 47) 34.

[91] P Schmitter, 'Imagining the Future of the Euro-Polity with the Help of New Concepts' in G Marks, FW Scharpf, P Schmitter and W Streeck (eds), *Governance in the European Union* (London, Sage Publications, 1996) 122.

This divergence of views about the goals and nature of integration was able to flourish in the expressly neutral language of the technocratic version of the Monnet method. Without a shared vision of a *finalité politique*, both old and new Member States were justified in approaching integration with more mundane national interests in mind. And decades of variable geometry, opt-outs and flexible approaches – designed to retain the breadth of the membership sometimes at the expense of its depth – served to give some participants a heightened sense of a Europe *à la carte*, from which they could pick and choose as they saw fit. Asymmetrical federations do exist, but like symmetrical federations, they also operate in conjunction with an assumption of loyalty and voice and provide for multilateral exit (if at all).[92] As a textual matter, the Constitution's withdrawal clause implied unilateralism.[93]

The scholarly warnings about forcing clarity were correct: dissensus was brought into sharper focus. Rather than a consensus-forming constitutional moment, the Convention demonstrated the persistence of the 'debate about ... the "highly controversial f-word of European federalism"'.[94] With some Member States unwilling to resolve core questions in favour of a European *demos* (no matter how thinly constructed as a cultural phenomenon), the Convention's federal aspirations were ill-fated. The French and Dutch referendums opposing ratification of the proposed Constitutional Treaty raised yet more fundamental concerns: Do voters *want* a European federation? Is a generalised European *demos* desirable? How can or should European integration continue?

IV. The Future of Federalisation: A Return to the Past

The discussion thus far has accepted and extended the claims made by earlier commentators about the incompatibility of the Monnet method with the challenges facing the European Union. But in the absence of a formal resolution of these issues, is the option of incremental federalisation really foreclosed? The Monnet method on its own may not be able to achieve federation, but in the right environment of elite political consensus, it could again move integration forward, in an explicitly federalist direction. And the withdrawal clause may be the critical mechanism to allow a new consensus to form.

After the failure of the Constitution to be ratified in popular votes in France and the Netherlands, Heads of State and Government eventually agreed to implement a number of treaty reforms through an intergovernmental conference, drafting a

---

[92] See eg *Reference re Secession of Quebec* [1998] 2 SCR 217.

[93] Shaw (n 63) (noting that other choices were available to the Convention for constructing a multilateral withdrawal clause, such as using the Canadian Supreme Court's solution devised in the *Québec Secession Reference*).

[94] N Stame, 'The European Project, Federalism and Evaluation' (2008) 14 *Evaluation* 117, 117.

document eventually ratified as the Treaty of Lisbon. Included in this Treaty was the Constitution's withdrawal clause, codified as Article 49A, and renumbered as Article 50 of the Treaty on European Union. Article 50, in the words of the German Bundesverfassungsgericht in its review of the Lisbon Treaty, demonstrated that '[i]f a Member State can withdraw based on a decision made on its own responsibility, the process of European integration is not irreversible'.[95] Thus, the clause merits its description as 'the ultimate elaboration of constitutional devices … conceived to cater for the needs of less integrationist states'.[96]

But by making *withdrawal* the mechanism by which to express displeasure, Article 50 can serve to isolate outliers. As Weiler suggested long ago, the option of withdrawal may make other mechanisms of recalcitrance less successful. For an outlier state, individual opt-outs from specific programs may be harder to negotiate. In this way, the withdrawal mechanism may serve to aid in redefining the group that makes up the European consensus; it makes it 'possible for a state to step out of, rather than hold up the integration process'.[97] This possibility was expressly noted in response to the drafting of the original clause in the Constitution. As Convention delegate Andrew Duff wrote: 'The Constitution makes a greater imposition on Member States, and some might not be able or willing to make the leap. That being so, it makes sense to permit a Member State to choose a looser partnership in preference to full membership.'[98] The United Kingdom is currently in the process of so extracting itself.

In a new political context of fewer Member States and more closely shared goals, a *federal* European integration project might yet inch forward. Like-minded Member States and integration-driven institutions may find new ways to promote 'ever closer union', in Monnet's step-by-step fashion. The federal pendulum may once again swing towards incrementalism. But even operating under a new integrationist consensus, incremental federalism cannot on its own achieve federation. Robust democratic and division-of-power protections will still require wholesale institutional redesign. To get there, the pendulum will be forced back towards formal federalisation and another constitutional convention.[99] Given the experience of the European Constitution of 2004, politicians seeking federation should be cautious and deliberate. The federal integrationist project may not survive a second failure.

---

[95] BVerfG, Judgment of the Second Senate of 30 June 2009, 2 BvE 2/08, para 329.

[96] Hillion (n 80) 10.

[97] Ibid, 1.

[98] A Duff, L Dini, P Helminger, R Lang and Lord Maclennan, *Suggestion for Amendment of Article: I-59 bis (New): Associate Membership*.

[99] Another approach to this challenge is to question the function and purpose of federal constitutions themselves. Bellamy and Castiglione suggest that 'constitutions can no longer operate as the apex of a normative hierarchy in which they frame and offer the basis for democracy, as is the case in the standard federal model … instead … they have to be seen as a part of a continuous series of dialogues and compromises'. R Bellamy and D Castiglione, 'Legitimising the Euro-"Polity" and its "Regime"' (2003) 2 *European Journal of Political Theory* 7, 22.

7

The Two Europes

NW BARBER*

There are two Europes: a pair of political entities that occupy the same territory, have identical membership, share almost all the same rules, and yet are divided by radically different understandings of the point of the European project. The first Europe is a fledgling state, a federal construct in which the Member States are non-sovereign regions within the polity. This vision is exciting: a Europe that can become a superpower, a Europe capable of rivalling America and China. The second Europe is a confederation of states, an international construct under the control of its sovereign Member States. This vision is also exciting: a form of confederation deeper and richer than any other in the modern world, a new form of that polity, a political unit built on the agreement of its constituent parts rather than the absolutism of a state constitution. One of the reasons for the success of the European Union lies in the avoidance of resolving the disagreement between these two visions. There is a sort of constructive ambiguity, a Grand Bargain, that permits people who subscribe to each vision to work together – aware that their disagreement might, one day, need to be fought out, but also aware that there is a great deal to be gained by postponing that moment of choice. Perhaps unintentionally, the Draft Constitutional Treaty undermined this compact, pushing Europe towards the first, state-focused, model. Worse still, once the Draft Constitution was rejected by France and the Netherlands (and looked likely to be rejected by other states in which a referendum was promised), much of the substance of the Draft Constitution was copied into the Lisbon Treaty, and became part of European Union law. It seemed that the European elite was unwilling to accept the verdict of the people. The dramatic story of the rise, fall, and resurrection, of the Draft Constitution is particularly unfortunate in that many important elements of the Draft Constitution – the practically significant parts of that document – need not have been controversial. There was no need to choose between the two Europes in 2004; constructive ambiguity could have been preserved.

* Parts of this chapter draw on NW Barber, 'The Constitution, the State, and the European Union' in J Bell and C Kilpatrick (eds), *Cambridge Yearbook of European Studies: Volume 8 2005–2006* (Oxford, Hart Publishing, 2006). With thanks to Maria Cahill, Dorota Leczykiewicz and Steve Weatherill for their helpful comments.

This chapter examines the two visions of Europe and illustrates the ways in which these rival visions were accommodated through constructive ambiguity. It then looks at the Draft Constitution and identifies the ways in which that document shifted the balance between these two visions, so challenging the compact on which the development of the Union had depended. The chapter concludes by drawing some very cautious and very weak connections between the Draft Constitution and the Brexit vote in the United Kingdom. If the Draft Constitution was the zenith of the state-model of the Union, Brexit may be its nadir; a reaction, a terrible over-reaction, against the centralisation of constitutional power within the European project.

I. Two Visions of Europe

Max Weber famously described the state as 'a human community that (successfully) claims the *monopoly of the legitimate use of physical force* within a given territory'.[1] Attention is often focused on the invocation of force within this definition, but, given that force need only be exerted when the state's authority is challenged, it could be argued that authority, not force, is the primary part of the definition.[2] A core characteristic of states is the interaction of claimed authority and raw power: states are *sovereign* entities. State sovereignty embodies an assertion of authority and, moreover, an assertion of authority that is, in some respects, effective.[3] The claims that are characteristic of sovereignty have an assertion of finality at their core.[4] Not only does the state purport to tell people how they ought to behave, it also asserts that the decisions of its institutions may only be legitimately challenged within its constitutional structures: the state, as a whole, has the final say about the rights and duties of its nationals and those within its territory. This sovereign claim is coupled with a requirement of effectiveness. For the state to exist in the world – and for the political ordering to be characterised by sovereignty – these claims must be effective to some extent. Whilst the claims of sovereignty are absolutes, the effectiveness of these claims is a matter of degree; no state is able to completely control conduct within its borders. Sovereignty, then, lies at the intersection of authority claims and power; it is a particular type of authority claim that has some practical power behind it.[5]

---

[1] M Weber, 'Politics as a Vocation' in HH Gerth and C Wright Mills (eds), *From Max Weber: Essays in Sociology* (London, Routledge, 1991) 78. I discuss the nature of the state at length in NW Barber, *The Constitutional State* (Oxford, Oxford University Press, 2011).

[2] As Weber recognised: M Weber, *Economy and Society* (G Roth and C Wittich, eds, California University Press, 1978) 903–04.

[3] I discuss the principle of sovereignty at greater length in NW Barber, *The Principles of Constitutionalism* (Oxford, Oxford University Press, 2018) ch 2.

[4] FH Hinsley, *Sovereignty*, 2nd edn (Cambridge, Cambridge University Press, 1986) 22–26.

[5] M Loughlin, *The Idea of Public Law* (Oxford, Oxford University Press, 2003) 81–82.

Federations are states. In a federation, a single constitution divides power between the centre and the regions.[6] All of the levels of government, the federal and the local, exercise delegated powers.[7] These powers are conferred by a constitution,[8] which normally claims to derive its legitimacy directly from the people as a whole.[9] In federations power is divided such that each level of government has the final decision about some matters.[10] Arend Lijphart goes on to identify a number of secondary characteristics of a federal state.[11] Federal states normally have written constitutions that are difficult to amend, a constitutional court that can police the boundaries between the regions and the centre, and a bicameral legislature, one chamber of which represents the regions.

Confederations, in contrast, are not states. Most political scientists understand confederations as political entities in which the central government is subordinate to the regional governments.[12] In a confederation, the centre and the regions lack the unifying constitution of a federation: the centre has its own constitution, and each of the constituent states has its own, underived, constitution. In Daniel Elazar's telling phrase, these are 'communities of polities'.[13] Confederations, unlike federations, are not states because the confederation, in contrast to its constituent states, does not claim the monopoly of the legitimisation of force, nor does it claim to possess supreme authority over people within its territory. Its authority is derivative, and the states may limit or remove the powers it possesses. Furthermore, the raw power of a confederation to enforce its decisions largely depends on the actions of its constituent states; it relies upon national enforcement structures to execute its decisions. In short, a confederation does not make the type of claims that are characteristic of a state: it does not claim sovereignty and could not, in any event, make good on such a claim.

Even if it is sharp in theory, the line between federations and confederations is blurred in practice. Whilst the existence of a single constitution in a federal state, in contrast to the multiple constitutions of confederal entities, provides a sharp theoretical division, this may not be of great practical significance.[14]

---

[6] See further Erin Delaney's contribution to this volume.

[7] D Elazar, *Exploring Federalism* (Tuscaloosa, University of Alabama Press, 1992) 39–41. See also RL Watts, 'Comparing Forms of Federal Partnerships' in D Karmis and W Norman (eds), *Theories of Federalism: A Reader* (Basingstoke, Palgrave Macmillan, 2005).

[8] Watts, 'Comparing Forms' (n 7) 240.

[9] J Weiler, 'Federalism without Constitutionalism: Europe's *Sonderweg*' in K Nicolaidis and R Howse (eds), *The Federal Vision* (Oxford, Oxford University Press, 2001) 56.

[10] See generally A Lijphart, *Patterns of Democracy* (New Haven, Yale University Press, 1999) ch 10; KC Wheare, *Federal Government*, 4th edn (Oxford, Oxford University Press, 1963) 33; D MacKay, *Federalism and the European Union: A Political Economy Perspective* (Oxford, Oxford University Press, 1999) ch 2.

[11] Lijphart, *Patterns of Democracy* (n 10) 186–91.

[12] Wheare, *Federal Government* (n 10) 33; C Hughes, 'Cantonalism: Federation and Confederacy in the Golden Epoch of Switzerland' in M Burgess and A Gagnon (eds), *Comparative Federalism and Federation* (Toronto, University of Toronto Press, 1993) 155.

[13] Elazar, *Exploring Federalism* (n 7) 50–54.

[14] Ibid, 11.

A constitution is not merely a legal document; it is the whole assemblage of rules that define the structure of the state. Some of these rules are legal, some are not. Sometimes the legal rules of the constitution fossilise, leaving an impression in the constitution once the effective rule has disappeared. The fossilisation of legal rules coupled with the emergence of new conventions may allow a state to move from one form of government to another, even without explicit constitutional amendment.[15] A confederation might grow into a federation as the boundaries between the competences of the centre and the states became more rigid. The relationships between the confederation's separate constitutions could become regulated by conventions – and, through these conventions, the distinct constitutions may combine into a single constitutional entity. The question of whether a given political entity is a confederacy of states or a strongly federated state may be impossible to answer in some instances.

A. The First Europe: Europe as State

Some of the founders of the European Union envisaged that it would, over time, become a state.[16] Both Jean Monnet and Altiero Spinelli, key figures in the creation of the European project, were explicit about their desire to create a federation.[17] Monnet believed that the logic of integration would propel Europe ever closer; that gradually, perhaps over a long period of time, economic union would lead to a political union, which would eventually bring a federation in all but name.[18] Spinelli was more direct, pushing for an explicitly federal structure from the start. Indeed, Spinelli was the animating force behind the 1984 Draft Treaty, a document that Andrew Duff describes as aiming to 'pitch forward the constitution in a federal direction'.[19] Spinelli's Draft Treaty did not become part of the European legal order, but it had a significant impact on Europe's constitutional development, with many of its ideas re-emerging in later treaties. It was also one of the documents that fed in to the deliberations of the Convention that drew up the Draft Constitution.[20]

There are aspects of the European legal order, aspects present before and after the Draft Constitution, that echo Monnet's and Spinelli's aspirations for statehood. Most obviously, perhaps, the jurisdictional claims made by the Court of Justice of the European Union resemble the claims that we might expect to find the supreme

---

[15] See Wheare's discussion of various constitutions which have shifted in nature over time: Wheare (n 10) ch 2.

[16] D Dinan, *Europe Recast: A History of the European Union*, 2nd edn (London, Palgrave, 2014) 10–13.

[17] Erin Delaney's contribution to this volume provides a powerful account of the federalist thought at the start of the European project.

[18] M Burgess, *Comparative Federalism: Theory and Practice* (London, Routledge, 2006) 228–29; A Duff, *On Governing Europe: A Federal Experiment* (Brussels, The Spinelli Group, 2017) 79–81.

[19] Duff, *On Governing Europe* (n 18) 111.

[20] Ibid, 195–97.

court of a state advancing.[21] The Court of Justice not only claims that EU law has supremacy over conflicting rules of national law,[22] it also claims that it, the Court, is entitled to provide definitive answers to all questions of EU law,[23] and, moreover, is entitled to determine what constitutes an issue of EU law.[24]

These three supremacy claims are not quite enough to meet Weber's definition of statehood. The Court of Justice does not claim comprehensive jurisdiction over the territory of Europe, and so does not claim that all exercises of legitimate power are legitimated by European institutions; there remain areas in which Member States act autonomously. But the Court of Justice does assert the right to determine whether or not EU law – and, consequently, its own jurisdiction – applies in these areas. If the claims made by the Court on behalf of the Union were accepted, the Court would have the final say on the legitimacy of all laws and state actions within the Union – even if, in the exercise of this capacity, it concluded that decisions about the legality of the act lay at the level of the Member States. On some under-standings of sovereignty, understandings that build on, but modify Weber's, this assertion of supremacy is sufficient to constitute an assertion of sovereign capac-ity; the Court of Justice, on behalf of the Union as a whole, is advancing authority claims that are characteristic of a state.[25]

The supremacy claims made by the Court are, perhaps, the most obvious, and important, element of the state-model within the European project, but others can also be identified. The introduction of citizenship in the Maastricht Treaty, for example, brought in a concept formed within the state into the European legal order.[26] At least part of motivation behind the introduction of citizenship was to bolster the apparent legitimacy of the Union, to persuade the people of Europe that the commands of Community institutions ought to be obeyed.[27] Where citizen-ship is established, the authority claimed by the state, its assertion of sovereignty, is an aspect of a particular form of constitutional relationship between the individual and state institution. Where state members are citizens, rather than subjects, they share in the control of the state and, in part because of this shared control, have a broad duty of loyalty towards the state. Of course, the formal aspects of citi-zenship might be in place without those characterised as citizens acknowledging this role, but it may have been hoped by the authors of the Treaty that the formal

---

[21] H Lindahl, 'Sovereignty and Representation in the European Union' in N Walker, *Sovereignty in Transition: Essays in European Law* (Oxford, Hart Publishing, 2003).

[22] Case 6/64 *Costa v ENEL* [1964] ECR 585.

[23] Art 234 (formerly Art 177).

[24] J Weiler, *The Transformation of Europe* in J Weiler, *The Constitution of Europe* (Cambridge, Cambridge University Press, 1999) 21. Case 314/85 *Foto-Frost v Hauptzollamt Lübeck-Ost* [1987] ECR 4199.

[25] I discuss the reasons for modifying Weber's account in Barber, *The Constitutional State* (n 1) ch 2, and its implications for sovereignty in Barber, *The Principles of Constitutionalism* (n 3) ch 2; see also L Green, *The Authority of the State* (Oxford, Clarendon Press, 1990) 78–83.

[26] See generally NW Barber, 'Citizenship, Nationalism and the European Union' (2002) 27 *European Law Review* 241.

[27] S O'Leary, *The Evolving Concept of Community Citizenship* (London, Kluwer, 1996) ch 1.

introduction of European citizenship would bring with it the emotional attachment sometimes experienced by individuals who are citizens at the national level.[28]

The introduction of citizenship in the Maastricht Treaty may have also
amounted to an attempt to recast the basis of legitimacy of the European Union.
The second vision of Europe, discussed below, grounds the legitimacy of the
demands of Europe in the agreement of its Member States: it is the decision of
these states to create and abide by the institutional structures of the Union that
renders authoritative the decisions made by those structures. In contrast, the introduction of citizenship points towards a model of Europe in which the legitimacy
of its institutions is derived directly from its people.[29] The elements of control and
responsibility, at the core of the concept of citizenship, circumvent the Member
States.

In addition to the supremacy claims advanced by the Court and the citizenship
provisions, there are a host of other features of the Union that can be interpreted
in a state-like manner.[30] There is the European Parliament, a body that is directly
elected by the people of Europe, there is the Council which, looked at in a certain
light, resembles the second chamber of a federal legislature, and there are the
Treaties, which resemble constitutional documents, establishing and constraining
these institutions.

B. The Second Europe: Europe as States

The second understanding of Europe regards the Union as a confederation of
sovereign states, who have agreed to act together for their mutual advantage.
A powerful scholarly articulation of this vision can be found in the work of Joseph
Weiler. Responding to calls for the European Union to move towards statehood,
Weiler warned of the centralisation of power that this would bring, and questioned whether the move was necessary.[31] For Weiler, a strength of the Union is
that it rests on the interaction of states, both with each other and with European
institutions.[32] Weiler contends that the principle of what he terms 'constitutional
tolerance' is a distinctive feature of the European system. Whereas in a federal state

---

[28] J Carens, *Culture, Citizenship and Community* (Oxford, Oxford University Press, 2000) ch 7;
J Weiler, 'To be a European Citizen: Eros and Civilization' in J Weiler, *The Constitution of Europe*
(Cambridge, Cambridge University Press, 1999).

[29] At the core of Mancini's argument for a federal Europe is the claim that only a federation could
bring the democratic structures needed to legitimate the Union: GF Mancini, 'Europe: The Case for
Statehood' (1998) 4 *European Law Journal* 29, 40.

[30] See more generally J Pinder, 'The New European Federalism: The Idea and its Achievements' in
M Burgess and A Gagnon (eds), *Comparative Federalism and Federation* (Toronto, University of
Toronto Press, 1993).

[31] J Weiler, 'Europe: The Case Against the Case for Statehood' (1998) 4 *European Law Journal* 43,
responding to Mancini, 'Europe: The Case for Statehood' (n 29).

[32] Ibid, 62.

regions are commanded to obey, in Europe Member States accept the constraints of membership. As Weiler puts it:

> The Quebecois are told: in the name of the people of Canada, you are obliged to obey. The French or the Italians or the Germans are told: in the name of the peoples of Europe, you are invited to obey.[33]

In each case the continuation of the polity depends on discipline, but in Europe this discipline depends on a continuing and voluntary act of subordination. For Weiler, this is a profound and valuable form of structuring, one that maintains distinct constitutional identities whilst, at the same time, requiring these entities to cooperate, interact and respect each other.[34]

This vision of Europe is one that is shared by many institutional actors within the Member States. Member State courts, in particular, have lined up to reject the supremacy assertions advanced by the Court of Justice. The German Constitutional Court has, perhaps, been the most articulate of the dissenters. In the period before the Draft Constitution, the German Court had advanced a different understanding of the force of EU law. In *Solange I*, that court rejected the supremacy of European Law as articulated by the European Court of Justice. The Court insisted on its duty to protect fundamental constitutional rights contained within the German Constitution: supremacy of European law could not be accepted until the European legal order had the capacity to protect these rights.[35] In the *Maastricht* decision, the Court rejected the Court of Justice's claim to have the final say over the meaning and scope of European law.[36] Whilst accepting that it was bound by the German Constitution to implement European law as best it could, the German Court stated that it would not accept surprising readings of the Treaty that had the effect of extending the Union's powers.[37]

Many, perhaps most, Member State courts have followed the model set by the German Constitutional Court, both before and after the fall of the Draft Constitution.[38] Most recently – but before the result of the 2015 General Election

---

[33] Weiler, 'Federalism without Constitutionalism' (n 9) 21.

[34] Ibid, 19–21. See also Weiler's writing on European Citizenship which expresses a similar idea: Weiler, 'To be a European Citizen' (n 28).

[35] *Internationale HandelsgesellschaftmbH v Einfuhr-und Vorratsstelle für Getreide und Futtermittel* [1974] CMLR 540.

[36] *Brunner v The European Treaty* [1994] CMLR 57. See M Zuleeg, 'The European Constitution Under Constitutional Constraints: The German Scenario' (1997) 22 *European Law Review* 19 for energetic criticism of the decision, and M Kumm, 'Who is the Final Arbiter of Constitutionality in Europe?' (1999) 36 *Common Market Law Review* 351.

[37] Ibid, paras 33, 48–49. The case law continues after the fall of the Draft Constitution: C Wohlfahrt, 'The *Lisbon* Case: A Critical Summary' (2009) 10 *German Law Journal* 1277.

[38] See among others: Italy: *Frontini v Ministero delle Finanze* [1974] 2 CMLR 372; France: *Nicolo* [1990] 1 CMLR 173; W Sadurski, 'Solange, Chapter 3: Constitutional Courts in Central Europe – Democracy – European Union' (2008) 14 *European Law Journal* 1. The Danish Supreme Court has recently handed down a strong decision following this line of cases: R Holdgaard, D Elkan and G Schaldemose, 'From Cooperation to Collision: The ECJ's *Ajos* Ruling and the Danish Court's Refusal To Comply' (2018) 55 *Common Market Law Review* 275.

that made the Brexit referendum likely – the United Kingdom's Supreme Court followed suit. In *R (HS2 Action Alliance Ltd) v Secretary of State for Transport*, the Supreme Court asserted that there were some parts of the United Kingdom Constitution that might be beyond the reach of EU law – that in the event of a conflict between at least some of these constitutional instruments and the demands of European institutions, domestic constitutional instruments would prevail. Equally importantly, echoing the German Constitutional Court, the United Kingdom Supreme Court made it clear that it was for the courts of the United Kingdom to decide on the scope and effectiveness of EU law, rejecting the jurisdictional supremacy claims made by European courts.

A further point worth making about the supremacy claims of the European Court of Justice is the practical weakness of European Institutions. Whilst the claims made by the Court are sweeping, the institutions of the Union are almost entirely reliant on Member States for the execution of their commands.[39] If EU law is effective because of the relationship officials and others within the Member States have with their domestic states and not because of their relationship with the Union, the Union fails to achieve the level of effectiveness characteristic of a sovereign entity. It may be this qualification that led Walter van Gerven to assert that the most important reason the Union is not a state is that its peoples do not wish it to gain statehood.[40] Even if people are doing as the European Union requires, they are not doing so solely *because* the European Union requires it.

The second model of Europe is also evident in the citizenship provisions. The original citizenship provision was introduced by the Maastricht Treaty in 1993 and simply asserted that nationals of Member States were European citizens. This was quickly modified by the Amsterdam Treaty in 1999 which included a provision making it clear that European citizenship complemented, and did not replace, national citizenship.[41] Whereas the Maastricht provision seemed to track our first model of Europe, the modified provision was more equivocal. It could be read as a compromise, or, even, it could be construed as a re-assertion of state sovereignty, as an insistence that national citizenship comes first, and European citizenship is secondary. This would reflect the reality of the law on citizenship. Citizenship of the Union continues to be dependent upon citizenship of one of the Member States, and European law does not require that Member States confer domestic citizenship on individuals – though it may require Member States to allow residency to family members of European Citizens.[42] Member States retain control over the conferral of citizenship, and what legitimacy the Union gains through the creation of citizenship remains mediated through those Member States.

---

[39] A Moravcsik, 'The European Constitutional Compromise and the Neofunctionalist Legacy' (2005) 12 *Journal of European Public Policy* 349, 370.

[40] W van Gerven, *The European Union: A Polity of States and Peoples* (Oxford, Hart Publishing, 2005) 37–39.

[41] The Lisbon Treaty later changed 'complementary' to 'additional'.

[42] Case C-135/08 *Rottmann v Freistadt Bayern* [2010] ECR I-1449, para 48.

As with the first model of Europe, many of the other features of the Union could be interpreted as tracking this confederal model. The Council consists of representatives of the Member States, the national balance of the Commission is carefully delineated, each Member State gets to appoint a judge to the Court. There is plenty of material that a dedicated confederalist could cite in a debate over Europe's true constitutional character.

II. The Grand Bargain and the Draft Constitution

Many scholars have noted that the Union stands between a federation and a confederation and possesses elements of each form of ordering.[43] This hybridity is partly accidental but is also, in part, the product of compromise, both explicit and tacit.[44] The citizenship provisions are an example of an explicit compromise; the text of the Treaty was amended to recognise the claims of the Member States. The dispute over the force of EU law is a tacit compromise: the European Court and the courts of the Member States both continue to advance rival supremacy claims but each side – normally – shows restraint. Steve Weatherill has issued a powerful warning to those tempted to fight for a single narrative about the location of constitutional authority within Europe. As Weatherill notes, this can only be achieved by suppressing diversity, and comes at a cost: such a narrative was eventually imposed in the USA, but required the bloodshed of a civil war.[45]

The ambiguity over the nature and future direction of Europe brings a significant asset. It permits adherents of the two, rival, visions of Europe to work together within the European project. This might be termed the 'Grand Bargain' of European integration. Whilst each side may profoundly disagree over the destination of the European project, they are able to agree on the vast majority of the substance of the current rules; there is agreement over the day-to-day legal obligations those within the Union are under. Each can interpret these rules within their very different models of Europe. Cass Sunstein has written of the value of incompletely theorised agreements within the law, where people agree with a proposition but may disagree over the reasons for endorsing that proposition.[46] The Grand Bargain may be

---

[43] eg D Elazar, 'The United States and the European Union: Models for Their Epochs' 55; Weiler (n 9) 55–58; A Moravcsik, 'Federalism in the European Union: Rhetoric and Reality' 176, 186. All of which are to be found in K Nicolaidis and R Howse (eds), *The Federal Vision* (Oxford, Oxford University Press, 2001). See also Burgess, *Comparative Federalism: Theory and Practice* (n 18) ch 9.

[44] The compromises between these visions forms a theme of Andrew Duff's excellent book on the emergence of the Union: A Duff, *On Governing Europe: A Federal Experiment* (London, The Spinelli Group, 2018).

[45] Steve Weatherill warns of the dangers of trying to impose a single narrative about the location of constitutional authority in Europe: S Weatherill, *Law and Values in the European Union* (Oxford, Oxford University Press, 2016) 229–30.

[46] C Sunstein, 'Incompletely Theorized Agreements' (1995) 108 *Harvard Law Review* 1733. *cf* J Rawls, 'The Idea of an Overlapping Consensus' in J Rawls, *Political Liberalism* (Columbia University Press, 1993).

an incompletely theorised agreement on a monumental scale: one of the century's most ambitious political projects, balancing on radically different understandings of that project's goal.

Sometimes constitutional ambiguity of this type is a liability. It may be that disputes become harder to resolve over time and postponing the moment of conflict will make that conflict more destructive. But sometimes the postponement of the moment of decision may avoid conflict entirely.[47] It could be that, one day, one of the two visions of Europe gains the support of the peoples of Europe: there is a clear winner between the two. Or it could be that the ambiguity could last indefinitely, perhaps reaching a point at which it is unnecessary to resolve the disagreement as each side has got what they wanted from the project.

A. The Draft Constitution as a Challenge to the Grand Bargain

The Draft Constitution presented a challenge to the Grand Bargain in a number of respects. First, and most prominently, the decision to label the document a 'constitution' appeared significant. In order to avoid 'semantic' disagreements, Valéry Giscard d'Estaing announced in the opening session of the Convention that the end-product would be labelled a 'constitutional treaty'.[48] This might have appeared a compromise of sorts, but the decision to include 'constitution' in the title of the document produced by the Convention was no mere slip of the pen. The immediate origins of the Draft Constitution can be traced back to a speech delivered by Joschka Fischer in 2000.[49] Fischer's vision for Europe was explicitly federalist; falling squarely within the first of our two models. He argued for a division of sovereignty between the Member States and the Union, with a European Parliament and a European Government exercising legislative and executive power within the new federation. The idea of a *constitution*, linked to the idea of a state, was part of the Convention project from the very beginning, and when the European Council, in Laeken, issued the declaration that laid the groundwork for the Convention, that declaration, it was said, read like a *constitutional* agenda rather than a mandate for classic treaty reform.[50] By labelling the resulting document a constitution, the

[47] On the possible uses of inconsistency, see NW Barber, 'Legal Inconsistency and the Emergence of States' in HP Glenn and L Smith (eds), *Law and the New Logics* (Cambridge, Cambridge University Press, 2017).

[48] P Norman, *The Accidental Constitution* (Brussels, Eurocomment, 2005) 63–64.

[49] Dinan, *Europe Recast* (n 16) 270–71; Norman, *The Accidental Constitution* (n 48) 12–13: Fischer called for a 'lean federation'.

[50] P Magnette and K Nicolaidis 'The European Convention: Bargaining in the Shadow of Rhetoric' (2004) 27 *West European Politics* 381, 388; Norman (n 48) 20.

Convention drew on this history, providing a clear and prominent link to Fischer's federalist vision.[51]

In addition to this label, the Draft Convention also included what we might call the 'dressings' of a constitution, a range of decorative constitutional statements that made the document look more like a state constitution. The Constitution specified a flag, an anthem, a special day, and asserted a temptingly Hegelian motto for Europe: 'Unity in Diversity'. These dressings were of little or no practical significance in themselves, but reinforced the impression the document was intended to amount to more than a mere international treaty.

Second, the resulting Convention provided a novel deliberative forum, inviting comparisons with the body that authored the American Constitution.[52] The very structure of the Convention seemed to imply that it was trying to achieve something that could transcend an international treaty. The Convention included a representative from each of the Member States, 30 representatives from the national Parliaments, 16 from the European Parliament, and two from the Commission. Representatives from the accession candidate countries were also able to take part in proceedings, and various other organisations were given observer status.[53] However, although considerable efforts were made to ensure different points of view were heard in the Convention, and efforts were made to engage people outside of the Convention, it was not an elected body, and its public profile was limited. Many of its representatives were appointed by the executives of the Member States, or by the Community Institutions.[54] And perhaps unavoidably, the process was dominated by the Chairman and Vice-Chairmen, who gave forceful direction to the debates and drafts.[55] To add a personal recollection, I do not recall the work of the Convention being given much prominence within the United Kingdom. I suspect that most people outside of the world of European politics and scholarship were unaware, completely unaware, that the Convention was taking place, and would have been surprised – to put it mildly – to hear that this body was intended to form a new constitution on their behalf.[56]

Third, the substance of the document reflected the state-model of Europe in some respects. Most obviously, the Draft Constitution contained a provision which

[51] As Renaud Dehousse contends, it was the decision to label the document a 'constitution' that made the resulting referendums all but inevitable: R Dehousse, 'The Unmaking of a Constitution: Lessons From the European Referenda' (2006) 13 *Constellations* 151, 151.

[52] M Rosenfeld, 'The European Convention and Constitution Making in Philadelphia' (2003) 1 *International Journal of Constitutional Law* 373; R Badinter 'A European Constitution: Perspectives of a French Delegate to the Convention' (2003) 1 *International Journal of Constitutional Law* 363.

[53] P Craig, *The Lisbon Treaty: Law, Politics, and Treaty Reform* (Oxford, Oxford University Press, 2010) 6–7.

[54] J Fossum and A Menéndez 'The Constitution's Gift? A Deliberative Democratic Analysis of Constitution Making in the European Union' (2005) 11 *European Law Journal* 380, 403.

[55] G Stuart, *The Making of Europe's Constitution* (London, Fabian Society, 2003) 14–26.

[56] Dinan (n 16) 274.

purported to give EU law primacy over the law of the Member States. Article I-6 stated that:

> The Constitution and law adopted by the institutions of the Union in exercising the competences conferred on it shall have primacy over the law of the Member States[57]

After the fall of the Draft Constitution this provision was dropped, and did not find its way into the Lisbon Treaty.[58] How the courts of Member States would have reacted to the provision can only be a matter of speculation. Perhaps national judges would have concluded that the provision only gave primacy to decisions which European institutions reach within the scope of the competences conferred on them by the Draft Constitution, and that a national court need not, therefore, attribute primacy to purported laws made in excess of conferred jurisdiction. Perhaps a divide might have been drawn between the law of Member States and their constitutional rules; with EU law taking primacy over national law, not over the national constitution.[59] But the inclusion of the primacy clause was a significant step, and, if the Draft Constitution had come into effect – particularly if it came into effect after a national referendum – it would have been hard for the courts of Member States to have retained, unmodified, their position on supremacy, discussed in the earlier part of this chapter. The primacy clause amounted to a challenge to Weiler's principle of constitutional tolerance, a principle that rested on the continuing consent of sovereign states.[60]

A further provision that nudged the Union towards a federal state, and one that did survive in the Lisbon Treaty, was Article I-60. This is now the notorious Article 50, which regulates the withdrawal of Member States from the Union.[61] Whilst the provision might seem designed to placate Eurosceptics, providing a path to exit from the Union, it is a provision that appears more federal than confederal. In a confederation a state can leave at any time. There is no need for a special process for exit; the confederation neither claims, nor possesses, the power to stop one of its sovereign constituent states from leaving. In a federation, in contrast, it is the national constitution that determines the capacity of regions to leave the federation.[62] Some federations give some territories a right of exit, some create structures through which a right might be conferred, whilst others allow no space for this possibility – but, as Jean Monnet noted long ago, in a federation

---

[57] Official Journal C310 (16 December 2004).

[58] Craig, *The Lisbon Treaty* (n 53) 146–51.

[59] PP Craig 'The Constitutional Treaty and Sovereignty' in C Kaddous and A Auer (eds), *Les Principes Fondamentaux de la Constitution Europeene* (Geneva, Bruylant, 2006).

[60] See J Weiler, 'A Constitution for Europe? Some Hard Choices' (2002) 40 *Journal of Common Market Studies* 563, 658–59.

[61] C Hillion, 'Accession and Withdrawal in the Law of the European Union' in A Arnull and D Chalmers (eds), *The Oxford Handbook of European Union Law* (Oxford, Oxford University Press, 2015).

[62] D Haljan, *Constitutionalising Secession* (Oxford, Hart Publishing, 2014), esp ch 8; R Weill, 'Secession and the Prevalence of Militant Constitutionalism Worldwide' (2019) *Cardoza Law Review* (forthcoming).

no region can leave by unilateral decision.[63] By including Article I-60 in the Draft Constitution, the Convention authored a document that purported to confer and regulate the Member States' right of exit.

Finally – though other provisions could also be examined – the Draft Constitution sought to introduce the Charter of Rights into EU law.[64] The Charter had been drawn up in 2000, but whilst it had been used by the Commission to review its legislation it was not yet legally binding.[65] The inclusion of the Charter in the Draft Constitution would have rendered it binding within EU law, though not applicable in national law that fell outside of this field. The Charter is a curious document.[66] It includes rights found within the European Convention on Human Rights (ECHR), but expresses these rights in different terms. The Charter made it clear that where there was an overlap with the ECHR the rights in the Charter should be given the meaning and scope of those in the ECHR – but left open the possibility that the Union might provide more extensive protection.[67] It also creates new rights not found in that document. Some of these – such as the prohibition on cloning or the protection of personal data – reflected technologic developments since the drafting of the ECHR in the 1950s.[68] Others reflect a growing ambition for the role of rights within the state. For example, the European Charter included the right of elderly people to participate in social and cultural life,[69] the right to a free work placement service,[70] and the right to a paid holiday,[71] amongst many other far-reaching rights.

It is worth noting that the version of the Charter included in the Draft Constitution did not include an important qualification later found in the Lisbon version, a qualification that sought to distinguish between 'principles' and other provisions in the Charter.[72] These 'principles' can, it seems, only be relied upon to interpret acts or be used as a basis on which to ground the legality of legislation. Though the legal effect of this provision is debatable, it seems that 'principles' cannot be relied upon as a ground to challenge legislation that would otherwise be valid or relied upon to require the production of new legislation.

Once again, the Charter pushed Europe towards the state-model. It mirrored the bills of rights commonly found within nation states, presenting Europe as the body with primary responsibility for their protection. Though the motivation to provide some form of rights protection at the Union level was understandable, it risked creating – and, after Lisbon, may well have created – constitutional confusion

---

[63] Duff, *On Governing Europe: A Federal Experiment* (n 44) 31–32.

[64] Norman (n 48) 68–71.

[65] P Craig and G de Búrca, *EU Law: Text, Cases, and Materials*, 6th edn (Oxford, Oxford University Press, 2015) 16.

[66] The original text is found in [2000] OJ C364/1.

[67] Art 52(3).

[68] Art 8 and Art 3(2).

[69] Art 25.

[70] Art 29.

[71] Art 31(2).

[72] [2012] OJ C362/391, Art 52(5).

within the legal orders of Member States. All Member States were also signatories to the ECHR. All the Member States also had domestic bills of rights in some form, which more or less closely tracked the ECHR. Consequently, at the time of the Draft Constitution, Member States already had two human rights systems operating within their territory – the domestic and the ECHR – and the Charter added a third system where states laws fell within the reach of EU law. There are, then, three relevant documents and three relevant sets of courts, all tied in a complicated relationship of mutual recognition and interaction in each Member State. Whilst this might be seen as a benefit for those looking to protect rights, allowing them to pick and choose between a range of documents and a range of courts, the uncertainties it brings incur at least two costs. First, the range of action of political institutions becomes less clear. Bills of rights serve to limit, with greater or less severity, the capacity of the democratic part of the constitution to make decisions. Given the importance of democracy to the legitimacy of the state, these restrictions should be exceptional and, so far as possible, clearly defined. Having multiple, overlapping, bills of rights runs the risk that legislators will be uncertain about their scope of action, impairing the functioning of democracy. Second, and building on this point, bills of rights should speak to citizens: the document is an expression of *their* rights, a recognition of their place within the state. Bills of rights can help encourage people to identify with the state by providing a constitutional articulation of some of the features of state-membership. Ironically, one of the motivations behind the creation of the Draft Constitution was to make the Union more comprehensible to, and less remote from, its citizens.[73] But by creating confusion around rights there is a risk that the capacity of bills of rights to play this role will be lost, and the various rights instruments will come to be seen merely as technical instruments used by lawyers in their challenges to state action, and not as documents intended to be read by citizens.

That the Draft Constitution challenged the Grand Bargain was noted by academics at the time. Joseph Weiler warned that the adoption of the Draft Constitution would move Europe away from the 'constitutional tolerance' that grounded the relationship between the Member States and the Union.[74] Whilst Pavlos Eleftheriadis, though more positively disposed towards the project, asserted that the constitutional nature of the Draft Constitution would entail profound changes to the Union's competences: national courts would be compelled to concede unqualified primacy to EU law, Directives would be give horizontal as well as vertical direct effect, and the Charter of Rights would gain domestic legal force.[75]

---

[73] G de Burca, 'The European Constitution Project After the Referenda' (2006) 113 *Constellations* 205, 206.

[74] J Weiler, 'A Constitution For Europe? Some Hard Choices' (2002) 40 *Journal of Common Market Studies* 563.

[75] P Eleftheriadis, 'Constitution or Treaty?' *Federal Trust Online Paper* 12/04.

One of the most surprising things about the Draft Constitution was the extent to which it included provisions that were unlikely to have much practical effect whilst being virtually certain to stir opposition to the project. The title of the document, the constitutional dressings, the primacy clause, were all features that were likely to irritate supporters of the confederal model of Europe – and, of course, infuriate those Euro-sceptics who were opposed to the European project. These were very prominent parts of a very bulky document, set out in the first few pages. It was always likely that these would be features that would be seized upon in any subsequent debates over the adoption of the document.

In retrospect, the Draft Constitution provides a textbook example of a premature attempt to resolve a constitutional disagreement. With the exception of the Charter of Rights – which, for good or ill, was a substantial change worth arguing over – the other state-like aspects of the document were unnecessary. Their impact on the substance of European law, those rules that shaped the conduct of the people of Europe, was likely to be slight. There was no pressing need, no crisis, that necessitated a choice between the two Europes at that moment. No broad social consensus had emerged that would have made the choice an easy one. By forcing the issue, the Convention challenged the Grand Bargain on which the development of Europe had rested to that point; and, by creating a conflict within the ranks of the supporters of the Union, risked weakening that project.

B. The Path to Brexit

Ideologically, Brexit stands as the extreme opposite to the Draft Constitution project. If the Draft Constitution was an attempt to push Europe towards federation, Brexit amounts to a push towards a radically loosened connection between the United Kingdom and the rest of the Member States. Any links between the Draft Constitution and Brexit must be drawn with exceptional caution; the Draft Constitution was rarely cited, if at all, in the Brexit debates, and it is likely that for most voters in the United Kingdom it was a distant memory. But there are some aspects of the Draft Constitution story that may have played a part in shaping the public mood that led to the Brexit vote. Whilst the content of the Draft Constitution may have caused lasting concern to some – amounting to a manifesto for a Europe they disliked – it could be that it was the process by which the document was produced and the manner in which the European elites responded to its rejection that were its lasting legacies.

In terms of process, as was discussed earlier, the Convention did make a genuine effort to include different voices in the process and to reach out to the public during the formation of the Draft Constitution, but these attempts to engage were of limited effect. For many in Europe, it must have seemed that this radical change, a change that looked to some like the abandonment of Member State sovereignty in the creation of new federal entity, was both a surprise and a *fait accompli*. It was a surprise, in that there was no obvious need for the creation of a new constitutional order. Many people, I suspect, were unaware this process was being undertaken. Once produced, it was presented as a *fait accompli* in that there seemed to be no process that would enable people to object to provisions or call for modifications.[76] The Draft Constitution was presented as a package that the peoples of Europe were expected to accept as a whole.

These two elements may have combined to reinforce a sense that there is a gap between the elite of Europe and its people. The Draft Constitution was the product of a very small section of European society, and allowed people outside of that set little capacity to engage with its production. There is an echo here, perhaps, of the Brexit referendum. In the referendums on the Draft Constitution and in the Brexit referendum, a very broad divide can be seen between those who had benefited from globalisation, often those with higher education qualifications and money, and those who are worried by globalisation, often the poorer part of society.[77] There is an irony in that the Draft Constitution aspired to help reduce Europe's democratic deficit, to draw people closer to the European project and improve democratic accountability.[78] But the manner of its creation and presentation may have achieved the opposite; giving the impression that Europe was an elite project, one that the rest of the people of Europe were expected to be grateful for, rather than participate in.

After the rejection of the Draft Constitution by the peoples of France and the Netherlands, much of that document was transferred into the Treaty of Lisbon.[79] The people of France and Netherlands were not given a second chance to vote on Lisbon. The Irish were, however, and rejected that Treaty in 2008 – but, a year later, voters were asked again and, with some assurances from the Union on the number of commissioners, Ireland's military neutrality and abortion laws, voted for the Lisbon Treaty.

As Professor Weatherill argues in his contribution to this volume, the reintroduction of much of the substance of the Draft Constitution into the Lisbon Treaty is problematic. This is not a comment on the content of the transferred provisions; whilst this chapter has focused on the constitutionally controversial aspects of the Draft Constitution, there were many other provisions in that document that were far less controversial. Instead, it is the manner in which these provisions entered into the Lisbon Treaty that might cause concern. The Draft Treaty was rejected by the peoples of France and the Netherlands, but those voters nevertheless ended up subject to many of the rules in that document. As Professor Craig argues in

---

[76] Dehousse, 'Lessons' (n 51) 158.

[77] On the Dutch referendum, see R Cuperus, 'Why the Dutch Voted No' (2005) 4 *Progressive Politics* 92, 101–02; on the French referendum, see Dehousse (n 51) 155–56; on Brexit: S Hobolt, 'The Brexit Vote: a Nation Divided, a Divided Continent' (2016) 23 *Journal of European Public Policy* 1259, esp 1265–70.

[78] A point put powerfully by MacCormick: N MacCormick, *Who's Afraid of a European Constitution?* (London, Imprint Press, 2005) ch 1.

[79] Dinan (n 16) 308–10; Craig (n 53) 23–25.

his chapter, the reasons for the French and Dutch rejections may have turned on local political issues rather than a careful assessment of the merits of the Draft Constitution, but the resurrection of the Draft Constitution in Lisbon may have added to the impression that the European project is only weakly linked to the wishes of its people.

III. Conclusion

Could it have been different? Could the Draft Constitution have been a success? It could certainly have been produced in a manner that engaged more directly and fully with the peoples of Europe. There could have been greater opportunities for people outside of the Convention to engage with the process. As Professor Nicolaïdis argues in this volume, more use could have been made of the internet, and more local meetings could have been organised. The style of the document should, perhaps, have been different: a shorter text that could be read and understood by the people it addressed might have proved more popular. But in the end, it was probably just not the right time for a challenge to be made to the Grand Bargain on which Europe's development rested. There was no need to choose between the two visions of Europe, and by attempting to force the choice, the Draft Constitution may have weakened the European project.

8

The Competence Catalogue in the Treaty Establishing a Constitution and the Treaty of Lisbon: Improvement, but at a Cost

STEPHEN WEATHERILL*

I. Introduction

The principal focus of this chapter is the matter of competence. The EU possesses only the competences conferred on it by its founding Treaties. Competences not so conferred on the EU rest with the Member States. The EU accordingly operates only within a limited domain, that mapped by its conferred competence, and it is the Member States, by ratifying the Treaties, which are the foundational source of its legitimate authority. The longstanding problem in the EU has been the poorly defined limits of the scope of conferred competence and, an associated problem, the tendency in practice for competences to 'creep' outwards to the detriment of national autonomy. This was an important agenda item at the Convention on the Future of Europe, which shaped the Treaty establishing a Constitution, and concrete proposals for reform emerged. The Treaty establishing a Constitution would have made important contributions to improving the pattern of competence definition and competence demarcation, both at the level of the substance of the rules and in the matter of institutional process. Those planned improvements to the EU's competence catalogue were sunk by the negative referendums in France and the Netherlands, but they were, with only negligible adjustment, retained during the negotiation of the Treaty of Lisbon, and they are today the basis of the EU system governing competence. In this sense, the Treaty establishing a Constitution exerted a clear and strong formative influence even after its demise.

* Law Faculty and Somerville College, University of Oxford.

The purpose of this chapter is, first, to summarise, in short, 'the competence problem' in the EU (section II). It then tells the story of the treatment of competence at the Convention on the Future of Europe, paving the way for the agreement of the Treaty establishing a Constitution (section III). It then examines the amending Treaty of Lisbon and, in particular, traces the contours which are plainly visible in that Treaty which were originally put in place by the (rejected) Treaty establishing a Constitution (section IV). The chapter offers comment in a generally approving fashion on the changes that were made, which were designed to make more intelligible the basic structure and nature of the EU's legislative competences, and observes how they, embedded in the TEU and TFEU, have been put into practice since the entry into force of the Treaty of Lisbon in 2009 (section V). I think the reforms were and are largely helpful to the functioning of the EU – so this is the improvement to which the title of this chapter refers.

Then, however, the chapter adopts a more critical perspective. The EU system governing competence today is incomparably superior to that which had been developed incrementally over time, under the cycle of revision of the original Treaties that culminated in the Treaty of Nice. The problem is not substance – the problem is process. The reforms envisaged by the Treaty establishing a Constitution were subsequently re-presented in almost exactly the same substance, if not exactly the same form, in the Treaty of Lisbon. The Treaty establishing a Constitution was rejected by referendums in two of the EU's founding Member States, yet the corpse was kept warm and its vital organs, of which the competence catalogue was one, were transplanted to the text of the Treaty of Lisbon, in respect of which no referendums (except in Ireland) were permitted. The problem, then, is subversion of the expressed will of the people of two Member States. This is section VI of the chapter. It is a powerful example of the deceptive pattern whereby much of the content of the Treaty establishing a Constitution was simply re-packaged as the Treaty of Lisbon and shoved through the ratification process largely unchanged, but via a route which avoided the irritation of asking the peoples of (most parts of) Europe whether they approved. This – alienation, disengagement – is the cost to which the chapter's title refers.

There are other aspects of the re-making of the Treaty establishing a Constitution as the (in substance, little changed) Treaty of Lisbon which invite similarly mournful assessment, but section VII steps outside this instance to show how a comparable narrative of evading popular explanation – let alone approval – blights the development of the Eurozone. The suspicion that 'more Europe' is being imposed on the peoples of Europe without their knowledge, let alone their consent, is not confined to the sorry tale of the demise and after-life of the Treaty establishing a Constitution.

The matter of competence, the principal concern of this chapter, is one platform on which to build this critique, and then, in section VIII of the chapter, to reflect on possible solutions. These focus on making more flexible the process of amending EU law. Section IX concludes.

II. The 'Competence Problem'

The legitimacy of the European Union is damaged if it trespasses beyond the sphere of the competences attributed to it by its founding Treaties, because this is to undermine the basic constitutional design whereby the EU does what it does according to the consensual transfer made by the Member States at time of accession to and revision of the Treaties. Moreover its legitimacy is damaged if it exercises competences attributed to it in a manner that unnecessarily interferes with the competences that remain in the hands of the Member States.

This phenomenon of what can conveniently be labelled 'competence creep' engages harm to both the EU's *formal* and its *social* legitimacy. Adherence to the *formal* rule that the EU's competences are limited to those conferred on it by its founding Treaties, as stipulated today by Article 5 TEU but always an (initially unwritten) principle underpinning the EU's legal order, is undermined by such trends, while *social* acceptance of the EU is diminished where it is seen to stretch to act in spheres where popular acceptance of its legitimate role is weak and where, worse still, it may do a poor job because it is institutionally and/or constitutionally ill-equipped to do what it pretends to do.

The core of the 'competence problem' lies in the gap between the purity of the assertion of limited competence contained in Article 5 TEU and the practical operation of the system established by the Treaties. There are a lot of bases for legislative action scattered across the Treaties, but two stand out as the most problematic in the matter of conferring a competence that in practice is deceptively wide. These are the pair of functionally-driven legal bases: they are today Articles 114 and 352 TFEU, but they have in some form always been in the Treaty. They have limits – in short, a tie to the making of the internal market under Article 114 and a tie to the EU's objectives under Article 352 – but these are limits that lack precision, and both legal bases have been exploited for the making of wide-ranging legislation in a great many areas which, crucially in practice, are not easily shown *not* to be connected to those broad and vague objectives. So for every *Tobacco Advertising* finding legislative use of (what is now) Article 114 invalid[1] and for every *Opinion on Accession to the ECHR* finding use of (what is now) Article 352 invalid[2] there are heaps of examples of legislative action based on the provisions where political will was strong but constitutional authority, though uncertain, was typically assumed and the matter left unchallenged. And today it is Article 114 that really matters. It requires the ordinary legislative procedure, entailing a qualified majority in Council combined with the support of the Parliament, whereas Article 352 is in practice sidelined because of the demanding requirement of unanimity in Council. And even where measures of legislative harmonisation have been challenged, they have commonly been sanctioned by the Court, which has crafted a

---

[1] Case C-376/98 *Germany v Parliament and Council* EU:C:2000:544.
[2] Opinion 2/94 EU:C:1996:140.

test which is broad and readily recycled by the legislative process.[3] It is in fact close to non-falsifiable.[4] The fear is that this constitutionally-flimsy control over legislative action tends to generate a centralising dynamic which lacks political legitimacy.

Also relevant to the critical account is the weak performance of the two structural principles of EU law which are meant to govern the exercise of a conferred competence – the principles of subsidiarity and of proportionality. Here too legislative practice readily claims compliance and the Court is very slow to intervene. From an economic perspective, subsidiarity might conceivably help to focus attention on the need for a proper accounting of the costs and benefits of choosing between centralised rules and local autonomy,[5] but this serves to highlight that subsidiarity's role is promoting the asking of the right sort of questions rather than providing definitive answers. In itself it is deficient in the necessary vigour to act as an operationally useful controlling mechanism. It does not generate a simple yes-or-no answer to the question 'should the EU do this?'. Partly for this reason the Court has found a way to check the compliance of EU measures with subsidiarity in principle without engaging in review in practice. For legislative harmonisation the Court asks whether the EU is better at producing common rules than its Member States – and of course it inevitably is.[6] Producing common rules is what the EU does. The political decision to act is in this way largely immunised from judicial review. In a functionally similar manner the Court, using a test which grants a high level of discretion to the decision-maker, has robbed proportionality of any real force in checking legislative ambition practised at EU level.[7]

An extra dimension to 'competence creep' lies in the often misperceived significance of the wider reach of negative EU law compared with positive EU law. The law of the internal market – free movement, competition law and non-discrimination – reach into areas that are not (at all or much) within the scope of the EU's legislative competence. They do not direct what shall be done (the province of positive law) but rather they prohibit practices that are incompatible with EU internal market law (in this sense, negative law). So, for example, sport was not even mentioned in the Treaty until 2009, and even now the legislative competence granted by Article 165 TFEU is slender, but this did not stop the Court challenging sporting autonomy where its exercise conflicted with the demands of the law of the

---

[3] eg on Art 114 Case C-380/03 *Germany v Parliament and Council* EU:C:2006:772; Case C-270/12 *UK v Council and Parliament* EU:C:2014:18; Case C-547/14 *Philip Morris Brands* EU:C:2016:325.

[4] S Weatherill, 'The Limits of Legislative Harmonisation Ten Years after *Tobacco Advertising*: how the Court's Case Law has Become a "Drafting Guide"' (2011) 12 *German Law Journal* 827; J Oberg, 'The Rise of the Procedural Paradigm: Judicial Review of EU Legislation in Vertical Competence Disputes' (2017) 13 *European Constitutional Law Review* 248.

[5] See, eg, R Van den Bergh, 'Farewell Utopia? Why the European Union should take the Economics of Federalism Seriously' (2016) 23 *Maastricht Journal of European and Comparative Law* 937.

[6] eg Case C-491/01 *R v Secretary of State, ex parte BAT and Imperial Tobacco* EU:C:2002:741; Case C-58/08 *Vodafone, O2 et al v Secretary of State* EU:C:2010:321.

[7] eg *Vodafone* (n 6).

internal market.[8] Similarly Article 153(5) TFEU excludes the right to strike from the legislative competence conferred by that Treaty provision, but this does not block the application of the free movement rules to trade unions taking industrial action which interferes with cross-border corporate mobility.[9]

In the background lurks a vital structural point. The Treaty does not declare particular sectors to be off-limits to the EU. Nor does it reserve particular functions to the Member States. Article 5(1) TEU's reference to the 'limits' of Union competence is not supported by clear and easily monitored rules – nor, arguably, by attentive institutions either. Competence control was founded on an assumption of *ex ante* restraint by the political institutions and *ex post* review by the Court. In principle, an act should not be adopted if it trespasses beyond the scope of the mandate conferred by the Treaty. Nor should a competence, even if established as attributed by the Treaty, be exercised if that would conflict with the principles of subsidiarity and/or proportionality. And if the rules are infringed the act is susceptible to annulment by the Court. But 'institutional incestuousness' prevails in the EU. The practice of competence monitoring is complacent and weak.

III. The 'Competence Solution': The Treaty Establishing a Constitution

Faced by problems associated with both the structure and presentation of the Treaty and the prevailing institutional culture in the EU, some revolutionary ideas were touted at the Convention on the Future of Europe.[10] These ranged from a 'hard list' of competences (exhaustive and tightly defined lists of the areas in which the Union is competent to act; or identification of areas off-limits to the Union and therefore remaining within the exclusive competence of the Member States); deletion of what are today Articles 114 and 352 TFEU as the principal motors of competence creep; granting a veto power to national parliaments; sterner judicial control of adopted or even proposed legislation, perhaps involving a freshly minted 'court of competence', comprising members drawn from not only the EU but also national judiciaries.

Whichever particular model is preferred, the basic aim is to block 'competence creep' and to confine the EU to an agenda which can be reliably identified in advance; and moreover to ensure the whistle can be blown quickly and uncontroversially if the boundary is crossed. The problem is that this will in turn impose significant costs measured in inflexibility. It will diminish the EU's capacity to act effectively in order to address (the rather wide range of) objectives assigned to it by its Treaty. This would, by fracturing the EU's problem-solving flexibility,

---

[8] Case C-415/93 *Bosman* EU:C:1995:463.

[9] Case C-438/05 *Viking Line* EU:C:2007:772; Case C-341/05 *Laval* EU:C:2007:809.

[10] S Weatherill, 'Competence Creep and Competence Control' (2004) 23 *Yearbook of European Law* 1.

weaken an important source of legitimacy. These anxieties were salient: the finally agreed plans were at the conservative end of the scale. The chosen solutions were clarification, transparency and extra monitoring by national parliaments, but not according to a veto.

So the solution proposed by the Convention on the Future of Europe, and endorsed by the Heads of State and Government in 2004, was composed of two parts. First, the agreed text sought to clarify and re-organise the Treaty rules governing competence. Second, it freshened the system for monitoring the existence and exercise of competence by bringing in new actors from outwith the uncritical EU institutional family – most of all, *national parliaments* were to be invested with the responsibility to stop creep according to a new *ex ante* monitoring system, the 'early warning system' and the so-called yellow card procedure. So, it was intended, the rules should be clearer, making misperceptions less excusable and their application easier. And, in the shape of national parliaments, an extra and previously excluded new monitor would be introduced into aspects of the 'competence debate'. After all national parliaments would have a real incentive to look critically at centralising tendencies promoted by the EU law-making process given their particular sensitivity to the political marginalisation consequent on such rhythms.

Article I-1 of the Treaty declared: that 'Reflecting the will of the citizens and States of Europe to build a common future, this Constitution establishes the European Union, on which the Member States confer competences to attain objectives they have in common.'

Title III of Part 1 was entitled *Union Competences*. It covered Articles 1-11 to 1-18. Article 1-11, *Fundamental principles*, provided:

1. The limits of Union competences are governed by the principle of conferral. The use of Union competences is governed by the principles of subsidiarity and proportionality.

2. Under the principle of conferral, the Union shall act within the limits of the competences conferred upon it by the Member States in the Constitution to attain the objectives set out in the Constitution. Competences not conferred upon the Union in the Constitution remain with the Member States.

3. Under the principle of subsidiarity, in areas which do not fall within its exclusive competence, the Union shall act only if and insofar as the objectives of the proposed action cannot be sufficiently achieved by the Member States, either at central level or at regional and local level, but can rather, by reason of the scale or effects of the proposed action, be better achieved at Union level.

The institutions of the Union shall apply the principle of subsidiarity as laid down in the Protocol on the application of the principles of subsidiarity and proportionality. National Parliaments shall ensure compliance with that principle in accordance with the procedure set out in that Protocol.

4. Under the principle of proportionality, the content and form of Union action shall not exceed what is necessary to achieve the objectives of the Constitution.

The institutions of the Union shall apply the principle of proportionality as laid down in the Protocol on the application of the principles of subsidiarity and proportionality.

The rest of Title III goes on to set out the types of competence conferred on the EU, and the areas of activity to which they attach. There are three principal types: exclusive, shared and supporting. In line with the longstanding structure of the Treaties, the fourth competence which in principle must exist – exclusive Member State competence – is mentioned (in Article 1-11(2), set out above) but its scope is left wholly unelaborated.

Anyone familiar with the current state of EU law in this area will immediately identify that both substantively and institutionally the similarities between the 'lost' scheme of the Treaty establishing a Constitution and the Lisbon Treaty's subsequent adjustments are very strong.

IV. The Treaties as Amended by the Lisbon Treaty

The structure of the Treaty establishing a Constitution is quite different from that of the Treaty of Lisbon. The Treaty establishing a Constitution would have been a new beginning and the Treaties would have been changed into a single text, divided into four Parts. Once this was abandoned in the wake of the French and Dutch referendums, the plan shifted back to the orthodoxy of incremental Treaty revision, and what we have today as a result of the reforms made by the Lisbon Treaty, the TEU and the TFEU, are simply the latest version of the much-amended original Treaties, dating back to the 1950s in the case of the TFEU and the 1990s in the case of the TEU. So the material dealing with competence spans both the TEU and TFEU, and it is more fragmented than the model of the Treaty establishing a Constitution. But the *content* is scarcely altered at all. After the structural adjustment, whereby the Lisbon Treaty, unlike the Treaty establishing a Constitution, is simply an amending Treaty is taken into account, and taking account too of the ruthless stripping-out of any 'constitutional' discourse and motifs, the similarities far outweigh the differences when one examines the treatment of competences.

Article 1 TEU declares that 'By this Treaty, the High Contracting Parties establish among themselves a European Union, hereinafter called "the Union", on which the Member States confer competences to attain objectives they have in common'. This is an echo of Article I-1 of the Treaty establishing a Constitution.

Article 4(1) TEU provides that 'In accordance with Article 5, competences not conferred upon the Union in the Treaties remain with the Member States'. This reference to the 'fourth competence' in the EU's constitutional architecture – exclusive Member State competence – appears twice, because Article 5(2) TEU makes the same point, and it is made again in Declaration 8 appended to the Treaties, *Declaration in relation to the delimitation of competences*. The Lisbon Treaty therefore uses belt-and-braces on this point. This is part of the defensive mood music of the Treaty in the aftermath of constitutional hubris. None of this recitation of the protection of exclusive Member State competence is new as a matter of law, but the explicit hammering home of these points in the Treaty reflects the political desire of the time to emphasise still further the *limited* nature of the EU's competences and powers. But, in line with past practice, nothing spells out exactly what falls within the zone of exclusive Member State competence.

The more detailed material on competence is divided between the TEU and the TFEU.

The master provision is now Article 5 TEU:

1. The limits of Union competences are governed by the principle of conferral. The use of Union competences is governed by the principles of subsidiarity and proportionality.

2. Under the principle of conferral, the Union shall act only within the limits of the competences conferred upon it by the Member States in the Treaties to attain the objectives set out therein. Competences not conferred upon the Union in the Treaties remain with the Member States.

3. Under the principle of subsidiarity, in areas which do not fall within its exclusive competence, the Union shall act only if and in so far as the objectives of the proposed action cannot be sufficiently achieved by the Member States, either at central level or at regional and local level, but can rather, by reason of the scale or effects of the proposed action, be better achieved at Union level.

The institutions of the Union shall apply the principle of subsidiarity as laid down in the Protocol on the application of the principles of subsidiarity and proportionality. National Parliaments ensure compliance with the principle of subsidiarity in accordance with the procedure set out in that Protocol.

4. Under the principle of proportionality, the content and form of Union action shall not exceed what is necessary to achieve the objectives of the Treaties.

The institutions of the Union shall apply the principle of proportionality as laid down in the Protocol on the application of the principles of subsidiarity and proportionality.

This is obviously a warm embrace of what was Article 1-11 of the Treaty establishing a Constitution.

Title 1 of Part 1 the TFEU is entitled '*Categories and Areas of Union Competence*', and it covers Articles 2 to 6 TFEU. It is, with only a few cosmetic changes, identical to the provisions of the Treaty establishing a Constitution. So it rests on specification of three types of EU competence – exclusive, shared, supporting – and areas of activity falling within these categories are listed. In addition, the role of national parliaments as monitors is recognised. Equally, and more concretely, the small number of 'new' legal bases for legislative action foreseen by the Treaty establishing a Constitution are absorbed in the Lisbon Treaty.[11]

Changes were few, and largely presentational. The eagle-eyed will note that Title III of Part 1 of the Treaty establishing a Constitution contained eight articles, whereas the combination of Article 5 TEU and the provisions in the TFEU yields only six articles. Two of the provisions were not taken over directly. Article I-16 in the Treaty establishing a Constitution deals with the common foreign and

---

[11] See Art 118 TFEU on Intellectual Property, Art 165 TFEU on sport, and Art 194 TFEU on energy.

security policy, and it is now to be found in an extended version in Article 24 TEU. Article I-18 Treaty establishing a Constitution was called the 'flexibility clause': it is the safety-net legal base that has been in the system since the very start, and it is now to be found in Article 352 TFEU. But overall the verdict is clear: the alterations favoured by the Treaty establishing a Constitution were largely imported without adjustment into the Treaty of Lisbon.

Under the Lisbon Treaty, national parliaments are to exercise the essence of the newly granted responsibilities which were already mapped out in the Treaty establishing a Constitution. Article 12 TEU, located in Title II on *Provisions on Democratic Principles*, deals with the role of national parliaments. They shall 'contribute actively to the good functioning of the Union'. The means envisaged to bring this about cover: receiving information from the Union's institutions and having draft legislative acts forwarded to them in accordance with the Protocol; and ensuring respect for the subsidiarity principle in line with the procedure set out in the Protocol; plus several other activities which I do not consider here because they are not directly relevant to issues of competence.

The Protocol on the role of national parliaments deals with the distribution of information to national parliaments. It allows the submission of a reasoned opinion in cases of suspected violation of the subsidiarity principle, and mandates a standstill period designed to give national parliaments a real practical opportunity to intervene, applicable in all but urgent cases. The standstill lasts eight weeks, which is two weeks longer than was provided for in the Treaty establishing a Constitution.

The Protocol on subsidiarity and proportionality absorbs this procedure in Article 6. Then, in Article 7, it puts flesh on the bones. The essence is unchanged from the Treaty establishing a Constitution's model. The vigour of the procedure is, however, slightly enhanced. Where reasoned opinions on non-compliance with subsidiarity represent at least one-third of all the votes allocated to national parliaments, the draft must be reviewed. The Commission may then maintain, amend or withdraw the draft, giving reasons for this. This is the yellow card. Where reasoned opinions on non-compliance with subsidiarity represent a simple majority of votes cast by national parliaments, then the Commission must review the proposal and, if it decides to maintain it, it must itself present a reasoned opinion dealing with its view why the proposal complies with the subsidiarity principle. These opinions are then made available to the Union legislator and shall be considered in the manner set out in Article 7(3) of the Protocol. This is the orange card, and it constitutes a more elaborate version of the consequences should the Commission choose to maintain its proposal in the face of objections registered by national parliaments than had been planned under the Treaty establishing a Constitution. Plainly the overall aim is to maximise the opportunity for dialogue and for the voice of the national parliaments to be heard effectively.

So, in the matter of national parliamentary involvement, the Lisbon Treaty envisages a slightly deeper intrusion than was foreseen by the Treaty establishing a

Constitution – eight weeks' 'standstill', not six, and an elaborated requirement of a formal Commission response in some circumstances where objections are raised. But, basically, the Lisbon Treaty adheres to the model proposed by the Convention on the Future of Europe and adopted in the Treaty establishing a Constitution. Most of all, what is today found in Articles 2 to 6 TFEU is in all material respects identical to the pattern of Articles 1-11 to 1-18 of the Treaty establishing a Constitution.

V. Practice Since the Reforms were Put in Place

The scheme governing competence which has prevailed since 2009 is not perfect. The definition of shared competence in Article 2(2) TFEU is at best clumsy and at worst wrong, and had to be (partially) rescued by Protocol 25 on the exercise of shared competence. The sharp divide between subsidiarity, which is monitored by national parliaments, and proportionality, which is not, is an error. The two principles are closely related and in some respects they overlap (for example, in judging the appropriate intensity of EU action) and to include one but not the other in the system for review by national parliaments risks triggering unhelpful demarcation disputes. More generally, it would be unwise to expect too much of the involvement of national parliaments. Their resources are finite and, given the absence of a red card, their incentives to engage are modest. Practice bears this out. In eight years, there have been only three yellow cards and no orange ones, and 88 is the highest number of reasoned opinions submitted in a single calendar year (in 2013).

However, overall the reforms are an improvement when compared with the pre-existing system. Articles 2 to 6 TFEU are far more accessible than what went before, in that they offer a description of what the EU does and how. The employment of national parliaments is well-intentioned: it is a model that rejects the more radical proposed changes advanced at the Convention and so accepts the basic structure of the EU as sound, but seeks to promote more dialogue about the worth of particular legislative proposals.

VI. Evasion

My broad anxiety is that the failure of the Treaty establishing a Constitution and the success (of sorts) of the Lisbon Treaty offers a glimpse of a nightmare:

> the EU has become too complicated and intransparent for voters to understand and, as a reaction, they reject the texts handed down for their approval by political élites, and so the texts are then converted into legally binding instruments through means that carefully avoid those voters (except the Irish). So deepens the lack of understanding; so grows popular resentment to an authoritarian sense of 'we know best'.[12]

---

[12] S Weatherill, *Law and Values in the European Union* (Oxford, Oxford University Press, 2016) 418.

There are two main consequences. If Treaty revision by referendum is too risky, it is done either by avoiding the need for a referendum or by avoiding the need for a Treaty revision. This simply increases the poison of popular resentment.

The Treaty of Lisbon was Treaty revision, but by evasion. The promises made to voters about participation in the ratification of the Treaty establishing a Constitution were broken through the trick of claiming that the deal was qualitatively different. It was not. The Treaty establishing a Constitution would have recast the system in four parts, imposing new clean lines on the Treaty in preference to the previous pattern of incremental revision, whereas the Treaty of Lisbon adheres to that old incremental model. But that is only *presentationally* significant: it did not and could not alter the fact that, at bottom, both texts were Treaties which sought to amend the working method of the EU. In particular the claims made in the Conclusions of the European Council Presidency in June 2007, at the moment of abandonment of the Treaty establishing a Constitution and the shift to what would become the Lisbon Treaty, deserve a sceptical hearing. The Conclusions declared that 'the constitutional concept which consisted in repealing all existing treaties and replacing them by a single text called Constitution is abandoned', and they heralded too the demise of an EU motto and flag – the 'symbols of the Union' mentioned in Article I-8. So the Lisbon Treaty is not the same as the Treaty establishing a Constitution. But in content, if not in structure, it is similar. And the 'constitutional concept' was in any event devoid of any formal legal significance.

It is commonly sneered that the EU overrides negative outcomes in national referendums by requiring that a second vote be held. And it is true that in Denmark, in the case of the Maastricht Treaty, and Ireland, in the cases of the Nice and the Lisbon Treaty, a second referendum did indeed follow a first, in all three cases causing a negative outcome to be superseded by a positive. But the allegation that this is to defy democracy does not hold water. The EU did not – could not – force Denmark or Ireland to hold a second referendum. Nor could the EU determine the outcome of the second referendum. Those states chose to do so and their people chose, after some strategically evasive clarifications were issued, to consent to ratification of the relevant Treaties. This was not defiance of democracy – it was democracy. The story of the ratification of the Lisbon Treaty was (everywhere except Ireland) quite different. A first vote having been held in France and the Netherlands (and promised elsewhere, including in the UK), a second vote was then withheld, on the spurious basis that the Lisbon Treaty was qualitatively different from the rejected Treaty establishing a Constitution. But it was not.

The consequence is deeper popular alienation from an elite-driven project. Were the competence catalogue the only area in which this unhappy trick could be observed, then the critique would lack vigour. But not so: competence is a particularly vivid example of how the Treaty establishing a Constitution's changes were simply re-packaged in the Treaty of Lisbon, in way designed to avoid the need for the popular approval which had been withheld by the French and the Dutch, but it is by no means the only one. One could readily adopt a similar critical perspective if one inspects other aspects of the reforms attempted by the Treaty establishing a Constitution and then made by the Treaty of Lisbon. The Union's accession to the European Convention for the Protection of Human Rights and Fundamental Freedoms was mandated by Article I-9(2) of the Treaty establishing a Constitution, subject to the proviso that 'accession shall not affect the Union's competences as defined in the Constitution'. The text of the lost Article I-9(2) is now found in Article 6(2) TEU in *exactly* the same wording, save only that the proviso refers to the 'Treaties' rather than the 'Constitution'. The Treaty establishing a Constitution would have made the Charter of Fundamental Rights binding, and located it as Part 2 of the text: the Treaty of Lisbon achieves the same legal result, albeit that it does not embed the Charter within the Treaties but rather cross-refers to it in Article 6 TEU as a separate text.

Institutional reforms such as the formal recognition of the European Council and the creation of the role of its President, the re-definition and clarification of the intricacies of qualified majority voting in Council, an enhanced role for what we now know as the High Representative of the Union for Foreign Affairs and Security Policy, and the reduction in the number of Commissioners are all to be found in the Treaty establishing a Constitution and, in lightly-amended form, in the Treaty of Lisbon, even if the last of these, reduction in the number of Commissioners, was in practice averted, largely to satisfy the voters of Ireland, by a convenient procedure allowing the European Council to set aside the reduction which itself is to be found in both the Treaty establishing a Constitution and the Lisbon Treaty.[13]

So too the provision permitting voluntary withdrawal from the Union was conserved. It was Article I-60 of the Treaty establishing a Constitution, and is now, in materially similar form, Article 50 TEU, although it is of course well under-stood that, given the intricate interdependence of the Member States of the EU combined with the way that the provision itself is loaded in favour of protecting the interests of remaining Member States rather than the quitter, no state with an astute sense of political context would invoke it without having first clearly agreed where it wishes to be two years hence.

In all these instances, which are not an exhaustive list, the reforms made by the Treaty of Lisbon are recognisably those agreed in the Treaty establishing a Constitution. The referendums in France and the Netherlands lost, Treaty revision was nonetheless achieved without referendums (except in Ireland).

VII. The Eurozone

Revising the Treaties while avoiding the need for a referendum is only one available way forward. Avoiding the need for a Treaty revision altogether is another route. The trick is to step outside the EU system. The European Stability Mechanism

---

[13] Art I-26(6) Treaty establishing a Constitution; Art 17(5) TEU.

(ESM) is founded on a free-standing international Treaty to which most, but not all, EU Member States are party. It exists formally outwith the EU legal order, but it is in substance unavoidably tangled up with the existing rather dense thicket of adjacent EU law, and it also makes use of EU institutions. The Court was asked in *Pringle* to decide whether this scheme complied with EU law – in particular, but not only, whether what was envisaged as a set of binding obligations under international law amounted to an unlawful undermining of obligations already undertaken as EU Member States.[14] It did not. The Court found that the design could survive condemnation as a violation of EU law, but the awkwardness involved is plain from its atypical reasoning. In particular, the Court adopted a narrow reading of existing EU competences on monetary policy in order to find they did not bar the Eurozone countries from agreeing the ESM Treaty. The ruling is not *wrong* – the legal texts are too ambiguous to permit any such confident finding[15] – but it is out of line with the Court's normally generous reading of the scope of EU's competences, and it suggests a Court nervous when asked to upset politically sensitive compromises even where, and perhaps especially where, they strain the architecture of the EU.

The content of the ESM is framed round a 'golden rule' that government budgets be balanced, which the parties are to incorporate into their domestic constitutions. Its institutional arrangements are more strongly intergovernmental in character than EU orthodoxy, as one would expect given its formal designation as an instrument operating outwith the EU, although the Commission and the Court are 'borrowed' in limited aspects. More broadly, the European Council has become increasingly powerful in the development of the Eurozone, not only setting the direction of general initiatives but also becoming heavily engaged in detailed policy preparation, thereby subverting normal EU assumptions and also disempowering national parliaments.[16] A gap between the growing power exercised by, and the cramped chains of accountability of, the Eurogroup has been persuasively diagnosed.[17]

A system that draws on legal orders at national, EU and international levels will typically generate boundary disputes and conflicts. But of more profound significance is the background reason *why* this arrangement, lurking on the edges of the EU system, has been put in place. The financial crisis which erupted in 2008 led to the adoption of the so-called six-pack, followed by the two-pack – a group of

---

[14] Case C-370/12 EU:C:2012:756.

[15] For sharply divergent views, see G Beck, 'The Court of Justice, the Bundesverfassungsgericht and Legal Reasoning during the Euro Crisis: The Rule of Law as a Fair-Weather Phenomenon' (2014) 20 *European Public Law* 539; M Everson, 'An Exercise in Legal Honesty: Rewriting the Court of Justice and the Bundesverfassungsgericht' (2015) 21 *European Law Journal* 474; P Craig, 'Pringle and the Nature of Legal Reasoning' (2016) 23 *Maastricht Journal of European and Comparative Law* 205.

[16] See, eg, M Dawson and F De Witte, 'Constitutional Balance in the EU after the Euro-Crisis' (2013) 76 *Modern Law Review* 817; N Scicluna, 'Politicization without Democratization: How the Eurozone Crisis is Transforming EU Law and Politics' (2014) 12 *International Journal of Constitutional Law* 545.

[17] P Craig, 'The Eurogroup, power and accountability' (2017) 23 *European Law Journal* 234.

Regulations and Directives adopted under the TFEU.[18] But more was needed. The United Kingdom in particular was opposed to the idea of adopting new Treaty arrangements designed to enhance the EU's competence in the field, while Germany in particular was not content with the adoption of secondary rules of EU law and demanded the security of binding Treaty commitments. The chosen solution was the establishment of the ESM. It was no doubt a clever compromise which brought short-term relief. But it added yet another layer of complexity and intransparency to the management of the relationship between the Member States of the EU. The risk is long-term damage: further alienation, so that blockages to reform of the system simply become still more stubborn.

VIII. The Case for, and Possible Patterns of, Reform

The argument is that Treaty revision on a scale that triggers requirements for national referendums is politically blocked because of the unreadiness among voters to offer approval, vividly demonstrated by the negative results recorded in France and the Netherlands which sank the Treaty establishing a Constitution. The consequence is that other routes to change are found. The Lisbon Treaty was an exercise in Treaty revision without referendums (except in Ireland); the ESM shows a readiness to step outside the EU system altogether in order to secure reform. The consequence is a deepening of prevailing intransparency and the exacerbation of the alienation of voters. The problem, then, is an inflexibility and resistance to change that is endemic to the EU's system, but a bigger problem than inflexibility and resistance to change is evasion of that inflexibility and duplicitous subversion of that resistance.

What might be done, if anything, to secure a more vibrant engagement of citizens in the EU's trajectory and fate? This prompts two immediate, albeit rather defensive, responses: first, that there is no silver bullet, but instead that a menu of adjustments should be concocted, and second, that the required intimate connection with improving the design of the system reaches far beyond the plausible ambitions of this chapter. However, some features of a system that would be more flexible, and so more open to revision, are visible. But none is cost-free.

The most obvious focus is revision of the Treaties, but the inquiry should also extend to revision of secondary legislation and of rulings of the Court of Justice.

Were the Treaties capable of revision by some species of majority vote, rather than requiring the support of all the Member States, there would be a much higher degree of flexibility in the system. Negative referendums would no longer need to be evaded – provided they were few, they would be overridden. This change scores very well in improving the effective operation of the EU Treaty system as a dynamic

---

[18] For a full account, see A Hinarejos, *The Euro Area Crisis in Constitutional Perspective* (Oxford, Oxford University Press, 2015).

process. Lifting the veto power of individual Member States would, however, harm the system's social legitimacy. It would deepen the well of resentment.

A more modest version of this strategy already exists: the readiness to perform Treaty revision without binding all Member States to new commitments undertaken. This is the route to opt-outs, of which many, incrementally accepted at times of periodic Treaty revision, litter the Treaty superstructure. Such 'variable geometry' makes it easier for states that are reluctant with the direction of travel to agree nonetheless that they will, duly protected by an opt-out, consent to more rapid movement by the other Member States. The Treaty provisions on enhanced cooperation, inserted with effect from 1999 by the Treaty of Amsterdam, were designed as a more coherent and principled basis for managing such trends, although it has turned out that there is little appetite to use them. There are interesting things to say about the normative desirability of a model that seeks to respond to the pressures of geographical and functional expansion by treating them not as antagonistic to cherished uniformity but instead as a realistic response to differing conditions and different preferences. 'Ever closer union' and 'integration' deserve a sceptical appraisal as preferred paradigms.[19] One size does not fit all. But this solution is not cost-free. Creating more layers and more concentric circles within which to understand a fractured European Union is likely to make the picture more confused and thereby to deepen intransparency and alienation.

It is easier to change secondary legislation than it is to change the Treaties, but it is still not easy. There may be scope for allowing revision by procedures that require a lower threshold than the qualified majority voting numbers permit under the ordinary legislative procedure and/or for greater reliance on delegated or implementing legislation. 'Sunset' clauses may have a place too. It should be appreciated that here, too, the existing shape of the *acquis* reveals how the pressures of geographical and functional expansion have led to high levels of differentiation. It has been calculated that, looking across patterns of 'instrumental differentiation', largely driven by temporary sensitivities about the consequences of the widening of the EU's geographical scope, and 'constitutional differentiation', built on permanent expression of scepticism about deepening the EU's functional reach, and factoring in policy area, timeline and identification of which Member States are involved, it was possible in 2012 to identify 194 distinct forms of differentiation.[20] Talk of a two-speed Europe vastly underplays the reality. There is evidently flexibility in this design, but none of this seems likely to cure the ills of intransparency and alienation. Quite the reverse.

Consideration of the place of rulings of the Court of Justice is also merited. A distinction should be drawn between rulings of the Court which interpret primary law and those which deal with the interpretation of secondary legislation.

[19] See, eg, A Von Bogdandy, 'European Law beyond "Ever Closer Union". Repositioning the Concept, its Thrust and the ECJ's Comparative Methodology' (2016) 22 *European Law Journal* 519.

[20] F Schimmelfennig and T Winzen, 'Instrumental and Constitutional Differentiation in the European Union' (2014) 52 *Journal of Common Market Studies* 354.

The latter are capable of adjustment by the EU legislative institutions, which, though not easy, is much easier than effecting change to rulings dealing with primary law, which requires Treaty revision. This occurs only periodically and only with the support of all the Member States, and it is no surprise that, given such blockages, Court rulings of such exalted significance have almost never been overturned through the Treaty-making process.[21] The anxiety is that this leads to 'over-constitutionalisation'. What is currently primary law is locked in and very hard to change, to the detriment of a vibrant political culture, and that status quo is locked in still more intricately by rulings of the Court. In *Viking Line* and *Laval*, the Court took a controversially narrow view of the permissibility of trade union action where it interfered with corporate cross-border mobility.[22] Once the Court had made its choice, the matter was beyond political readjustment. It was an interpretation of primary law, and in principle primary law may be altered only by changing the Treaty. In fact, a political route was attempted: the Commission's proposal for a clarifying Regulation in the wake of the judgments, though modest in its scope, ran into the sand as there was no adequate consensus among the Member States and the EU institutions about which priorities should prevail.[23] The problem has attracted wonderfully vivid criticism – Turkuler Isiksel laments the locking away of the matter of defining the scope of freedoms in the EU market in 'the forbidding crypt of constitutional entrenchment',[24] while for Damian Chalmers the EU is guilty of 'overresponsibilisation', and the Court is part of this centralising malaise.[25] True, the scale of the problem of 'over-constitutionalisation' should not be exaggerated. *Viking Line* is exceptional, not the norm, and the Court is normally attentive to the importance of leaving space for political processes at EU and at national level.[26] But the complaint has salience, and the danger is that such a lock-in generates resentment directed at the technocratic suppression of democratic contestation which it entails, and leads to a push back towards the national(ist) arena. And added to the concern is the occasional tendency of the Court to identify principles that are not formally primary law but which acquire a similarly hard-to-change status. One may cite the dubious credentials of the horizontally applicable principle forbidding discrimination based on age discovered by the Court in *Mangold*[27] and the principle of state liability which the Court mysteriously declared was 'inherent' in the Treaty in *Francovich*.[28]

---

[21] A separate, though intriguing, line of inquiry asks whether in areas of ambiguity the Court is tempted to interpret primary law in light of legislative initiatives. Interpretation of primary law 'by analogy' with secondary legislation which is not applicable to the case is found in eg Case C-165/16 *Toufik Lounes* EU:C:2017:862.

[22] *Viking Line* (n 9); *Laval* (n 9).

[23] See the now withdrawn 'Monti II' legislative proposal of the Commission, COM (2012) 130.

[24] T Isiksel, *Europe's Functional Constitution* (Oxford, Oxford University Press, 2016) 103.

[25] D Chalmers, 'The unconfined power of European Union law', *European Papers* available at www.europeanpapers.eu/en/e-journal/unconfined-power-european-union-law.

[26] S Weatherill, '*Viking* and *Laval*: The EU Internal Market Perspective' in M Freedland and J Prassl (eds), *EU Law in the Member States: Viking, Laval and Beyond* (Oxford, Hart, 2014).

[27] Case C-144/04 EU:C:2005:709.

[28] Joined Cases C-6 and C-9/90 EU:C:1991:428.

One could champion an easier means to change Court rulings even where they interpret primary law, for example through a modified – that is, harder to achieve – version of the ordinary legislative procedure. It would doubtless be uncommon because it would require a high level of agreement that the Court requires rebuke. *Viking Line*, largely welcomed by Central and Eastern European Member States, did not generate antipathy on that scale, and there has never been any appetite to interfere with *Francovich* or indeed audacious precursors such as *Van Gend en Loos*[29] and *Costa v ENEL*[30] because all the Member States gain from the effect of rulings which make more credible the commitments they have all made. Incendiary rulings that generate widespread negative reactions are rare. But allowing for the possibility of reversal outside the process of Treaty revision opens up space for democratic contestation.

Overall, then, the aim is to put the EU on a diet: to slim down the matters that are locked in at the level of primary law and generally to make the system more amenable to change, thereby to release more space for politics rather than law at EU and at national levels.

This is a menu of reforms that merits consideration. But I advance it with no optimism. There are large numbers of Europeans dismayed by the imposition of austerity in the Eurozone, shaken by the convulsions of the refugee crisis and content, even eager, to retreat to national(ist) solutions and the politics of exclusion who have no sympathy at all for the prescription that more democratic contestation at EU level will reinvigorate their attachment to the process. The very opposite, increased resistance to the EU's pretensions, may be the result.

IX. Conclusion

The decision of the peoples of France and the Netherlands to reject the Treaty establishing a Constitution might be thought mistaken, but it was no existential threat to the EU. By contrast the reaction to it – agreement and ratification of the functionally similar Treaty of Lisbon without resort to popular approval (except in Ireland) – was a serious blunder born of short-term make-do-and-mend politics. Its longer-term implications remain to become fully visible, and will in any event be hard to track with forensic confidence given the many other political events that have shaped and continue to shape the EU. But if the problem lies in an EU that has become too complicated and intransparent for voters to understand and which provokes them, if given a chance, to reject texts handed down for their approval by political élites, then Brexit too is part of this baffled backlash. The substantive changes made by the Lisbon Treaty were an improvement, but they came at a cost which cannot yet be quantified.

[29] Case 26/62 EU:C:1963:1.
[30] Case 6/64 EU:C:1964:66.

9

The Charter of Fundamental Rights and the EU's Shallow Constitutionalism

DOROTA LECZYKIEWICZ

The chapter assesses the extent to which the EU's 'shallow' constitutionalism has been 'deepened' by giving the Charter of Fundamental Rights a formal legal status, equal to the EU Treaties, by the Lisbon Treaty; a solution adopted also, albeit in a different way, by the Constitutional Treaty.[1] The Charter started its life as a 'solemn proclamation' of the European Parliament, the Council and the Commission, but notably not of the Member States' governments, in Nice in 2000.[2] In a declaration on 'the future of the Union' attached to the Treaty of Nice, the status of the Charter was mentioned as one of the issues which 'a deeper and wider debate about the future of the European Union' was meant to address.[3] It was the Laeken Declaration which for the first time used the word 'Constitution' to describe the document that the future of the European Union should need.[4]

---

[1] Art 6(1) TEU, as amended by the Treaty of Lisbon of 2007, which entered into force in December 2009. and Part II of the Treaty Establishing a Constitution for Europe, signed on 29 October 2004, OJ, C 310, 16 December 2004.

[2] The Charter was drafted by a Convention consisting of 'representatives of the Heads of State and Government and of the President of the Commission, and members of the European Parliament and national parliaments'. Representatives of the European Court of Justice participated as observers. Already at the Cologne European Council meeting on 3–4 June 1999, where it was decided that the Charter should be drafted, a decision was taken that it would not be adopted as a treaty and that '[t]he European Council will propose to the European Parliament and the Commission that, together with the Council, they should solemnly proclaim on the basis of the draft document a European Charter of Fundamental Rights'. Decision as to the Charter's formal force was to be made 'later' (see also the conclusions of the Nice European Council Meeting of 11 December 2000).

[3] Declaration on the future of the Union attached to the Treaty of Nice (Declaration No 23).

[4] See Presidency Conclusions, European Council Meeting in Laeken, 14 and 15 December 2001, Sn 300/1/01 Rev 1, Annex I, 'Laeken Declaration on the Future of the European Union', p 24: 'The question ultimately arises as to whether this simplification and reorganisation [of the EU Treaties] might not lead in the long run to the adoption of a constitutional text in the Union. What might the basic features of such a constitution be? The values which the Union cherishes, the fundamental rights and obligations of its citizens, the relationship between Member States in the Union?'

A section in the Laeken Declaration entitled 'Towards a Constitution for European Citizens' explicitly mentioned the question of 'whether the Charter of Fundamental Rights should be included in the basic treaty'.[5] The Constitutional Treaty duly included the Charter as Part II of its text. After the Dutch and the French referendums and the period of 'constitutional reflection' it became clear that if the Charter was to survive as a binding document it could not be incorporated into the text of the Treaties. Instead, Article 6(1) TEU refers to 'the Charter of Fundamental Rights of the European Union of 7 December 2000, as adapted at Strasbourg, on 12 December 2007' as a source of rights which the Union 'recognises' and states that the document is to have 'the same legal value as the Treaties'. In this way the Charter has become part of the written layer of the EU constitution. Its legal character is one of the lasting elements of the failed constitutional project's legacy.

To assess what form of constitutionalism, 'shallow' or 'deep', the EU adopted before the binding Charter of Fundamental Rights I will first examine the way in which the EU Treaties were 'constitutionalised' before the formal process of drafting the Treaty establishing a Constitution for Europe started in 2001. I will observe that during this period the Court of Justice of the EU, as it is now called ('the CJEU' or 'the Court'), was making decisions as to the depth with which fundamental constitutional principles should be imbedded in the EU constitution. I will argue that in all its central aspects, the constitutionalisation to which the EU was subjected by the creative activity of the CJEU lacked the deeper engagement with fundamental constitutional principles and was thus insufficient to vest the EU with the required normative legitimacy. This constituted a moral and political bar to the EU becoming a 'state'.[6] I will then move on to discuss the extent to which the drafting of the Constitutional Treaty should be seen, as overtly intended by the signatories of the Laeken Declaration, as a process of 'constitutionalising' the EU (in a deep sense). I will argue that one of the key arguments in favour of seeing the creation of the Constitutional Treaty as a process of 'constitutionalising' the EU, or of deepening the EU's existing constitution, is precisely the role this Treaty ascribed to a bill of rights. I will then look more closely at the text of the Charter to identify if and how the constitutional weaknesses of the EU were acknowledged and reflected in it, and what invitation, if any, the text of the Charter extends to the Court of Justice to develop the EU's constitutional tradition in the direction delineated by values of limited government and individual liberty.

This assessment will lead me to the conclusion that the Charter of Fundamental Rights and the case law of the Court interpreting and applying this document so far has failed to deliver on this document's constitutional promise. I will claim that

---

[5] Laeken Declaration, p 24.

[6] The only form of a 'state' the EU can become is a 'constitutional state'. While nation states can be either constitutional or not, ie they may implement or not the values of post-revolutionary constitutionalism, the EU in order to become a state needs first to constitute legitimate authority by both being democratically legitimised and offering a system of government which is limited and protective of liberty.

despite the central role of bills of rights in the process of state-building (where 'state' is meant to denote a polity with a special kind of a relationship with its citizens),[7] the Charter's contribution to EU's deep constitutionalism is limited, which is a result of flaws in both its text and the interpretive activity of the Court of Justice of the EU. Consequently, the Charter does not successfully constrain and direct the CJEU, in particular by tackling the Court's expansionist and integrationist tendencies. The post-Lisbon jurisprudence of the Court, with one or two notable exceptions, is either consolidating the EU's shallow constitutionalism or constituting constitutional regress. In order to substantiate this claim, the chapter will review the case law of the Court of Justice and give examples of constitutional disappointments that the Charter should have prevented but, largely due to the Court's interpretation of this document, failed to do so. These will in particular concern the expansion of the scope of Union law beyond its previously delineated boundaries, including the expansion of the jurisdiction of the Court of Justice to review national measures against EU standards of 'fundamental rights', and the improper use of the principle of proportionality in the context of fundamental rights review of EU acts. I will conclude the chapter by briefly discussing the connection between the Charter's limited role in deepening EU constitutionalism and the outcome of the Brexit referendum.

I. The EU's Institutional Constitution between 'Deep' and 'Shallow' Constitutionalism

The failure of the Constitutional Treaty project meant that the EU lost an opportunity to become equipped with a documentary constitution. Instead, its legal and political foundations continue to reside in international treaties. These treaties, now the Treaty on the European Union and the Treaty on the Functioning of the European Union, have been subjected to extensive, elaborate and quite autonomous interpretation by the EU's judicial institution, the Court of Justice. Under the EU constitution, the CJEU is not only the sole authoritative interpreter of the Treaties and the sole judicial controller of EU institutions under the procedure of judicial review, but is also the ultimate creator of the standards of EU 'legality' and the catalyst of institutional values and practices.[8] So while the EU does not partake in the tradition of documentary constitutionalism (the big 'C' constitutionalism), it is often regarded as possessing a constitution that consists primarily of two elements, the EU Treaties and the case law of the Court of Justice. I will describe such a constitution as an 'institutional constitution'.

---

[7] L Siedentop, *Democracy in Europe* (New York, Columbia University Press, 2001) ch 5 'Why Constitutions are Important'.

[8] See D Leczykiewicz, '"Constitutional Justice" and Judicial Review of EU Legislative Acts' in G de Búrca, D Kochenov and A Williams (eds), *Europe's Justice Deficit? Beyond Good Governance* (Oxford, Hart Publishing, 2014) 97.

The main feature of institutional constitutionalism is the centrality of law in the formation and development of those institutional practices considered to be of constitutional importance. Thus, institutional constitutionalism is not a neutral term. It relates strongly to the rule of law ideal, and while it can be described as unduly state-centric, it also ties in with a set of values, or constitutional foundations, important to scholars working within a multi-level or global constitutionalism tradition.[9] It does not presuppose any particular place for the economic, societal and political elements.[10] Instead, it implies a causal connection between the content and wording of the written texts and the institutional practice which surrounds them, on the one hand, and the richness or the robustness of the constitutional discourse in a given polity, on the other.[11] It presupposes that a deeper and richer constitutional discourse, if such was desired, can be inspired by the process of, and be the product of, drafting a new set of texts performing the function of the written layer of a constitution.

It is not the purpose of this chapter to discuss the extent to which the creation and the workings of the Convention that drafted the text of the Constitutional Treaty contributed to the enrichment of the EU's constitutional discourse. Nor do I want to assess the extent to which the binding Charter of Fundamental Rights, which includes provisions on political participation, social organisation, EU economic freedoms and socio-economic rights, helps to broaden the characteristically narrow approach to EU constitutionalism, as involving the creation of legal rights primarily of an economic kind. The central argument in the chapter focuses, instead, on the contribution of the Charter of Fundamental Rights, both independently and through the case law of the CJEU, to the quality of the EU constitution. The frame of reference will be provided by a distinction between 'shallow' and 'deep' constitutionalism, where 'shallow' constitutionalism means the existence of formal structures and procedures, while 'deep' constitutionalism means respect for core constitutional values, such as democracy, individual liberty and equality.

This frame of reference departs from the post-revolutionary tradition of 'constitutionalism', where discontinuity with the previous political order means that the new values have to be expressly articulated in order to form part of the constitutional framework.[12] Within this tradition, a polity will only have a

---

[9] N Walker, 'Postnational Constitutionalism and the Problem of Translation' in JHH Weiler and M Wind (eds), *European Constitutionalism beyond the State* (Cambridge, Cambridge University Press, 2002) 27.

[10] N Walker, 'European Constitutionalism and European Integration' [1996] *Public Law* 266.

[11] Walker points out that the term 'constitution' necessarily implies 'the existence of a discrete and self-contained entity – a polity or a political community – as an object of constitutional reference', which includes a number of 'framing registers': juridical, politico-institutional, authorising and social, as well as discursive, as 'a kind of frame of frames'. N Walker, 'Reframing EU Constitutionalism' in JL Dunoff and JP Trachtman (eds), *Ruling the World? Constitutionalism, International Law, and Global Governance* (Cambridge, Cambridge University Press, 2009) 149, 151–52.

[12] C Möllers, 'Pouvoir Constituant–Constitution–Constitutionalism' in A von Bogdandy and J Bast, *Principles of European Constitutional Law* (Oxford, Hart, 2009) 169, 171–72, contrasts post-revolutionary constitutions whose objective is to found an entirely new order, for which the

constitution if it explicitly asserts fidelity to constitutional values. In contrast, in order to be able to assess the extent to which values play a crucial role in the institutional version of the EU constitution and what hierarchy emerges from the analysis of the case law of the CJEU, I propose to describe a system practising respect for democracy, liberty and equality as an instance of 'deep constitutionalism', while a system which pays no attention to these constitutional values or locates them below other considerations, such as effectiveness and jurisdictional autonomy, as an instance of 'shallow' constitutionalism. The focus on the EU's judicial institution, the CJEU, is justified by two considerations. First, it was the CJEU which first 'constitutionalised' the EU Treaties, by asserting the 'constitutional' character of the EC/EU Treaties, and thereby setting the EU on a constitutional trajectory.[13] Secondly, the CJEU is an institution possessing a high degree of institutional autonomy, given the vague wording of the Treaties and the incomplete nature of the constitutional settlement in the EU Treaties. Thus, while the EU Treaties may be accused of not doing enough to instil the deep form of constitutionalism in EU structures, the written text cannot be seen as preventing the creation of the deeper layer of EU constitutionalism. In such circumstances, the judicial institution is expected to enhance whatever constitutional standards the documentary constitution already offers, and thus can be attributed blame when 'deep' constitutionalism does not emerge.[14]

II. The Principle of Limited Government and the Charter of Fundamental Rights

The process of constitutionalisation is often described as 'a set of processes that ... involves the attempt to subject all governmental action within a designated field to the structures, processes, principles, and values of a "constitution"'.[15] Thus, 'constitutionalisation' means the process of 'limiting government' and 'constitutionalism' would then be 'a theory of limited government ... concerned mainly with the norms which modern constitutions should contain'.[16] This understanding

---

proclamation of constitutional values is particularly important, and constitutions which merely juridify the existing political practices, in particular those aimed at constraining power.

[13] Case 294/83 *Parti Ecologiste 'Les Verts' v European Parliament* [1986] ECR 1339, para 23: 'It must first be emphasized in this regard that the European Economic Community is a community based on the rule of law, inasmuch as neither its Member States nor its institutions can avoid a review of the question whether the measures adopted by them are in conformity with the basic constitutional charter, the Treaty.'

[14] It could be argued that the normative legitimacy of the entire EU project depends on its capacity to undertake and intensify constitutional commitments. From this it follows that the role of the EU's constitutional court is to strengthen adherence to constitutional values.

[15] M Loughlin, 'What is Constitutionalisation?' in P Dobner and M Loughlin (eds), *The Twilight of Constitutionalism?* (Oxford, Oxford University Press, 2010) 47.

[16] Ibid, 55. See also Paul Craig's forth meaning of 'constitutionalism' in P Craig, 'Constitutions, Constitutionalism, and the European Union' (2001) 7 *European Law Journal* 125, 128.

is in line with a view frequently expressed in EU constitutional scholarship that a system of divided, and thus limited, powers between the EU and the Member States constitutes 'the essence of [EU] constitutionalism', as embodying the principle of 'limited government operating under the rule of law'.[17] More importantly, however, this understanding is also in line with the perspective of the signatories of the Laeken Declaration, which initiated the drafting of the Constitutional Treaty. Indeed, the Laeken Declaration and the documents prepared by the European Convention identified, directly or indirectly, a number of constitutional weaknesses from which the EU had been suffering vis-à-vis the principle of limited government. They included a lack of transparency and respect for the limits of EU competences and the non-binding nature of the Charter of Fundamental Rights. Removing these weaknesses was one of the reasons for constitutionalising the EU in a documentary sense through the adoption of a constitutional text.[18]

The concept of limited government in a multi-level political structure like the EU inevitably needs to encompass two dimensions; the federal and the individual. The federal dimension concerns the division of powers between the EU and the Member States and finds its expression in the principles of conferral, mutual respect and sincere cooperation.[19] The second dimension relates to the republican idea that a certain level of individual liberty should be established. This creates tensions with the principle of democracy and is usually resolved by creating a set of rights which protect individual liberty and which cannot be (unduly) infringed by a majoritarian vote, the so-called 'constitutional rights'. In the EU, the role of 'constitutional rights' is performed by 'fundamental rights', poorly defined and under-theorised as a concept,[20] but unquestionably acting as constraints

---

[17] K Lenaerts, 'Constitutionalism and the Many Faces of Federalism' (1990) 38 *American Journal of Comparative Law* 205 ibid.

[18] Declaration 23 attached to the Treaty of Nice called only for 'a deeper and wider debate about the future of the European Union', although already at this stage the following questions were posed: 'how to establish and monitor a more precise delimitation of powers between the European Union and the Member States, reflecting the principle of subsidiarity.' The Declaration recognised also 'the need to improve and to monitor the democratic legitimacy and transparency of the Union and its institutions, in order to bring them closer to the citizens of the Member States'.

[19] See Art 4 TEU: '1. In accordance with Article 5, competences not conferred upon the Union in the Treaties remain with the Member States. 2. The Union shall respect the equality of Member States before the Treaties as well as their national identities, inherent in their fundamental structures, political and constitutional, inclusive of regional and local self-government. It shall respect their essential State functions, including ensuring the territorial integrity of the State, maintaining law and order and safeguarding national security. In particular, national security remains the sole responsibility of each Member State. 3. Pursuant to the principle of sincere cooperation, the Union and the Member States shall, in full mutual respect, assist each other in carrying out tasks which flow from the Treaties.'

[20] The problem with 'fundamental rights' is that it is not clear whether it is meant to be the EU's equivalent of 'constitutional rights'. While fundamental rights are recognised to constitute constraints on EU and Member States' power it is debatable that they all do so in the same way as national constitutional rights, and that the imposition of limitations on each fundamental right requires the same strong justification. It is also not clear whether the Charter can be taken as a document codifying EU fundamental rights, given the fact that 'general principles of EU law' continue to be an independent source of EU fundamental rights (see Art 6(3) TEU). The Court has also never unequivocally clarified

on EU action with negative consequences for individual freedoms and interests.[21] EU fundamental rights currently arise from two sources: 'general principles of law', inspired by the European Convention on Human Rights (ECHR) and state constitutional traditions, and the Charter of Fundamental Rights, the EU's distinctive and largely autonomous bill of rights.[22] Despite the fact that the Charter is not actually incorporated into the EU Treaties,[23] since Lisbon, the Charter has been treated as one of the foundational documents of the EU, and has been given the same status as the Treaties in the EU's legislative and judicial review processes.

There are multiple reasons for conceptualising the Charter as a constitutional document.[24] Some of them relate to the need to equip the EU with firmer moral foundations,[25] to strengthen the bond between EU citizens and EU institutions,[26] or rebalance the EU's economic tilt.[27] As Maduro observed in 2003, the Charter is torn between two constitutional ideas: on the one hand, the Charter is a codification of existing principles, consolidating the status quo and providing the EU with a more transparent bill of rights; whilst on the other hand, the Charter is an exercise in transformation, a new beginning for EU fundamental rights and a reshaping of the EU's constitutional landscape more generally.[28] My own view, now vindicated by the Court's case law, has always been that the Charter will have a transformative, as well as a consolidating effect. More importantly, the supporters of the Constitutional Treaty saw the vesting of the Charter with formal legal status as a way of addressing some of the EU's constitutional weaknesses.[29]

---

what the relationship between the Charter and 'general principles' is and which of the two has a higher constitutional status.

[21] Case 11/70 *Internationale Handelsgesellschaft mbH v Einfuhr- und Vorratsstelle fur Getreide und Futtermittel* [1970] ECR 1125, para 4. Case C-402/05 P & C-415/05 P *Yassin Abdullah Kadi and Al Barakaat International Foundation v Council and Commission* [2008] ECR I-6351, para 283.

[22] Preamble to the Charter states that the Charter merely 'reaffirms … the rights as they result, in particular, from the constitutional traditions and international obligations common to the Member States, the European Convention for the Protection of Human Rights and Fundamental Freedoms, the Social Charters adopted by the Union and by the Council of Europe and the case-law of the Court of Justice of the European Union and of the European Court of Human Rights'. See also, the Charter's Art 52(3) and (4).

[23] See n 1.

[24] *Cf* S Douglas-Scott, 'The EU Charter of Fundamental Rights as a Constitutional Document' (2004) 1 *European Human Rights Law Review* 37.

[25] The European Parliament expressed the hope that 'the establishment of a binding European list of fundamental rights will confer a more secure legal and moral basis on the process of European integration'. European Parliament resolution on the drafting of a European Union Charter of Fundamental Rights (C5-0058/1999 – 1999/2064(COS)), Point 2.

[26] G de Búrca and B Aschenbrenner, 'European Constitutionalism and the Charter' in S Peers and A Ward (eds), *The European Union Charter of Fundamental Rights* (Oxford, Hart Publishing, 2004) 3, 19.

[27] S Weatherill, 'The Internal Market' in S Peers and A Ward (eds), *The EU Charter of Fundamental Rights* (Oxford, Hart Publishing, 2004) 183, 201.

[28] M Poiares Maduro, 'The Double Constitutional Life of the Charter of Fundamental Rights in the European Union' in T Harvey and J Kenner (eds), *Economic and Social Rights under the EU Charter of Fundamental Rights* (Oxford, Hart Publishing, 2003) 269, 277.

[29] Laeken Declaration (n 4) p 24. See also European Parliament resolution on the drafting of a European Union Charter of Fundamental Rights (C5-0058/1999 – 1999/2064(COS)), where the

It is thus in this light that the Charter and the case law of the CJEU which it has attracted will be examined.

III. First-order versus Second-order Constitutional Principles of the EU

The European Union is founded on international treaties subjected to interpreta-tion of the Court of Justice of the EU, whose adjudicative output is frequently described as a process of their 'constitutionalisation'. This process has a number of dimensions, the most important of which include the 'legalisation' of the EU's decisional processes, ie the introduction of legal accountability mechanisms and the vesting of individuals with rights enforceable against EU institutions. By 'legalising' the EU the Court converted an international organisation operating primarily on the political plane into a legal entity, a 'community of law', where both EU institutions and the Member States have to conform to rules.[30] Yet, the status of the CJEU as a constitutional court depended not only on the 'legalisa-tion' of the European Economic Community but also on its 'supranationalisation', ie the creation of doctrines which enabled the Court to review national laws and practices in the light of EU law and which obliged national courts to give prec-edence to that law in the event of conflict with national rules and practices. For this purpose, the Court converted an interpretative competence envisaged in the Treaties (now Article 267 TFEU) into a review competence and introduced the principles of primacy and direct effect of EU law. Both of these changes would not have been possible if the Court saw its role as a mere guardian of the histori-cal political consensus expressed through the Treaties. It is interesting that it is predominantly these supranationalising transformations that are regarded as 'constitutionalisation' of the Treaties.[31]

Already in the 1990s, in a famous article 'European Constitutionalism and its Discontents', Joseph Weiler drew scholarly attention to the concept of constitu-tionalism with which the Court had been working. Weiler argued that the Court's understanding of this process involved a transformation of the EC/EU leading to greater effectiveness, autonomy and authority of the European legal order, but not to greater accountability and transparency of the organisation.[32] Weiler

---

Charter is described as 'a basic component of the necessary process of equipping the European Union with a constitution' (Recital V).

[30] See AG Darmon in Case 222/84 *Johnston, Marguerite Johnston v Chief Constable of the Royal Ulster Constabulary* [1986] ECR 1651, point 3.

[31] C Timmermans, 'The Constitutionalisation of the European Union' (2001–02) 21 *Yearbook of European Law* 1, 3. See also GF Mancini, 'The Making of a Constitution for Europe' (1980) 26 *Common Market Law Review* 595; E Stein, 'Lawyers, Judges, and the Making of a Transnational Constitution' (1981) 75 *American Journal of International Law* 1.

[32] JHH Weiler and JP Trachtman, 'European Constitutionalism and Its Discontents' (1996–97) 17 *Northwestern Journal of International Law and Business* 354, 357.

insists that EU constitutionalism should be seen as a two-fold transformation: the vesting of the European legal order with effectiveness, autonomy and authority, but also with normative legitimacy, achieved through greater accountability and transparency. I will use this two-dimensional approach to constitutionalisation to distinguish between two forms of supranationalisation of an international organisation. On the one hand, we have supranationalisation which is not accompanied by a process of subjecting the international organisation to the constitutional principle of limited government ('shallow' constitutionalism). If, on the other hand, the process of supranationalisation has been accompanied by practices leading to the embedding of constitutional values, in particular to a proper engagement with the principle of limited government, and these values are treated as hierarchically superior to those that strengthen the international organisation's supranational character, I will conclude that we are in the presence of 'deep' constitutionalism.

It is unquestionably the case that the process of the EU's supranationalisation has been accompanied by engagement with constitutional values. It is not, however, the case that these values possess the status of first-order principles of the EU. In the most dominant conception of EU constitutionalism, shared by both judges of the Court of Justice and the majority of EU scholars, the central elements of the EU constitution are the doctrines of direct effect, supremacy, effectiveness, effective judicial protection, the general principles and, more recently, EU citizenship.[33] Only in the second order do we find principles such as conferral, national procedural autonomy, proportionality of EU action, or respect for constitutional identity of the Member States.[34]

The fact that the Court itself sees EU constitutional principles organised in a form of hierarchy is visible in the infamous *Melloni* judgment and reconfirmed by the Full Court in Opinion 2/13 on the EU's Accession to the ECHR.[35] *Melloni* concerned a conflict between Spanish constitutional standards protecting the right to a fair trial and the effectiveness of the EU arrest warrant regime. In paragraphs 59–60 the Court of Justice held that:

> it [was] an essential feature of the EU legal order [that] rules of national law, even of a constitutional order, [could not] be allowed to undermine the effectiveness of EU law on the territory of that State ... where an EU legal act calls for national implementing measures, national authorities and courts remain free to apply national standards of protection of fundamental rights, provided that the level of protection provided for by

---

[33] Timmermans, 'The Constitutionalisation of the European Union' (n 31) 3. See also Mancini, 'The Making of a Constitution for Europe' (n 31); Stein, 'Lawyers, Judges, and the Making of a Transnational Constitution' (n 31); JHH Weiler, 'The Transformation of Europe' in *The Constitution of Europe* (Cambridge, Cambridge University Press, 1999) 10, 18–31.

[34] This is not to say that these principles do not form part of the EU constitution. Instead, what is argued here is that the process of constitutionalisation is traditionally associated much more closely with direct effect, supremacy etc than with, eg, the operationalisation of the principle of conferral.

[35] Case C-399/11 *Stefano Melloni v Ministerio Fiscal*, Judgment of the Grand Chamber of 26 February 2013; Opinion 2/13 of the Full Court of 18 December 2014 on the Accession of the European Union to the European Convention for the Protection of Human Rights and Fundamental Freedoms.

the Charter, as interpreted by the Court, and the primacy, unity and effectiveness of EU law are not thereby compromised.

It follows that between respect for national constitutional standards, a constitutional principle of the EU, and effectiveness of EU law, it is the latter which is given priority in the event of conflict. Thus, EU principles which contribute to 'primacy, unity and effectiveness' of EU law have a privileged status. They, and not the protection of fundamental rights, are the first-order principles.

The weakness of the constitutional principles contributing to the idea of limited government is not, I believe, the sign of their deficient normative potency or irrelevance in the European Union's constitutional mosaic. The Laeken process confirmed the central significance of the division of competences, which was motivated by a broader concern about a lack of effective limits on the EU's legislative and control powers. Protection of individual liberty and creation of a proper European system of rights could be seen as the objective standing behind the decision to make the Charter formally binding.[36] After all, it is for the first time that all EU fundamental rights, as included in the Charter, and not only those granted by the EU Treaties, are meant to be protected as 'rights', and not only as 'principles'. Thus, it is curious that in the Laeken process, which was so attentive to the values of limited government, so little space was devoted to one of the main sources of the EU's constitutional deficiencies – the adjudicative activity of the Court of Justice. This is also true about the Charter of Fundamental Rights itself. No consideration was given to the principle of federalism (as the first aspect of limited government) in the transformation of the Charter into a binding document, despite the fact that it is both EU institutions and the Member States which are bound by its provisions.[37] Through the Charter the Court of Justice has received a stronger mandate not only to invalidate EU acts but also to review Member State action. The Charter is also ambiguous in its commitment to individual liberty, given the fact that it permits limitations of rights also when they are not necessary in a democratic society.[38]

IV. The Principle of Federalism

A. The Principle of Federalism in the EU Treaties

The principle of federalism is associated mainly with the US Constitution, where the federal government is required to respect the powers of the states

---

[36] Annex IV to the Conclusions of the Presidency at Cologne European Council meeting on 3–4 June 1999 states that 'Protection of fundamental rights is a founding principle of the Union and an indispensable prerequisite for her legitimacy'.
[37] See Art 51(1) of the Charter.
[38] See Art 52(1) of the Charter.

and regulate only to the extent that it is granted competence to do so by the Constitution.[39] This looks indistinguishable from the European principle of conferral, or conferred/attributed powers. According to Article 5(2) TEU:

> Under the principle of conferral, the Union shall act only within the limits of the competences conferred upon it by the Member States in the Treaties to attain the objectives set out therein. Competences not conferred upon the Union in the Treaties remain with the Member States.

The central function of the EU Treaty's principle of conferral is to ensure that when the EU acts it does so only on a basis explicitly granted to it by the Treaties.

There are two problems with such a formulation of the principle of federalism. First, the Treaty formulation of the principle of conferral and its interpretation by the Court of Justice marginalise what is the central function of this principle – prevention of over-centralisation. The principle does not in fact create a presumption in favour of Member States' power. This task is carried out, very ineffectively, only by the principle of subsidiarity.[40] It is noteworthy that during the Laeken process there was awareness of the fact that a principle of conferral, focusing exclusively on what the EU is permitted to do and not specifying also what it is prohibited to do, was an incomplete principle of federalism. Hence, one of the proposals was to incorporate a list of competences reserved for the Member States. While such a solution could never work in practice, it captured the gist of the EU's constitutional weakness. No matter how many times the Treaties say that 'competences not conferred upon the Union in the Treaties remain with the Member States' (Article 4(1) to be then repeated in Article 5(2) TEU), it does not oblige the EU (and especially the Court of Justice) to respect the autonomy of the Member States. Respect for the autonomy of the Member States is not, according to Article 2 TEU, one of the values on which the Union is founded, unless we claim that such respect is commanded by that article under the rubric of 'pluralism'.[41] Article 4(2) TEU does require that the EU show the Member States respect, but only as to their equality before the Treaties and their 'national identities, inherent in their fundamental structures, political and constitutional'. The same provision requires the EU to respect the states' 'essential functions'. While these are not listed exhaustively the non-exclusive list is telling; it includes 'the territorial integrity of the State, maintaining law and order and safeguarding national security'. Only that. It is interesting that despite its modest formulation Article 4(2) TEU has been used by national constitutional courts (in particular the German Constitutional

---

[39] The doctrine of enumerated powers of the US Congress, as listed in Art I, S 8 of the US Constitution. According to the 10th Amendment to the US Constitution: 'The powers not delegated to the United States by the Constitution, nor prohibited by it to the States, are reserved to the States respectively, or to the people.'

[40] See G Davies, 'Subsidiarity: The Wrong Idea, in the Wrong Place, at the Wrong Time' (2006) 43 *Common Market Law Review* 63.

[41] The Union's motto of 'United in Diversity', appearing in Art I-8 of the Constitutional Treaty, was removed from the Lisbon Treaty.

Court) to justify their review of the EU's observance of the principle of conferral.[42] This development was, in my view, entirely predictable in a system which, despite the ambitions of the Laeken process, inadequately protects Member States' powers against their encroachment by Union institutions.

But, the functional weakness of the Constitutional Treaty's formulation of EU competences, replicated in the Lisbon Treaty, is not the only flaw of the EU's constitutional design. Another one is the failure properly to recognise in the EU's 'constitutional charter' that EU competences include not only what could be described as 'positive competences', a power to legislate, but also negative competences, a power to preclude national laws and practices that are incompatible not only with express Treaty rules but also with 'the law', whose observance the Court of Justice is empowered to ensure.[43] So, not only is the creative role of the Court of Justice not explicitly subjected to the principle of conferral but its review powers are not restricted to fields where the EU has legislative competences. If the principle of conferral were properly to express the value of federalism it would control the Court's interpretive power by placing on it a higher burden of proof in cases where the Court moves away from a literal or historical meaning and creates for the EU (and itself) new ways of influencing outcomes and organising the regulatory space.

How defunct the EU Treaties are in ensuring respect for Member States' autonomy is visible also in the way the Court applies the supplementing principles of subsidiarity and proportionality. Already their inclusion in the Treaties is telling. Conferral was not enough, the EU had to be asked to respect also subsidiarity (the Union is permitted to act 'only in so far as the objectives of the proposed action cannot be sufficiently achieved by the Member States', Article 5(3) TEU) and proportionality (the content and form of Union action shall not exceed what is necessary to achieve the objectives of the Treaties, Article 5(4) TEU) but their ineffectiveness to contain EU action is notorious. The subsidiarity/proportionality Protocol is a further sign of their weakness, as is the Protocol on the role of national parliaments in policing compliance with the principle of subsidiarity, which could be interpreted as a manifestation of the Member States' distrust towards the Court of Justice.[44]

B. The Lisbon Treaty: Depillarisation

The Lisbon Treaty, following the Constitutional Treaty, significantly expands the review powers of the Court of Justice. It does so not only by equipping the Court with new review standards (the Charter) but also by removing the three pillars

---

[42] See the order of the German Constitutional Court in the *Honeywell* case, BVerfG, 6 July 2010 – 2 BvR 2661/06, paras 59 and 97.

[43] Art 19(1) TEU.

[44] See Protocol No 1 and No 2 to the Lisbon Treaty.

and extending the Court's jurisdiction onto the former third pillar, where fundamental rights have particular potency.[45] Naturally, the highly constrained jurisdiction of the Court of Justice in criminal matters was in itself a source of the EU's constitutional weakness. The most problematic, from the constitutional perspective, was a total bar on access of individuals wishing to challenge EU acts adopted in the second pillar and severe restrictions on their access to the Court in the third pillar.[46] As I have explained elsewhere, these limits of the Court's jurisdiction meant that the EU system did not offer a 'complete system of remedies' against EU acts, a doctrine which is the foundation of the Court's (self-proclaimed) exclusivity of the competence to annul EU acts.[47] This gave rise to concerns in particular with regard to the so-called 'restrictive measures', ie acts adopted by the EU on security concerns against specified individuals, mainly those who were suspected of terrorist activity.[48] Restrictions on the Court's jurisdiction led to the one-time significant *Segi* litigation, in which the Court of Justice was at pains to extend its jurisdiction to offer individuals at least some protection against EU acts freezing their assets.[49]

The Treaty of Lisbon, following the Constitutional Treaty, has to a large extent addressed these concerns. By depillarising the EU, it brought within the Court's jurisdiction former third-pillar acts and also some of former second-pillar acts.[50] But depillarisation, as far as the Court's jurisdiction is concerned, is a double-edged sword. Yes, the Court has gained more powers to control compliance of EU institutions with fundamental rights but also new competences to review national acts. Moreover, integrationist jurisprudence does not quite fit these new fields. It is plainly apparent that the internal market requires a high level of uniformity of

---

[45] Before the Lisbon Treaty, the EU was composed of 3 pillars: the European Community, the Police and Judicial Cooperation in Criminal Matters (the third pillar) and the Common Foreign and Security Policy (the second pillar). The Constitutional Treaty was to be the first one to remove those pillars and merge them into one. The Community method, which includes full jurisdiction of the Court, was to be extended onto the other 2 pillars.

[46] Before the Treaty of Lisbon, in the third pillar the Court had jurisdiction only to give preliminary rulings and only when the Member State from which a reference was to be sent accepted its jurisdiction (Art 35 EU). Individuals could not bring direct actions or actions for damages. Individuals could never challenge common positions and could request referrals only from national courts of last instance.

[47] For more on this, see D Leczykiewicz, "'Effective Judicial Protection' of Human Rights After Lisbon: Should National Courts Be Empowered to Review EU Secondary Law? (2010) 35 *European Law Review* 17. According to the Court's case law, national courts cannot be permitted to invalidate EU acts because this would undermine its powers and the uniform application (effectiveness) of EU law (Case 314/85 *Firma Foto-Frost v Hauptzollamt Lübeck-Ost* [1987] ECR 4199, para 20).

[48] These acts were sometimes adopted as non-reviewable, third-pillar common positions, implementing UN Security Council resolutions. In other cases, the EU used a mixed legal basis, combining Community provisions on capital and the general competence-conferring provision of Art 308 EC (now Art 352 TEU).

[49] Case C-355/04 P *Segi, Araitz Zubimendi Izaga and Aritza Galarraga v Council* [2007] ECR I-1657.

[50] Former second-pillar acts, ie those adopted as part of the EU's Common Foreign and Security Policy (CFSP), generally remain outside the scope of the Court's jurisdiction. Arts 24(1) TEU and 275 TFEU provide that, by way of exception, the Court of Justice may monitor if implementation of the CFSP does not affect the exercise of other EU competences and review the legality of decisions providing for restrictive measures against natural or legal persons adopted by the Council.

EU rules' application. But to prioritise uniformity of application and effectiveness in criminal matters and cases concerning parental rights would be an aberration. Uniformity and effectiveness simply cannot be the fundamental values of what is now the Area of Freedom, Security and Justice (AFSJ) (immigration, the combating of crime and judicial cooperation). The objective of ensuring effective cooperation among courts of different Member States cannot trump fundamental rights considerations, such as those concerning access to court, the right to fair trial, or the protection of children.[51]

And yet, in the Court's case law concern for effectiveness of EU AFSJ policies overrides fundamental rights considerations. The Court, when confronted with a choice between enhancing effectiveness of an EU regime of judicial cooperation and protecting the best interest of the child, decided to prioritise the former.[52] It decided to uphold the European Arrest Warrant Framework Decision,[53] despite blatant violations of the principles of legality and equality.[54] The presumption of mutual trust among the Member States' courts in matters of law and order is, in the Court's case law, almost irrebuttable, forcing national courts to stand by and watch how fair trial rights or the best interest of the child are being violated by courts of other Member States. It is thus questionable if depillarisation and expansion of the Court's jurisdiction on criminal and family matters in a system which places uniformity and effectiveness above fundamental rights in its hierarchy of constitutional values was a correct development.[55]

C. The Charter of Fundamental Rights and Competence Sensitivity

The 2000 version of the Charter already contained a provision which made it explicit that the Charter did not grant the EU any new powers.[56] A similar provision was included in the slightly modified 2003 version, which became Part II of

---

[51] For more on this point, see D Leczykiewicz, 'Human Rights in the Area of Freedom, Security and Justice' in M Fletcher, E Herlin-Karnell and C Matera (eds), *The European Union as an Area of Freedom, Security and Justice* (London, Routledge, 2016) 57.

[52] Case C 195/08 PPU *Inga Rinau* [2008] ECR I-5271; Case C 403/09 PPU *Jasna Detiček v Maurizio Sgueglia* [2009] ECR I-12193.

[53] Council Framework Decision 2002/584/JHA of 13 June 2002 on the European arrest warrant and the surrender procedures between Member States – Statements made by certain Member States on the adoption of the Framework Decision, OJ L 190, 18.7.2002, p 1.

[54] Case C-303/05 *Advocaten voor de Wereld VZW v Leden van de Ministerraad* [2007] ECR I-3633. For more on this, see D Leczykiewicz 'Constitutional Conflicts and the Third Pillar' (2008) 33 *European Law Review* 230.

[55] See, still relevant, J Coppel and A O'Neill 'The European Court of Justice: Taking Rights Seriously?' (1992) 12 *Legal Studies* 228. See also, S Douglas-Scott 'The Rule of Law in the European Union – Putting the Security into the Area of Freedom, Security and Justice' (2004) 29 *European Law Review* 219.

[56] See Art 51(2) in the version of the Charter of 2000: 'This Charter does not establish any new power or task for the Community or the Union, or modify powers and tasks defined in the Treaties.'

the Constitutional Treaty.[57] The modification was presented as responding to the concerns surrounding the first proclamation of the Charter in 2000.[58] Even though the Charter of 2000 did not have a formal binding force it still stated in its Preamble that it reaffirmed 'the rights as they result, in particular, from the constitutional traditions and international obligations common to the Member States, the Treaty on European Union, the Community Treaties, the European Convention for the Protection of Human Rights and Fundamental Freedoms, the Social Charters adopted by the Community and by the Council of Europe and the case-law of the Court of Justice of the European Communities and of the European Court of Human Rights' *'with due regard for the powers and tasks of the Community and the Union and the principle of subsidiarity'* (my emphasis). The Convention preparing the Constitutional Treaty, following the working group's recommendation, included a reference to subsidiarity also in Article 51(1) regulating the Charter's scope of application, and not only in the Preamble. It also added, again following the working group's recommendation, paragraph 6 to Article 52 distinguishing 'rights' from 'principles' in the Charter, which was connected expressly to the desire to respect the principle of subsidiarity.[59]

The 2007 version of the Charter, made binding by the Lisbon Treaty, states, like the Constitutional Treaty, that the Charter 'does not extend the field of application of Union law beyond the powers of the Union or establish any new power or task for the Union, or modify powers and tasks as defined in the Treaties' (Article 51(2)). Explanations relating to the Charter, prepared by the Praesidium of the European Convention, and referred to in the Preamble to the 2007 version of the Charter and in post-Lisbon Article 6(1) TEU, state that Article 51(2) means that

> [t]he fundamental rights as guaranteed in the Union do not have any effect other than in the context of the powers determined by the Treaties' and that 'the Charter may not have the effect of extending the field of application of Union law *beyond the powers of the Union as established in the Treaties.*[60]

[57] Art II-111: 'This Charter does not extend the field of application of Union law beyond the powers of the Union or establish any new power or task for the Union, or modify powers and tasks defined in the other Parts of the Constitution.'

[58] See the Final Report on Working Group II, p 5.

[59] Ibid, 5 and 8. Art 52(5) states that provisions of the Charter which contain principles 'shall be judicially cognisable' only in the interpretation of 'legislative or executive acts taken by institutions, bodies, offices and agencies of the Union implementing the principles and in the ruling on legality of these acts, and in the interpretation of the acts of Member States applying the principles in the process of implementing Union law'. It follows that without legislative implementation at EU and/or national level Charter 'principles' are not justiciable, or not fully justiciable, in domestic courts. Moreover, Charter 'principles' can produce effects only through influencing interpretation (ie not 'directly') and only when the case concerns application of acts adopted to implement the principles. Charter 'rights', on the other hand, are 'judicially cognisable' also in situations other than interpretation of legislative and executive acts implementing them, ie they can be used to interpret also other acts of the Member States or to assess compatibility of Member States' acts with EU law. Regardless of the intentions of the working group, the introduction of a stricter distinction between 'rights' and 'principles' does not address the Member States' concerns that the Charter extends the Court's powers because the Charter does not define which of its provisions contain 'rights' and which contain 'principles'.

[60] 'Explanation on Article 51 – Field of Application', Explanations relating to the Charter of Fundamental Rights, OJ C303, 14.12.2007, p 17 (emphasis added).

Moreover, the European Council meeting in Brussels in June 2007, ending the two-year period of uncertainty following the Dutch and the French referendums, added a further safeguard in Article 6(1) TEU and a declaration (Declaration No 1), both of which more or less repeat Article 51(2) of the Charter. The UK and Poland clearly thought that these safeguards were insufficient because in their Protocol on the application of the Charter (Protocol No 30) they used a different formulation. We read in the Protocol that the Charter

> does not extend the ability of the Court of Justice of the European Union, or any court or tribunal of Poland or of the United Kingdom, to find that the laws, regulations or administrative provisions, practices or action of Poland or of the United Kingdom are inconsistent with the fundamental rights, freedoms and principles that it reaffirms (Article 1(1)).[61]

It should be observed that the statement that the Charter does not extend the competences of the Union, as a description of this document's effect, is simply false. It would be possible to accept that the Charter indeed did not extend the EU's legislative competences. It is not true, however, that it does not extend its negative competences, in particular the capacity of the Court of Justice to render ineffective national rules incompatible with, and thus 'precluded by', EU law. The Charter introduces a whole range of new standards against which national laws and practices can be assessed. While these new standards may or may not have already been part of 'common constitutional traditions of the Member States' or the case law of the Strasbourg Court, unless they became translated into EU rights through the vehicle of 'general principles', they did not constitute standards which the Court could use against national measures. The translation into EU rights was not a straightforward task. Although the CJEU was free to 'invent' new 'general principles' and was not forced to use the lowest common denominator, introduction of a new general principle was a visible case of judicial activism, easily subjected to external scrutiny.

The Charter, by expressly incorporating many new rights into EU law, makes the Court's task much easier. Moreover, as the post-Lisbon case law of the Court confirms, it removes the need to refer to external sources, such as national constitutions or the European Convention on Human Rights, when EU fundamental rights are invoked. Despite the wording of Article 52(3) and (4), which seemingly obliges the Court to give Charter rights the same meaning and scope as the corresponding ECHR rights, or interpret rights resulting from the constitutional

---

[61] It should be noted that this provision, while superior in its the wording to Art 51(2) of the Charter, is still drafted with insufficient understanding of how EU law operates, and is thus ineffective. The advantage of the Protocol is, however, that it points directly to the source of the possible extension of EU powers, namely the Court of Justice. However, the Protocol does not address the British concerns (see below), and despite the impression which the British government at the time wanted to create, it does not constitute an opt-out from the Charter. See D Leczykiewicz, 'The EU Charter of Fundamental Rights and its Effects', UK Constitutional Law Blog.

traditions common to the Member States in harmony with those traditions, the Court's references to these external sources in its fundamental rights jurisprudence have dropped since Lisbon.[62] The Charter is applied largely as a document without a past, and thus without restricting baggage, giving the interpreter unlimited possibilities in the filling of its provisions with content. However, where this fits the Court's objectives, the Charter suddenly recovers its past, albeit in a fragmentary way because consisting exclusively in the Court's own case law. It is not so much that the Charter gives the Court a fresh start but the fact that the Court is no longer required to legitimise its creativity vis-à-vis the more imbedded national constitutions or the case law of the European Court of Human Rights (ECtHR) that best demonstrates the transformative role of the Charter for the division of powers between the EU and the Member States.

D. The Court of Justice and the 'No New Competences' Principle

All these changes in the division of powers between the EU and the Member States can be attributed to the text of the Charter, as endorsed by the Member States. However, I would like to propose a different interpretation of the causal connections. It is true that the Charter does not do enough to constrain the Court.[63] But it does not mandate the Court to extend its review capacity, either. Instead, it gives the Court tools to repudiate its previous expansionist approach. The Charter, taken literally, has a narrower scope of application than the pre-existing 'general principles' of fundamental rights. It applies to the Member States 'only when they are implementing Union law' (Article 51(1)), while 'general principles' applied 'within the scope of Union law', ie also where the Member States were derogating from Treaty provisions or when they acted in exercise of discretion left to them by EU secondary law.[64] While Explanations to the Charter shift, seemingly without significance, between the term 'implementing Union law' and 'acting within the scope of Union law',[65] it is simply incorrect to present the two as equivalent. An act involving 'implementation of Union law' presupposes the existence of a substantive provision of EU law, either in the Treaty or in legislation, which the Member

---

[62] G de Búrca, 'After the EU Charter of Fundamental Rights: The Court of Justice as a Human Rights Adjudicator?' (2013) 20 *Maastricht Journal* 168, 173–75.

[63] It is true that already the wording, and not necessarily just the application, of the so-called horizontal provisions of the Charter (Arts 51–54) 'reveal[s] tensions which reflect deeper problems in the European Union's constitutional nature'. S Douglas-Scott, 'The Charter of Fundamental Rights as a Constitutional Document' (n 24) 49. Yet, some of these 'problems' are attributable also to the Court because they result from its earlier case law.

[64] Case C-260/89 *Elliniki Radiophonia Tiléorassi AE and Panellinia Omospondia Syllogon Prossopikou v Dimotiki Etairia Pliroforissis and Sotirios Kouvelas and Nicolaos Avdellas* [199] ECR I2925; Case 5/88 *Hubert Wachauf v Bundesamt für Ernährung und Forstwirtschaft* [1989] ECR 2609.

[65] See n 60.

State is putting into effect in the domestic context in the case at hand. If the Charter was binding on the Member States 'only when they are implementing Union law' Member States would not be subjected to scrutiny against Charter standards in situations where they applied domestic provisions not serving as implementing acts for EU law. Moreover, they would not be bound by the Charter when applying domestic provisions impacting upon the effectiveness of some substantive provisions of EU law, and instead such domestic provisions could be precluded only if they were incompatible with those substantive provisions, not the Charter.[66] In particular, it would not be possible to apply against the Member States EU fundamental rights merely because they acted in a field which is thematically covered by some EU legislation or because the national rules in question make Treaty rights (such as free movement or citizenship) less effective.

The Court decided not to use the opportunity provided by the Charter to restrict the scope of application of EU fundamental rights, or at least of the Charter itself, to Member States' acts 'implementing Union law'. It held in *Fransson* that '[t]he applicability of European Union law entails applicability of the fundamental rights guaranteed by the Charter'.[67] It is difficult to discern from the judgment on what ground exactly this conclusion is reached. The Court insists that EU fundamental rights 'are applicable in all situations governed by European Union law'[68] but it does not explain why the Charter should have the same scope of application despite the fact that a different wording is used in Article 51(1) and what are the criteria of deeming a situation 'governed by European Union law'.[69] On the facts, the situation was held to be 'governed by European Union law' because the tax penalties and the criminal proceedings to which the applicant was subjected were 'connected in part to breaches of his obligations to declare VAT' and the VAT Directive makes the Member States responsible for effective collection of VAT due on its territory.[70]

The Court's unwillingness to respect Member States' powers is also visible in its interpretation of Article 53 of the Charter. This provision states that 'Nothing in the Charter shall be interpreted as restricting or adversely affecting human rights and fundamental freedoms as recognised, in their respective fields of application, by Union law ... and by Member States' constitutions'. The field of application of Union law (and thus of the Charter of Fundamental Rights) is, as we have seen in *Fransson*, interpreted broadly. Conversely, the field of application of Member States' constitutions is interpreted curiously narrowly, which is visible in the Court's

---

[66] It would thus be apparent, as the wording of Art 51(1) of the Charter suggests, that the scope of Union law is broader than the scope of application of the Charter.

[67] Case C-617/10 *Åklagaren v Hans Åkerberg Fransson*, Judgment of 26 February 2013, para 21.

[68] Ibid, 19.

[69] The only argument which is given to support the conclusion that the scope of the Charter's application should be the same as the pre-existing 'general principles' of fundamental rights is that such a 'definition of the field of application of the fundamental rights of the European Union is borne out by the explanations relating to Article 51 of the Charter' (n 60). *Fransson* (n 67), para 20.

[70] Ibid, paras 24–25.

rejection in the *Melloni* judgment of the interpretation of Article 53 that would permit Member States implementing EU secondary law to apply fundamental rights protected by their constitutions, and give priority to them over provisions of EU law when the national standard is higher.[71]

V. Individual Liberty

A. The EU as a Regulatory State

In the US Constitution, protection of liberty is elevated to the status of a governmental task and one of the reasons why the federation is created. The role of the federal government is, inter alia, to protect (negative) liberty of citizens by constraining the states and by providing another element to the checks and balances system. The European Union was not created with the same fundamental ambition, even though its law grants individuals new freedoms and exerts deregulatory pressures on the Member States. As Weatherill has frequently reminded us, the EU's internal market programme, or the EU's legislative programme more generally, is 'an exercise in re-regulation'. From the start the EU has been a locus of regulatory power and facilitated the spread of 'regulatory state'.[72] As I have explained above, the EU in its first-order constitutional principles shows preference to the regulatory values of efficiency and effectiveness over other, more typical, constitutional values. Nevertheless, the EU is sometimes presented as a liberal polity.[73] The EU legislator does not enjoy 'parliamentary sovereignty'; EU legislation is subjected to review by the Court of Justice.

Scharpf has argued that the EU's liberal constitution is strong because the Court is 'more immune from political correction than the constitutional court of any democratic state'.[74] While this may be true and the position of the Court has on some occasions been antagonistic towards legislative institutions (for example, by undermining the legislative consensus or by incorporating values into the interpretation of legislative acts which did not drive their adoption), it is also the case that the Court of Justice in reviewing EU acts is largely deferential to the legislative institutions. This attitude has been facilitated, rather than discouraged, by the principle of proportionality, which was introduced by the Court into EU law not in order to guarantee that 'individual freedom of action [is not] limited beyond the degree necessary in the public interest',[75] but rather in order to justify EU acts which were prima facie infringing fundamental rights.

---

[71] *Melloni* (n 35), paras 56–57.
[72] G Majone, 'The Rise of the Regulatory State in Europe' (1994) *West European Politics* 77.
[73] See FW Scharpf, 'Legitimacy in the Multilevel European Polity' MPIfG Working Paper 09/1, p 8.
[74] ibid.
[75] AG Lamothe in Case 11/70 *Internationale Handelsgesellschaft mbH v Einfuhr- und Vorratsstelle für Getreide und Futtermittel* [1970] ECR 1125.

Already in the *Nold* judgment in 1974, in the first phase of developing its fundamental rights jurisprudence, the Court held that rights 'are protected by law subject to limitations laid down in accordance with the public interest'.[76] However, the Court's pre-Lisbon case law might suggest that only some rights could be legitimately limited by EU law. Between 1974 and 2000 the Court denied EU fundamental rights the character of 'unfettered prerogatives' only when it spoke about the right of property and freedom of trade. Claims that the whole category of EU fundamental rights did not constitute 'unfettered prerogatives' first appeared in 2000 (the year the Charter was declared) and intensified after 2009 (when the Lisbon Treaty making the Charter formally binding was on its way to being ratified). In 2009, the right of the defence was for the first time described as a right which could be limited.[77] This approach was later extended to the right to an effective remedy.[78] Interestingly, however, where the Court was making this move, it felt obliged, quite uncharacteristically for itself, to refer to the case law of the ECtHR, as if in search of further legitimisation.[79]

It follows that the EU, in the case law of its court, has never implemented a liberal theory of rights.[80] No clear vision emerges from the Court's case law as to what individual liberties EU citizens can successfully assert. It is not even clear if there is any scope of individual freedom, however small, guaranteed to them by EU law because there is just a handful of cases where the Court was prepared to

---

[76] Case 4/73 *J Nold, Kohlen- und Baustoffgroßhandlung v Commission* [1974] ECR 491, para 14. It is important to note that *Nold* concerned the rights of ownership, with respect to which the Court could plausibly claim that '[i]f rights of ownership are protected by the constitutional laws of all the Member States … far from constituting unfettered prerogatives, must be viewed in the light of the social function of the property and activities protected thereunder'.

[77] Case C-394/07 *Marco Gambazzi v DaimlerChrysler Canada Inc. and CIBC Mellon Trust Company* [2009] ECR I-2563, para 29.

[78] Case C-279/09 *DEB Deutsche Energiehandels- und Beratungsgesellschaft mbH v Bundesrepublik Deutschland* [2010] ECR I-13849, para 45.

[79] Ibid. See also, the Court's judgment of 26 July 2017 in Case C-348/16 *Moussa Sacko v Commissione Territoriale per il riconoscimento della protezione internazionale di Milano*, paras 39–40:

An interpretation of the right to be heard, guaranteed by Article 47 of the Charter, to the effect that it is not an absolute right is confirmed by the case-law of the European Court of Human Rights, in the light of which Article 47 of the Charter must be interpreted, as the first and second paragraphs of that article correspond to Article 6(1) and Article 13 of the European Convention for the Protection of Human Rights and Fundamental Freedoms signed in Rome on 4 November 1950 (judgment of 30 June 2016, Toma and Biroul Executorului Judecătoresc Horaţiu-Vasile Cruduleci, C-205/15, EU:C:2016:499, paragraphs 40 and 41 and the case-law cited). … In that regard, the Court has previously stated that Article 6(1) of that convention does not impose an absolute obligation to hold a public hearing and does not necessarily require that a hearing be held in all proceedings. It has held, similarly, that neither the second paragraph of Article 47 of the Charter nor any other provision thereof imposes such an obligation (judgment of 4 June 2015, *Andechser Molkerei Scheitz v Commission*, C-682/13 P, not published, EU:C:2015:356, paragraph 44, which refers to the judgment of the ECtHR, 23 November 2006, *Jussila v Finland*, CE:ECHR:2006:1123JUD007305301, § 41).

[80] See, eg, the philosophy of Ronald Dworkin. R Dworkin, *Taking Rights Seriously* (Harvard, Harvard University Press, 1978).

hold that the 'substance' or the 'essence' of a EU fundamental right was violated.[81] This raises a question as to whether EU regulatory powers have ever been formally restricted by fundamental rights, or whether the only function of the 'general principles' of fundamental rights is to show national constitutional courts and the ECtHR that review against human/constitutional rights is carried out at the EU level. However, this need to appease national constitutional courts and the ECtHR was fundamental in steering the Court of Justice when invoking 'general principles' in a 'constitutional dialogue' with its national counterparts. Moreover, 'general principles' had been grounded in 'common constitutional traditions of the Member States'. A stark departure from the level of protection offered by states, in particular their shared conviction as to what is the maximum level of interference with a right, guided the case law of the CJEU and served as a constraint on the EU legislator and the Commission.

B. The Role of the Charter of Fundamental Rights in Protecting Individual Liberty

The contribution of the Charter to protecting individual liberty against the EU depends on whether the Charter can be an effective instrument of policing EU regulatory measures beyond the level already secured by Member States' constitutions and the ECHR. It should be remembered here that neither the Member States' constitutions nor the ECHR have a formal status among EU law sources. They informed the Court's review of EU acts as 'soft law' measures. The Court's reputation depended on showing respect for the European Convention on Human Rights. The Court's status depended on the acquiescence of national constitutional courts, which was difficult to solicit without paying at least some regard to the limits imposed on regulatory powers by national constitutions. Moreover, it was only because of the content of national constitutions, which contained human rights/fundamental rights provisions, that the Court had the competence to review national and EU acts against these standards.[82]

---

[81] It is far more common for the Court to invalidate EU acts, on the rare occasion that it happens, on the ground that they violate the principle of proportionality, and not because they infringe the essence of the right. See, eg, Joined Cases C-293/12 and C-594/12 *Digital Rights Ireland Ltd v Minister for Communications, Marine and Natural Resources and Kärntner Landesregierung*, Judgment of the Grand Chamber of 8 April 2014.

[82] This was because the EC Treaty did not contain a provision on fundamental rights. The Court thus had to derive its authority to adjudicate fundamental rights cases from the fact that it had a duty to ensure that 'the law' was observed and that 'the law' included the protection of fundamental rights. By invoking 'the law' the Court could not refer to 'Community law' at the time. So it must have relied on the state concept of 'the law' that included such protection. This explains also why national constitutional traditions were identified as the source of the general principles of (now Community) law protecting fundamental rights. Case 11/70 *Internationale Handelsgesellschaft mbH v Einfuhr- und Vorratsstelle für Getreide und Futtermittel* [1970] ECR 1125, para 4: 'respect for fundamental rights

The role of the Charter in enhancing the protection of individual liberty against the EU is limited and, in some respects, its adoption can be regarded as constitutional regression. This is because the Charter of Fundamental Rights has removed the previously existing structural safeguards protecting fundamental rights against excessive interference by the so-called public interest measures. Charter provisions which look like bulwarks against excessive interference, Article 52(1) and 52(3), in fact have legitimised the Court in treating as limitable rights which were not so treated before the Charter. It is notable that the question of limitations was not a subject of any deliberation in the working group responsible for preparing a report on the incorporation of the Charter into the Constitutional Treaty. Instead, despite its dubious constitutional credentials, the 2000 version of the Charter was taken as the starting point and a provision which permitted limitations on Charter rights was never subjected to any scrutiny in the working group.[83]

In this way two seemingly protective but in fact damaging provisions were incorporated into the binding version of the Charter. Article 52(1) is more problematic because the mistake is already in the wording of the provision, while Article 52(3) has proved damaging only as a result of its use by the Court of Justice. Let us look first at 52(1). It states that:

> Any limitation on the exercise of the rights and freedoms recognised by this Charter must be provided for by law and respect the essence of those rights and freedoms. Subject to the principle of proportionality, limitations may be made only if they are necessary and genuinely meet objectives of general interest recognised by the Union or the need to protect the rights and freedoms of others.

What is wrong with this provision? First of all, it is based on a presupposition that *all* rights and freedoms recognised by the Charter may be limited. Secondly, it does not require that the limitation has to have a legislative source – it may in fact result from the Court's case law (the Court's interpretation of the Treaty). Thirdly, it legalises the use of the principle of proportionality not only to principles but also to rights. Thus, despite the fact that the Charter guarantees a number of 'rights' and makes a clear distinction between 'rights' and 'principles', the central significance of that distinction is not applicability or non-applicability of the principle of proportionality but the limited 'judicial cognisability' of 'principles' not implemented by Union or national legislation (Article 52(6)). As a result, fundamental rights in the EU may be compromised not only by the need to protect the rights

---

forms an integral part of the general principles of law protected by the Court of Justice. The protection of such rights, whilst inspired by the constitutional traditions common to the Member States, must be ensured within the framework of the structure and objectives of the Community.'

[83] The working group was of the view that 'the content of the Charter represented a consensus reached by the previous Convention, and endorsed by the Nice European Council' and that '[t]he whole Charter – including its statements of rights and principles, its preamble and, as a crucial element, its "general provisions" – should be respected by this Convention and not to be re-opened'. Final report of Working Group II 'Incorporation of the Charter/accession to the ECHR' CONV 354/02, 22 October 2020, p 4 (emphasis added). The report contains no discussion of Art 52(1).

of others but also by the desire to pursue a policy objective.[84] The only trump card available to individuals is an argument based on 'the essence of the right' they wish to invoke. According to Article 52(1) the essence of a right should always be respected ('the inviolable essence'). Yet, what belongs to the inviolable essence in the case of each right is not defined in the Charter and is up to the Court of Justice.

It is also difficult to see Article 52(1) as a win for democracy over liberalism, or collectivism over individualism. It is true that in the domestic context limitations of rights are perceived as a way of ensuring a balance between constitutional prerogatives of individuals and democratic decision-making. The institution introducing limitations, and obliged to comply with the principle of proportionality, is the national parliament, traditionally possessing strong democratic credentials. Moreover, in the domestic context constitutional courts (to the extent they have the power to review legislative acts) have the tendency to side with constitutional rights rather than with policy objectives pursued by the legislature. The situation is different in the EU, where the legislator (the Commission, the Council and the European Parliament) enjoy much weaker democratic legitimacy and where the Court has a tendency to be deferential towards political institutions. This is confirmed by the fact that the part of Article 52(1) speaking of the essence of the rights and freedoms which has always to be respected. This is confirmed by the fact that the part of Article 52(1) speaking of the essence of the rights and freedoms which has always to be respected is used by the Court is used by the Court almost exclusively when it reviews national measures for their compatibility with the Charter.[85]

Article 52(3) states that '[i]n so far as the Charter contains rights which correspond to rights guaranteed by the Convention for the Protection of Human Rights and Fundamental Freedoms, the meaning and scope of those rights shall be the same as those laid down by the said Convention'. Again, this provision could easily be presented as guaranteeing that the level of protection of fundamental rights in the EU should not go below the one set by the ECtHR. The Explanations, moreover, state that the aim of this provision is to ensure that 'the meaning and scope of those rights, including authorised limitations, are the same as those laid down by the ECHR'. But the Explanations are quick to point out that ECHR standards need to apply 'without adversely affecting the autonomy of Union law and of the Court of Justice of the European Union'. This is curious, given the fact that the main point of a provision like Article 52(3) would be precisely to restrict the autonomy of the court responsible for fundamental rights adjudication and bind its case law, at

---

[84] This has had a particularly momentous consequence for conflicts between social rights and EU market liberalisation policies or between fair trial rights and the EU's objective to foster judicial cooperation. The wording of Art 52(1) is also different from many similar provisions in national constitutions because the provision does not include a requirement that the limitation be 'necessary in a democratic society'.

[85] See, eg, Case C-426/11 *Mark Alemo-Herron v Parkwood Leisure Ltd*, Judgment of 18 July 2013. Exceptions include *Digital Rights Ireland* (n 81) and Case C-283/11 *Sky Österreich GmbH v Österreichischer Rundfunk*, Judgment of 22 January 2013. When the Court reviews EU acts it often starts with the principle of proportionality, instead of, as the logic of Art 52(1) would suggest, the question of the inviolable essence. What is the right's inviolable essence is then not given separate consideration.

least as far as the minimum standard is concerned, to the external source. That the drafters of the Explanations might have problems with reconciling concern for the Court's independence with the desire adequately to protect fundamental rights is visible in the Explanations' next paragraph, where it is insisted that the reference to the ECHR covers both the Convention and the case law of the ECtHR, and that '[i]n any event, the level of protection afforded by the Charter may never be lower than that guaranteed by the ECHR'.[86]

It is interesting to observe what kind of use the Court has actually made of Article 52(3). So far the Court has not chosen to use Article 52(3) to justify a departure from its earlier interpretative line and offer EU fundamental rights more protection than enjoyed before the Charter was made formally binding. Instead, the Court refers to the case law of the Strasbourg Court only when it wants to legitimise a restriction imposed by the EU legislator which the Court did not have the chance to assess beforehand, or which national constitutions protect more stringently. Just like Article 52(1), Article 52(3) makes it easier for the Court to rubber-stamp legislative limitations. This is, naturally, the incorrect use of Article 52(3) and the ECHR. The ECHR is a document which introduces minimum standards, so even if it permitted limitations on the same grounds as a EU act, it cannot be used to demonstrate the act's compliance with *EU law*. After all, the Strasbourg Court often refrains from imposing stricter standards in order to respect the states' margin of appreciation. Moreover, compliance with the ECHR is a prerequisite of EU acts' compatibility with the Charter and not its guarantee. Review against Article 52(1) and against Article 52(3) cannot be merged into one.[87] Finally, as long as the EU is not a party to the ECHR there is no way of policing the Court's selective approach to the ECtHR's jurisprudence. The obligation to follow the Strasbourg Court's case law, which at the moment is a hollow one, would become real if the Luxembourg Court's judgments could be assessed for their compatibility with the ECHR by the Strasbourg Court. But Opinion 2/13 of the Court of Justice has effectively closed down the possibility of the EU becoming a party to the ECHR.[88] At paragraph 170, the Court speaks of the necessity to guarantee that 'interpretation of ... fundamental rights be ensured within the framework and the structure of objectives of the EU'. In the Court's view, EU fundamental rights cannot be protected in accordance with the ECHR because the Convention does not take into account the special constitutional framework of the EU. In this way, Opinion 2/13 reveals the Court's

---

[86] 'Explanations on Article 52 – Scope and interpretation of rights and principles', Explanations relating to the Charter of Fundamental Rights, OJ C303, 14.12.2007, p 17.

[87] For an example of the Court merging the two questions see the *Sacko* case (n 79).

[88] Opinion 2/13, *Accession of the Union to the ECHR*, Opinion of the Full Court of 18 December 2014. The opinion speaks extensively of the necessity to preserve the autonomy of EU law in the context of fundamental rights. In para 177 of the Opinion, the Court holds that '[f]undamental rights, as recognised in particular by the Charter, must ... be interpreted and applied within the EU in accordance with the constitutional framework referred to in paragraphs 155 to 176 above' (supremacy, direct effect, conferral, sincere cooperation and other principles mentioned by the Court). The EU's constitutional framework precludes, in the Court's view, the EU's accession to the ECHR on terms included in the Draft Accession Agreement.

true intentions as regards Article 52(3). If this provision was to be taken seriously, accession to the ECHR would not be considered a threat to the existing constitutional arrangement in the EU, of which Article 52(3) is part.

C. National Constitutional Tradition as a Bar to EU Action in Breach of Fundamental Rights

One additional constraint which the Charter attempted to impose on the Court's treatment of fundamental rights, especially when invoked against EU institutions, was the reference, in two different places, to Member States' constitutions. Article 52(4) speaks of 'the common constitutional traditions of the Member States' in the light of which the resulting rights should be interpreted. Article 53, already cited once above, states that '[n]othing in the Charter shall be interpreted as restricting or adversely affecting human rights and fundamental freedoms as recognised, in their respective fields of application, by Union law … and by Member States' constitutions'. This provision can be given a modest interpretation, according to which the Charter could not be used to undermine national standards of protection, but the Court would be permitted to ask national courts to undermine these standards if this course of action was supported by other arguments. Alternatively, the provision could be given a generous interpretation, according to which the Charter would empower national courts, in certain situations, to refuse to apply the principles of primacy and effectiveness of EU law. The latter interpretation would mean that EU citizens would not lose any human rights as a result of their situation being covered by EU law, and that national courts would not be forced to violate their own constitutions in order to comply with EU obligations.

The principle of primacy of EU law is not restricted to ordinary national rules. It also covers national constitutions. National constitutional and supreme courts have adopted different positions in response to the Court's claim of primacy of EU law and supremacy of the Court's jurisdiction within the scope of EU law. Famously, however, national courts have generally subscribed to primacy of EU law in practice by grounding it in their own constitutional provisions and doctrines, creating only limited exceptions to it, and by practically accepting the Court's rulings and their consequences. The Court of Justice has also taken steps to avoid conflict with national constitutions by tactically restricting the scope of Union law (*Grogan*) or accepting national constitutional standards as the point of reference (*Omega*), or allowing the national courts independently to decide the issue of proportionality.[89] In *Melloni*,[90] the Court famously decided not

---

[89] Case C-159/90 *The Society for the Protection of Unborn Children Ireland Ltd v Stephen Grogan* [1991] ECR I-4685; Case C-36/02 *Omega Spielhallen- und Automatenaufstellungs-GmbH v Oberbürgermeisterin der Bundesstadt Bonn* [2004] ECR I-9609.
[90] See n 35.

to use any of these instruments and proclaimed that national constitutions did not constitute any restriction on EU action. In the Court's view, applicability of an EU act meant that the situation was within the field of application of Union law, where the Court recognised only one set of fundamental rights standards, that stemming from the Charter and the Court's own case law. Because these standards were not violated in the case of the EAW Framework Decision, there was no reason for the national court not to execute the arrest warrant. Primacy, unity and effectiveness of EU law were given a higher stance than national constitutional provisions protecting human rights.

As I explained above, the *Melloni* judgment and Opinion 2/13 on the EU's accession to the ECHR best exhibit what the Court believes are the foundational, irrefutable principles of the EU, which could not be compromised by any other value, including respect for national constitutional traditions (or national constitutional identity) or for rights of an individual (see paragraphs 188 and 189 of Opinion 2/13). The Court has made it explicit that accession to the ECHR cannot mean that the Member States will possess new powers to lay down higher standards of protection than those set (by the Court) through the Charter. It is also telling that the Court does not mind the effectiveness of the EU regime being undermined *in casu*, as long as EU law remains supreme in principle. It accepts that fundamental rights may require that Member States depart from rules laid down by a legislative act and take upon themselves additional obligations.[91] In the follow-up case law to the *Melloni* judgment, the Court has allowed the national courts to take into account fundamental rights considerations and refuse to execute a European arrest warrant that formally complied with the requirements set out in the Framework Decision.[92] But the Court was not able to bring itself to say that, on certain occasions, human rights may require that primacy and effectiveness of EU law will suffer. This was an implicit acknowledgement, perhaps, that overtly undermining national courts' domestic authority as protectors of human rights is not good for the broader legitimacy of the EU.

VI. Brexit and the Charter of Fundamental Rights – The *N.S.* Case

Does the binding nature of the Charter, pushed through by the Lisbon Treaty despite the failure of the Constitutional Treaty project, have any relevance for the UK's EU membership referendum? The Charter has often been presented in the

---

[91] Joined Cases C-411/10 and C-493/10 *N. S. v Secretary of State for the Home Department and M. E. v Refugee Applications Commissioner and Minister for Justice, Equality and Law Reform* [2011] ECR I-13905.

[92] Joined Cases C-404/15 and C-659/15 PPU *Pál Aranyosi and Robert Căldăraru*, Judgment of 5 April 2016.

UK as a dangerous document, which should be opposed not because the UK does not share the values of EU fundamental rights, but rather because the Charter will enable the EU Court to impose on Britain higher social standards and undermine the UK's regulatory model.[93] Danger was seen to be coming from two independent sources. The first one was the wording of the Charter itself, which included Title IV 'Solidarity', guaranteeing such rights as worker's right to information and consultation, collective bargaining and action, protection against unjustified dismissal, the right to fair and just working conditions, protection of family life, the right to healthcare and the right of access to services of general economic interest. The Title included also provisions on social security and social assistance, environmental protection and consumer protection. Article 2 of the Polish/UK Protocol on the Charter was intended to deter the most far-reaching implications of including in the Charter a title which could challenge national social and economic policies. Hence, the Protocol lays down that 'nothing in Title IV of the Charter creates justiciable rights applicable to Poland or the United Kingdom except in so far as Poland or the United Kingdom has provided for such rights in its national law'. Of course, this does not prevent the Court from reviewing UK laws and practices for compliance with Title IV, especially in areas where the EU has already legislated (such as working time) and where EU legislation, not the Charter, could be portrayed as the source of rights.[94] On the whole, however, the Court responded to Member States' concern over the inclusion of the Solidarity Title with much understanding. In the *AMS* judgment (on reference from France) it ruled that Article 28 of the Charter contained only a principle and could not apply directly (on this occasion to a horizontal situation) without a legislative concretisation at the EU or national level.[95]

The other perceived source of danger was the expansion of the Court's general authority to subject national laws and practices to review against EU law. The UK was probably the only government which appreciated that incorporation of new standards into EU law meant expansion of the Court's power to render ineffective Member States' measures, thereby restricting their autonomy independently to regulate the issues touched, even very remotely, by some EU regulation. That is why Article 1 of the Protocol speaks directly to the ability of the Court of Justice to find national laws and practices inconsistent with the Charter (although its wording stills makes it practically ineffective as a method of excluding applicability of the Court's post-Lisbon fundamental rights case law to Poland and the UK).

---

[93] See the statement by Tony Blair made to the Liaison Committee on 18 June 2007 and reported in the House of Commons' European Scrutiny Committee's 35th Report, para 52: 'First we will not accept a treaty that allows the charter of fundamental rights to change UK law in any way.'

[94] See eg, Case C-219/14 *Kathleen Greenfield v The Care Bureau*, Judgment of 11 November 2015, which uses Art 7 of the Working Time Directive to refer to Art 31(2) of the Charter of Fundamental Rights. The case is a reference from the UK.

[95] Case C-176/12 *Association de médiation sociale v Union locale des syndicats CGT*, Judgment of 15 January 2014.

That the Court can use the Charter to review UK laws and practices against provisions of Title IV has been exemplified by a number of cases.[96]

As to the applicability of the Charter in the UK in principle, this question was one of the issues considered in the context of a reference submitted by the Court of Appeal in the famous *N.S.* case.[97] The case concerned the consequences of human rights violations in Greece for the operation of the European Common Asylum System, in particular the question of whether any additional obligations stemmed from the Member State's duty to respect EU fundamental rights for a state in which an asylum application had been lodged and where the applicant was present but which under the general rules was not the 'responsible' state. On the facts, the Court had to decide whether the UK and Ireland were obliged to give effect to EU rules on the responsible state and transfer applicants back to Greece where it had been established that such a transfer would expose the asylum seeker to a risk of having their fundamental rights violated. The Court decided to create a duty for the state where the asylum application was lodged, which knew or had to have known of the systemic deficiencies in the 'responsible state', to accept responsibility for the asylum application and keep the individual concerned on its territory.[98] In order to arrive at this conclusion the Court heavily relied on Article 18 of the Charter of Fundamental Rights, which, in a much more direct and unequivocal manner than international instruments and EU legislative law, lays down the right to asylum.[99] The UK government (at various stages of the proceedings) put forward two arguments which would block applicability of the Charter and the imposition on it of an obligation to consider itself 'the responsible state' in the specified 'exceptional circumstances'. The first of these arguments concerned the scope of application of the Charter, ie the interpretation of Article 51(1). The UK government argued that the relevant provision of EU Regulation provided for discretionary powers of the Member States exercisable on humanitarian grounds. Thus, the Member State was not 'implementing Union law' (or derogating from it) where it used that power, which, in the UK government's view, brought the situation outside the scope of Union law. The Court's reply was brief. The Member State relying on the Regulation to assume the position of the responsible state was implementing Union law because the Regulation set out the consequences of becoming the responsible state.

The second argument concerned the Polish/UK Protocol on the Charter. Before the High Court, the Home Secretary at the time (Labour) argued that the Charter did not apply in the UK. Cranston J in the High Court agreed with

---

[96] See, eg, Case C-539/12 *Z.J.R. Lock v British Gas Trading Limited*, Judgment of 22 May 2014, Case C-426/11 *Mark Alemo-Herron and Others v Parkwood Leisure Ltd* (n 85), Case C-300/11 *ZZ v Secretary of State for the Home Department*, Judgment of 4 June 2013, and Case C-260/11 *The Queen, on the application of: David Edwards, Lilian Pallikaropoulos v Environment Agency, First Secretary of State, Secretary of State for Environment, Food and Rural Affairs*, Judgment of 11 April 2013.

[97] Joined Cases *N. S. and M. E.* (n 91).

[98] Ibid, paras 96–97.

[99] See Leczykiewicz, 'Human Rights in the Area of Freedom, Security and Justice' (n 51).

this argument. In paragraph 155 of his judgment he held that '[g]iven the Polish and United Kingdom Protocol, the Charter [could not] be directly relied on as against the United Kingdom although it [was] an indirect influence as an aid to interpretation'.[100] Theresa May, who became the new Home Secretary in David Cameron's Cabinet, accepted before the Court of Appeal that this argument was unfounded and that fundamental rights set out in the Charter could be relied on as against the UK. She submitted that Cranston J 'erred in holding otherwise'.[101] Nevertheless, the Court of Appeal decided to ask the Court of Justice whether the UK obligations were 'in any respect modified by the Protocol (No. 30) on the application of the Charter to Poland and to the United Kingdom'. The Court pointed out that Article 1(1) did not call into question the applicability of the Charter in the UK or in Poland and that Article 6 TEU 'require[d] the Charter to be applied and interpreted by the courts of Poland and of the United Kingdom …'. However, the Court added, quite counterfactually, that 'the Charter … [did] not create new rights or principles'.[102] This statement had a two-fold objective. First, it was meant to demonstrate that the Protocol would be ineffective even if it was an opt-out, and that there was no need to react violently to the Court's ruling because applicability of the Charter is not such a big deal after all. And this is indeed how the judgment was received by academics. The wording of the Protocol did not warrant an interpretation which would enable the UK to be exempted from the Charter. Yet, the British public could think that the EU Court had cheated them out of the Charter opt-out, which the Blair government so courageously secured.[103] There is some evidence that the concern over the Court's power to scrutinise UK governmental decisions, whether real or perceived, played a role in the Brexit vote. The extent to which the Court of Justice is able to communicate with the public is limited and thus it is difficult for this institution to directly convince EU citizens of its legitimacy. But the CJEU could clearly have done more to show that it respects the Member States' 'fundamental boundaries'.[104] It is quite improbable that any particular judgment of the Court would have averted Brexit. I do believe, however, that greater engagement with fundamental constitutional values would

---

[100] *R (on the application of S v Secretary of State for the Home Department) v Amnesty International Limited, The Aire Centre (Advice on Individual Rights in Europe), United Nations High Commissioner for Refugees* [2010] EWHC 705 (Admin).

[101] Para 8 of the respondent's (Home Secretary's) notice, cited by Lord Neuberger in the judgment of the Court of Appeal deciding to refer the case to the CJEU.

[102] Joined Cases *N. S. and M. E.* (n 91) para 119.

[103] See the Presidency Conclusions of the Brussels European Council 21/22 June 2007, a revised version, 11177/07 REV 1. For a summary of how the Polish/UK Protocol on the Charter was presented in the British media, see C Barnard, 'The "Opt-Out" for the UK and Poland from the Charter of Fundamental Rights: Triumph of Rhetoric over Reality?' in S Griller and J Ziller (eds), *The Lisbon Treaty: EU Constitutionalism without a Constitutional Treaty?* (Vienna, Springer, 2008) 257, 277–78.

[104] JHH Weiler, 'Fundamental Rights and Fundamental Boundaries: Common Standards and Conflicting Values in the Protection of Human Rights in the European Legal Space' in R Kastoryano (ed), *An Identity for Europe. The Relevance of Multiculturalism in EU Construction* (New York, Palgrave Macmillan, 2009) 73.

have influenced the broader discourse and the citizens' perceptions and at least indirectly enhanced the EU's social and political acceptance.

VII. Conclusion

The purpose of this chapter was to assess the transformative role of the Charter of Fundamental Rights in the EU Constitution. I have argued that neither the content of the Charter of Fundamental Rights nor the case law of the Court interpreting and applying this document enabled the document to deliver on the constitutional promise that a written bill of rights constitutes. I have carried out this analysis by making a distinction between 'deep' and 'shallow' constitutionalism and explained why the Charter's contribution to deep constitutionalism is limited. The main problem with the Charter is that it does not successfully constrain and direct the CJEU and thus does little to counteract the Court's expansionist and integrationist tendencies. As a result, the EU remains deficient vis-à-vis two most fundamental constitutional principles – the principle of limited government and of individual liberty, and the Charter could be regarded as deepening these shortcomings. While it is difficult to prove that the Charter's failure as a constitutional document played any role in the Brexit referendum, the EU's first bill of rights does emerge as a lost opportunity to strengthen the EU's constitutional credentials in areas which, among others, captivated the British public.

10

The EU Constitution, Sovereignty and the Problem of Primacy

I. Introduction

It is a trite comment that the EU 'Constitution' is a misnomer. Its proper appellation, the 'draft Treaty for the Establishment of a Constitution for Europe' or 'draft Constitutional Treaty' (DCT), is less misleading and conveys the 'creative' ambiguity intended by those who drafted it.

Legally, the DCT was a treaty, ratified in the same way as previous reform treaties; it confirmed that the EU derived its powers by conferral from the Member States and did not proclaim an autochthonous source for the EU's powers. And, in common with previous EU reform treaties, the DCT continued to be fraught with potentially conflicting principles and concepts: the principles of conferral and subsidiarity versus the principles of supremacy and loyal cooperation, or the overreaching EU competence to harmonise national rules to facilitate the operation of the single market versus national policy prerogatives in areas of potential cross-border economic significance. By the same token, the DCT carried these conflicts to a higher level: it affirmed the position of the Member States as *Herren der Verträge*[1] and, at the same time, by the very use of the term 'constitution' staked a claim that the EU was, or was developing, into a state-like entity which at a supranational level exercises sovereign rights. The DCT does not proclaim an autochthonous source for the EU's political and law-making powers – an assertion which would be incompatible with the principle of conferred powers. However, the very use of the term 'constitutional' in the DCT suggests a new stage in the EU integration process and the acceptance by Member States of the Court of Justice of the EU's (CJEU) reference to the EU Treaties as EU's constitutional architecture

---

* SOAS University of London, & Barrister, 1 Essex Court (Chambers of The Rt Hon Sir Tony Baldry), Temple London.
[1] Trans: Masters of the Treaties.

which has no basis in the EU Treaties, international law or the national constitutions of EU Member States.

The term 'Constitutional Treaty' was the creation – ingenious in some respects – of Giscard d'Estaing, who calculated that, to ensure ratification, the DCT could and should be passed off to the public in the garb of yet another EU reform treaty. Once ratified, the terminology would change and, if only for ease of reference, the DCT could and would generally be referred to as the 'EU Constitution' by the EU institutions, pro-EU interest groups and the media and thereby, by monolithic rhetoric and the integrationist will of the majority of national governments, become gradually accepted as a self-standing source of EU law and policy-making. Words, as Wittgenstein said, are deeds, and the way legal documents and discussions are framed and perceived influences expectations and opinions about their function and scope, and the powers they bestow. The fact that the EU could claim to have a constitution approved 'democratically' by Member States in accordance with their national constitutions, would embolden the EU and integrationist Member States, and dishearten the reluctant by an avalanche of constitutional and legitimation theory propounded by overwhelmingly pro-EU and partly EU-funded academic commentary and, crucially, the media. Although the DCT was abandoned following referendums in the Netherlands and France, the ingenuity of Giscard's thinking may be gauged from the fact that, notwithstanding its failure, the DCT did indeed quickly come to be referred to almost exclusively as the first, albeit failed, EU Constitution, notably so in the academic literature.

Giscard, detached as he was from popular opinion, sentiments and concerns, of course, crucially underestimated the difficulties associated with blending out the constitutional aspects of the DCT during the ratification process, which could be – and were – perceived as a threat to national sovereignty. According to post-referendum surveys, concerns about further loss of national sovereignty were an important, although not the principal, motive of no-voters in the French referendum,[2] whilst in the Dutch referendum campaign and vote the sovereignty issue assumed central importance.[3] A symbol of this pervasive threat to national

---

[2] European Commission, *Flash Eurobarometer – The European Constitution: Post-referendum survey in France*, Flash EB 171, June 2015, p 17. 5% of 'no' voters expressed concern about 'loss of sovereignty'. To these may be added the added the following motives which all revolve around or overlap with the 'loss of sovereignty' theme: 'I am against European integration' (4%), 'Not democratic enough' (3%), 'I do not want a European political union/a European federal State/the "United States" of Europe' (2%), 'The draft goes too far/ advances too quickly' (3%). Taken together, these motives were not nearly as important to French as to Dutch voters, but they still represent the second most important congeries of motives for the 'no' vote in the French referendum.

[3] European Commission, *Flash Eurobarometer – The European Constitution: Post-referendum survey in the Netherlands*, Flash EB 172, June 2015, p 15. 19% of 'no' voters expressed concern about 'loss of sovereignty'. As above, to these may be added the following motives which revolve or overlap with the 'loss of sovereignty' theme: 'I am against European integration' (8%), 'Not democratic enough' (5%), 'I do not want a European political union/a European federal State/the "United States" of Europe' (5%), 'loss of Dutch identity' (3%), 'The draft goes too far/ advances too quickly' (6%), 'Europe is evolving too fast' (5%). Taken together, these sovereignty-related motives represent by far the single most significant motive for the 'no' vote in the Dutch election.

sovereignty in the DCT was the so-called primacy clause.[4] The EU institutions, national governments, jurists and the judicial establishment throughout the EU were at pains to emphasise that that clause no more than summarised the position developed by the CJEU. Those campaigning against adoption of the DCT, however, could, and did, point to its prominent place at the core of the new text, and, in more rarefied discussions, drew parallels with the interstate commerce clause and doctrine of pre-emption in the US Constitution which had been used by the US Supreme Court to strengthen and expand the powers of federal institutions at the expense of those in the States. Rightly or wrongly, the primacy clause was portrayed by critics as more than a mere codifying clause, as an aspirational declaration and a justiciable provision of intent which would entrench the CJEU's claim to exercise a quasi-supreme court jurisdiction over all areas of national law not only within the scope, but at the intersection of, EU law; a clause which would fuel and legitimate further integrationist ambitions of the EU institutions, including the CJEU and those Member States most intent on integration. This may explain why the primacy clause became the most prominent casualty of the double referendum rejection of the DCT and why it was subsequently relegated to an ignominious declaration annexed to the Treaty of Lisbon. As this chapter demonstrates, however, the removal of the primacy clause from the Treaty text did not prevent the further development of an increasingly hierarchical relationship between the CJEU and national constitutional courts, most notably in Germany.

II. Sovereignty

The term 'constitution' remains intimately linked to the concept of sovereignty. Carl Schmitt famously remarked that 'Sovereign is he who decides on the state of exception'.[5] Schmitt's characterisation of sovereignty acknowledges the legal and political elements of sovereignty. It is one thing for a constitution to define the powers of government and who has the right to suspend it (state of emergency), and another thing to have the will, power and general acceptance to exercise them. Where the designated sovereign lacks any of these attributes to exercise legal sovereignty, he lacks political sovereignty. The state of exception need not be narrowly conceived, as by Schmitt,[6] as the power to suspend the constitution, but

---

[4] Art. I-6 DCT which stated: 'The Constitution and law adopted by the institutions of the Union in exercising competences conferred on it shall have *primacy* over the law of the Member States'. (Emphasis added)

[5] C Schmitt, *Politische Theologie* (Munich, Dunker Humblot, 1934) 11.

[6] Schmitt overstates the extent to which liberal constitutional political systems are rule-governed and probably also the degree to which the operations of law, especially constitutional law, can be detached from the gravitational sphere of politics. See D Dyzenhaus, *Carl Schmitt's Critique of Liberalism* (Durham, Duke University Press, 1998) 44–47.

as extending to the more common[7] 'exceptional' constitutional situation where the relevant legal documents do not clearly allocate powers between the different institutions or different layers of government or their courts, but final authority must be located somewhere. Here the decision on the exception refers to the power to resolve competence[8] disputes. In relation to unresolved competence disputes, both (1) the issue of legal sovereignty accompanied by the lack of will and/or of power to exercise it, and (2) the issue of who has legal sovereignty, can only be resolved politically. Sovereignty is asserted by he who steps in and is able to assert himself, even against the letter of the constitution.

Schmitt's concept of sovereignty is thus ultimately political in Hobbes' sense: he is sovereign who is accepted as such. However, legal sovereignty remains important in the sense that, in conditions of modern constitutionalism, it is important for political authority to be seen as legitimate, ie in accordance with law. An assertion of political sovereignty in opposition to clearly legal sovereignty is therefore commonly accompanied by constitutional amendment, a constitutional revolution or, more precariously, by *contra legem* judicial interpretation of the constitution – an interpretation which reflects political reality to which an ever compliant judicature submits. An assertion of political sovereignty in conditions of undefined legal sovereignty requires no formal confirmation. Where the assertion is accepted by other relevant parties, including those with a conflicting claim to it, it will become the authoritative unwritten constitutional norm itself which is legitimated by the judicature.

Within the EU, an assertion of political over legal sovereignty occurs whenever the EU institutions claim and exercise powers which, according to the principle of conferral (Art 5 TFEU) and/or national constitutional law, are reserved to Member States, and that overreach into national sovereignty is accepted politically and/or judicially by Member States.

III. The Problem of *Kompetenz-Kompetenz*

The concept of *Kompetenz-Kompetenz*, which is related to the issue of primacy, in broad terms poses the question of who is legally sovereign. In the strict sense it refers to the question of who – generally a supreme or supranational court[9] – decides on the state of common exception, ie who has the final say in disputes concerning the allocation of competences between different layers of government in constitutionally- or treaty-governed political entities such as federal states, confederations or supranational organisations. In federal states, the *Kompetenz-Kompetenz*

---

[7] Not considered by and probably regarded as uncommon by Schmitt for the aforementioned reasons, namely, that he overstated the tendency of liberal constitutions to articulate institutional arrangements clearly and unambiguously in terms of legal norms.

[8] The term 'competences' is best translated as designated or authorised powers.

[9] Not all countries have a supreme or constitutional court, eg Finland, and in some constitutions the relevant powers are vested in the President or some other body.

is typically vested in a supreme or constitutional court at the federal, and not the state, level of government, which over time favours the accretion of power at the federal level at the expense of the constituent regional states. The prime example of such political centralisation through the judicial backdoor is the United States.[10]

Within the EU, the issue of *Kompetenz-Kompetenz* is focused on the question of which court decides the boundaries of the EU's legislative and executive competence: the CJEU on the basis of the exclusive jurisdiction granted to it in the EU Treaties to review and interpret Union law, or the national constitutional courts with reference to the overriding requirements of national constitutional laws.

In international law, the answer is clear. The Member States are sovereign and, according to the Vienna Convention on the Laws of Treaties (VCLT), are able to withdraw from, or suspend the operation of, the EU Treaties in case of violation of 'a rule of its internal law of fundamental importance' (Article 46), 'a material breach' (Article 60) or 'a fundamental change of circumstances' (Article 62). The VCLT applies to the EU Treaties notwithstanding the fact that the EU is not a party to the VCLT[11] and although the CJEU does not apply its methods of treaty interpretation. A withdrawal or suspension would be justified if the EU institutions manifestly exceed their powers as conferred in the Treaties and/or acted in breach of national constitutional law.

The CJEU, however, began referring to the EU Treaties as the EU's own constitutional charter long before the DCT was drafted. The CJEU has also long claimed the *Kompetenz-Kompetenz* to decide competence disputes between the EU institutions and its Member States, and first staked its claim to be the ultimate arbiter over the limits of the EU's powers in connection with the principle of the supremacy of Union law which it developed in a series of cases from the early 1960s.[12] In such competence disputes, as well as other cases involving the fundamental interests of the EU, the CJEU has adopted a pronounced *communautaire* or pro-Union approach. This approach is characterised by the CJEU's refusal to follow a clear interpretative methodology and its reliance instead on an ultra-flexible process which allows it to favour whichever criterion from an open-ended range of interpretative criteria – especially literal, contextual, purposive and meta-teleological criteria – best justifies an expansive reading of the EU's competences. The pro-Union tendency inherent in the Court's approach is powerfully illustrated by the CJEU's asymmetrical approach to the judicial review of national versus EU law: in infringement actions brought against Member States the CJEU has,

---

[10] To a lesser extent the same process can be observed in post-war Germany, Australia and Canada.

[11] Art 5 Vienna Convention on the Law of Treaties: 'The present Convention applies to any treaty which is the constituent instrument of an international organization and to any treaty adopted within an international organization without prejudice to any relevant rules of the organization.'

[12] Case C-26/62 *NV Algemene Transport- en Expeditie Onderneming van Gend & Loos v Netherlands Inland Revenue Administration* [1963] ECR-1; Case C-6/64 *Flaminio Costa v ENEL* [1964] ECR-585; Case C-11/70 *Internationale Handelsgesellschaft mbH v Einfuhr- und Vorratsstelle für Getreide und Futtermittel* [1970] ECR-114.

in many hundreds of cases, upheld the Commission's initial finding of a national breach of EU law, whereas in ultra vires actions brought by Member States against the EU institutions for the annulment of a general EU legislative act, the CJEU dismissed the action in all but a couple of cases.[13]

The CJEU's claim to be the sole arbiter over the scope of the Union's powers has been challenged by a number of national constitutional courts. Although amongst these the Czech and, arguably also, the Polish constitutional courts have been the most consistent and have not shied away from refusing to apply a CJEU decision,[14] the 'national perspective' on the issues of primacy, legal pluralism and *Kompetenz-Kompetenz* in the relationship between Union law and national law has nowhere been judicially more comprehensively and rigorously analysed than in the judgments of the German Federal Constitutional Court (FCC). This explains the focus in this chapter on the jurisprudence of the German FCC which still commands overwhelming political and public domestic respect – despite the fact that its judges are political appointees[15] – and thus is well placed to enforce the national constitution's requirements against EU-overreach should it wish to. Conversely, its failure to protect Germany's constitutional position and its furtherance instead, in collaboration with the CJEU, of EU integration by judicial stealth and in opposition to the wording of the EU Treaties provides a powerful legitimating function for further integrationist steps, certainly within Germany but also beyond. The FCC's reluctance to uphold German constitutional law has also emboldened the CJEU in its drive to further integration through the judicial backdoor. The FCC developed its analysis in a series of seminal judgments which go back to the 1970s.

---

[13] Case C-376/98 *Germany v Parliament and Council (Tobacco Advertising)*; Joined Cases C-293/12, *Digital Rights Ireland Ltd v Minister for Communications, Marine and Natural Resources* and C-594/12, *Kärntner Landesregierung*, Judgment of 8 April 2014.

[14] P Craig and G de Burca, *EU Law – Text, Cases and Materials* (Oxford, Oxford University Press, 2015) 305–09. The Danish and the Spanish constitutional courts also rejected the CJEU's claim that EU law is supreme over the law of the land, although the Spanish judges recently reversed their original position when they accepted the CJEU's preliminary ruling in *Melloni* (Constitutional Court *(Tribunal Constitucional) Decision of 13/02/2014, case no 26/2014*). The more deferential Portuguese Constitutional Court accepted the supremacy of EU law but subject to a reserve national fundamental rights jurisdiction (see M Kumm and VF Comella, 'The Primacy Clause of the Constitutional Treaty and the Future of Constitutional Conflict in the European Union' (2008) 3(2–3) *International Journal of Constitutional Law* 473, 475).

[15] It is a peculiar fact of contemporary societies, certainly in Western Europe and North America, that judges, especially constitutional judges, generally enjoy a very high degree of public esteem and confidence. The reasons for this include the traditionally high social status of the professions, especially the legal and medical professions, the fact that judges and lawyers are able to claim specialist expertise not open to the legally unqualified and to dress up their decisions and opinions in the specialist language of law so that laymen are largely excluded from discussion, that this allows judges, especially constitutional judges, to present political choices as decisions based on impersonal decisions constrained by methodological constraints, and, perhaps above all, that judges, unlike politicians, are largely exempted from media and public criticism, reinforced by the fact that the media rarely have the expertise, time and inclination to communicate legal argumentation to a wider audience. In Germany, high regard for the FCC is amplified, as almost everything else in Germany's political life is coloured, by Germany's agonistic history in the 20th century.

IV. The Pre-DCT Cases

In the *Solange I* case, the FCC ruled in 1974 that, in the hypothetical case of a conflict between Community law and the fundamental rights guarantees under the German Basic Law – Germany's Constitution in all but name[16] – constitutional rights take precedence over any conflicting norm of EC law. The FCC thus impliedly rejected the position of the doctrine of the primacy of Community law as laid down by the CJEU, although on the facts of the case the FCC held that the relevant provision of Community law did not conflict with the German Constitution.[17]

The FCC very significantly widened its analysis in *Brunner v Treaty on European Union (Maastricht Judgment).*[18] In this case, the FCC embedded its earlier human rights focus in a more comprehensive analysis of the relationship between EU law and German constitutional law as well as a historically and sociologically sensitive theory of democratic legitimacy. In a politically charged judgment, the FCC made clear that Germany's acceptance of the supremacy of Union law was limited by at least four factors:

1.   the need for democratic legitimation by means of parliamentary assent;
2.   the concept of a *demos* as the expression of the 'spiritual, social and political' identity of a people which understands itself as 'one' for the purposes of collective self-government – there is a national, but not an EU-wide, *demos*;
3.   the constitutional guarantee of fundamental rights; and
4.   the basic principle of legal certainty as one of the constituents of the rule of law which underlie the principle of the limited and specific conferral (*begrenzte Einzelermächtigung*) of sovereign rights to the EU.

---

[16] Formally, Germany does not have a Constitutional but a Basic Law or *Grundgesetz*. When the Federal Republic was established it was decided that the adoption of a constitution should be postponed until the reunification of the country. When reunification occurred, it was regarded as unnecessary, perhaps also too risky and certainly politically 'inconvenient' to replace the Basic Law with a publicly endorsed constitution. To all intents and purposed the Basic Law now functions as a de facto constitution although it was never formally adopted as such nor endorsed by a popular vote.

[17] The FCC later moderated its stance in the light of the CJEU's development of a doctrine of protection for fundamental rights (Case C-4/73 J. *Nold, Kohlen- und Baustoffgroßhandlung v Ruhrkohle Aktiengesellschaft*) and in *Solange II* (BVerfGE 73, vom 22 Oktober 1986, 2 BvR 197/83) ruled in 1983 that, in view of this development and for as long as the Community generally ensured an effective protection of fundamental rights the FCC would no longer exercise its jurisdiction to decide on the application of secondary Community legislation. However, the FCC neither said that it no longer had such jurisdiction nor did it rule out that it might resume exercising its jurisdiction should the conditions for its suspension no longer be in place. *Solange II* therefore did not substantially modify the substance of the FCC's judgment in *Solange I*, namely, that the power of the national government to transfer sovereign rights extends only so far and no further than is compatible with the basic structure of the Basic Law. On the facts, the FCC once again found there had been no breach of the complainant's procedural or substantive rights under the Basic Law.

[18] BVerfGE 89, 155 vom 12. Oktober 1993, 2 BvR 2134, 2159/92; *Brunner v European Union Treaty* [1994] CMLR 57.

The unifying principle central to the four strands of argument, the FCC opined, is the principle of conferral which means that the EU has no autochthonous law-making powers and ensures that the requirements of the German Constitution act as a side-constraint on any future transfer of further powers to the EU. Through the act of conferral of sovereign powers by parliamentary assent, the Union acquires the indirect democratic legitimacy it would otherwise lack. It does so via the legitimating medium of national political institutions which are, however, subject to limits set by their own constitutions. The principle of conferral thus both allows for a degree of European integration but it at the same time limits the powers of the European Union by reference to the overriding requirements imposed by the liberal-democratic basic order guaranteed by the German Constitution. The principle of conferral thus safeguards the democratic-majoritarian foundation of the German Constitution through the need for German parliamentary assent as a precondition for every step in the process towards European integration, and it protects the German Constitution's twin demands for the protection of fundamental rights and of the rule of law by reserving to the FCC the jurisdiction to strike down any unconstitutional legislation or acts irrespective of whether it has been adopted by the organs of the European Union or by the German Parliament.

It was against the background of this stand-off between the CJEU on the one hand and national constitutional courts, in particular the German FCC, on the other that the issue of *Kompetenz-Kompetenz* came to be more widely discussed again during the Convention on the Future of Europe. When Convention President Giscard d'Estaing presented the proposed draft Constitutional Treaty, concern amongst opponents of European federalism all over the EU was focused on the loss of national sovereignty symbolised by the proposed codification of the principle of supremacy. Critics feared, as supporters of the DCT hoped, that the formal elevation of the judge-made supremacy principle to treaty status would not only raise the CJEU to the status of a quasi-federal court but finally resolve the *Kompetenz-Kompetenz* rivalry in favour of the CJEU or, at any rate, that national constitutional courts should and would henceforth be more hesitant to review EU legislation.[19]

Theoretically, these expectations seemed exaggerated. Although the DCT proposed to introduce a new primacy clause, it also affirmed the principle of conferral as the key foundation of the EU's law-making powers. De iure the EU would have remained a treaty-based organisation with limited powers. However, the DCT was intended by the Convention Praesidium to be more than yet another EU amending treaty: it was drafted not by an Intergovernmental Conference but a Constitutional Convention loosely modelled on the Philadelphia model, and the choice of the term 'constitutional treaty' too indicated ambitions beyond a mere consolidation and streamlining of the existing treaties. Moreover, the very ambiguity of the term 'constitutional treaty' was perceived not simply as a vanity project

---

[19] Kumm and Comella, 'The Primacy Clause of the Constitutional Treaty' (n 14) 477–78.

on Giscard's part to ensure his legacy and with purely symbolic significance, but as an ingenious dissimulation. The text could be sold to the public as a consolidation treaty to facilitate ratification. Once ratified, the term 'treaty' would quickly recede into the background and be replaced in political, media and, eventually, everyday parlance by 'the EU Constitution' as the novel basis for a more tightly integrated federal EU with its own quasi-federal institutions.

At this point Giscard d'Estaing's analogy with the Philadelphia Convention would not have been entirely fanciful: the EU would have given itself a constitution drafted by representatives from the EU institutions and national government and parliamentary representatives and ratified by the people in the majority of Member States, which would have enhanced and extended the Union's legitimacy. Faced with a new and even more assertive 'constitutional' court of the EU charged with enforcing the primacy of Union law and an EU Constitution drafted, inter alia, by representatives from all national governments and parliaments, it is indeed unlikely that national constitutional courts would have had the political appetite to risk a judicial confrontation with the CJEU and, in many cases, their own national governments.

The DCT was abandoned following a double referendum defeat in two founding members of the EU (then the EEC). The EU, however, never takes 'no' for an answer, and, while the term 'constitution' was abandoned, most of the centralising and other changes envisaged in the DCT were subsequently reformulated and incorporated into the Lisbon Treaty[20] which reformed the EU treaty framework. Unlike about 90 per cent of the DCT text, however, the primacy clause which as part of the sovereignty debate had been a decisive factor in the Dutch and French referendums did not survive and was demoted to a declaration annexed to the Lisbon Treaty subject to additional apparent or real clarifications.[21] Did the abandonment of the term 'constitution' and the demotion of the primacy clause slow the integrationist momentum behind the constitutional project and embolden national constitutional courts to be more assertive in their relation with the CJEU? The answer seems to be a clear and clean 'no' with one or two qualifications,[22] and is best illustrated by the FCC's post-Lisbon *Euro rescue* case law.

V. The Lisbon Judgment

The FCC's initial reaction, however, seemed assertive. Following a constitutional complaint challenging the compatibility of the Lisbon Treaty with the German Basic Law, the FCC ruled that, subject to minor amendments of the German

---

[20] Date of entry into force: 1 December 2009.

[21] The primacy clause was demoted from treaty article to an annexed declaration (Declaration 10 of the Treaty of Lisbon).

[22] See below.

ratification act, the Lisbon Treaty was constitutional.[23] However, the underlying reasoning of the so-called Lisbon judgment was interpreted in the academic literature as imposing strict limits on the course and scope of further EU integration.[24] For the FCC not only affirmed but extended its claim to review EU law beyond the principles outlined in its *Maastricht* judgment. Essentially, the FCC held it had the right to disapply any EU legal or executive act on two distinct grounds: (1) *ultra vires* review, which focuses on the formal constraints imposed by the transfer of powers from the Member States to the EU, and (2) *identity* review, which goes further and emphasises the substantive requirements of German constitutional and national identity.

A. Ultra Vires Review

Regarding the first type, the FCC broadly followed its earlier reasoning: the EU lacks democratic legitimacy because there is neither an EU-wide *demos* nor a unified European political culture to legitimate its supranational institutions and decisions. Moreover, as a treaty-based organisation, the EU derives its powers by conferral from the sovereign Member States subject to their national constitutions interpreted by national constitutional courts. In these circumstances, where the EU lacks the democratic authority and legal sovereignty for autochthonous law-making, it must not, through the CJEU, be permitted to define and control the limits of its own treaty powers. Otherwise it could simply ignore and extend the boundaries of its conferred competences. *Ex hypothesi*, the EU institutions can only be construed as acting within their powers if their actions do not conflict with the national constitutions of any of the EU's Member States. The question of whether the EU has acted ultra vires may therefore only be answered by the national courts interpreting those constitutions.[25]

The FCC also re-emphasised the principle of legal certainty as the basis for the conferral of national powers to the EU: to minimise legal uncertainty over the scope of the Union's powers, any transfer of competences from the national to the Union level, the FCC affirmed, had to be for a limited and specific purpose (*Prinzip der begrenzten Einzelermächtigung*). If a Union institution exceeds these limited competences, the FCC reserves the right and indeed the constitutional duty to issue a declaration of invalidity under German law, just as the FCC has the authority to block any EU amending treaty which does not clearly define and limit the powers transferred to the EU.[26]

---

[23] Judgment on 30 June 2009, Bundesverfassungsgericht, BVerfG, 2 BvE 2/08.

[24] See, eg, D Thym, 'In the Name of Sovereign Statehood: A Critical Introduction to the *Lisbon judgment* of the German Constitutional Court' (2009) 46 *Common Market Law Review* 1795–22.

[25] 2 BvE 2/08, paras 208 et seq, 234–36.

[26] 2 BvE 2/08, paras 234, 236.

B. Identity Review

In addition to the formal constraints on the EU's powers imposed by the principle of conferral, the FCC opines in the Lisbon judgment, the EU must respect the national identity of its Member States including the integrity of their national constitutions and a minimum core of national sovereignty.[27] This is the kernel of the FCC's identity review which is rooted in the idea that, sociologically, culturally and therefore politically, democracy is embedded in national and not supranational and multilingual life forms. Until such time as the emergence of a common political culture at European level, democratic legitimacy ultimately 'remains connected ... to patterns of identification which are related to the nation-state, language, history and culture'.[28] By these patterns a '*demos*' is constituted, which may be defined as a people regarding itself 'as one' for the purposes of jointly governing the political affairs of its members.

The existence of these patterns of identification is inevitably a matter of self-perception and degree, but their subjective absence in the minds of the governed means that there is no *demos*. Their large-scale absence at the level of the EU, the FCC concludes, means there is no 'one European people'.[29] For this reason the European Parliament cannot claim 'democratic legitimisation'. The European Parliament cannot be regarded as a fully democratic legislature because it does not represent the will of a single European people which does not exist. National parliaments, in these circumstances, retain the primary legitimising function for as long as they represent identifiable and politically self-conscious peoples based on a common political culture constituted, inter alia, by shared language, culture, values and common collective historical experience.

The emergence of a recognisable European people alone, the FCC insists, could confer democratic legitimacy on common European institutions of government. Democracy is meaningful if and only if the essential decisions affecting key policy areas are taken by institutions that have a high degree of democratic legitimacy. The FCC identifies five areas of competence where a further transfer of national power to the EU would be incompatible with the concept democratic government:[30]

1. the military and police monopoly on the domestic and external use of force;
2. criminal law;
3. fundamental fiscal decisions;
4. the guarantee of a just social order; and
5. decisions central to the preservation of national culture, in particular family law, the school and education system and the status of religious communities.

---

[27] 2 BvE 2/08, paras 235–36.
[28] 2 BvE 2/08, para 251.
[29] 2 BvE 2/08, para 286.
[30] For the Court's discussion of these 5 essential elements of democratic self-government, see 2 BvE 2/08, at paras 252 et seq.

The FCC describes these areas as the inalienable core of sovereignty in which the democratically accountable and legitimated national political institutions must retain sufficient political scope for effective freedom of action (*Handlungsspielraum*). Central to such parliamentary freedom of action, without which sovereignty and democracy lose their meaning, is the principle of budgetary autonomy.[31] EU membership, the FCC opines, must not place such financial obligations on Member States so as to deprive their national parliaments of the budgetary autonomy for the effective political regulation of the economic, cultural and social framework determining the 'living conditions' of the individual nations that make up the European Union. 'Ought', in other words, implies 'can'. For as long as nation states alone have sufficient democratic legitimacy to determine the 'living conditions' of their electorates, they must retain the financial autonomy to make meaningful decisions in the areas of social, fiscal and economic policy. The principle of national budgetary autonomy, the FCC concludes, imposes an absolute limit on the transfer of powers to Brussels: Member States must not confer powers that would allow the Union fundamentally to affect their ability to pursue an independent social, fiscal or economic policy.[32]

The Lisbon judgment was greeted with dismay by integrationists all over the EU who suggested that the FCC, in spelling out the specific constitutional limits of the integration process which it had not previously done, had asserted an outdated view of sovereignty which was likely to enhance the prospect of future judicial conflict at the highest level over the precise scope of EU legal and political integration.[33] The FCC, it seemed, had drawn what many commentators thought an absolute line in the sand beyond which EU integration could not proceed for the foreseeable future.

However, no matter how persuasive as a matter of legal and political theory the Lisbon judgment may be, especially in its analysis of the interrelationship between democratic legitimacy and the limits of supranationalism, the FCC soon took fright at the boldness of its own conclusions and, under a new President,[34] Andreas Voßkuhle, rapidly qualified and, in practice, substantially relaxed the standards of both the Court's ultra vires and identity jurisdiction.

The first step in this ongoing ignominious rear-guard action was the FCC's *Honeywell* decision.[35] In this case the FCC, in obvious departure from its exacting Lisbon standards laid down less than 12 months before, stated that before

---

[31] See, eg, 2 BvE 2/08, para 256.

[32] See, eg, 2 BvE 2/08, paras 256–58.

[33] See, eg, *Thym*, 'Sovereign Statehood' (n 24).

[34] In Germany, the judges of FCC are elected in equal numbers by a non-transparent process involving a special parliamentary election committee formed by the lower house (Bundestag) and the upper house (Bundesrat). This effectively guarantees the 2 larger parties (CDU/CSU and SPD) control over the composition of the FCC. Federal constitutional judges are de facto political appointees.

[35] *Honeywell*, BVerfG, 2 BvR 2661/06 6 July 2010, Absatz-Nr (1–116).

declaring an EU act to be ultra vires, it would afford the CJEU 'the opportunity to interpret the Treaties, as well as to rule on the validity and interpretation of the acts in question, in the context of preliminary ruling proceedings according to Article 267 TFEU, insofar as it has not yet clarified the questions which have arisen'.[36] Post-*Honeywell*, the judgment made clear, the FCC would no longer autonomously exercise its ultra vires control but do so in 'dialogue and collaboration' with the CJEU. However, the *Honeywell* judgment did not commit the FCC to accept and follow any preliminary ruling issued by the CJEU.

VI. The Euro Crisis Judgments

The principle of parliamentary budgetary autonomy soon assumed centre stage in the FCC's decision to uphold the various Greek aid packages and the purportedly temporary European Financial Stability Facility (EFSF), which was handed down in September 2011. Notwithstanding the clear guidelines in the Lisbon judgment, the FCC held that the Bundestag's budgetary autonomy was not to any decisive extent diminished by Germany's assumption of total loans and guarantees for other Eurozone countries of up to €170bn, despite the fact that this was 60 per cent of Germany's entire 2011 federal budget of €306bn.[37]

A. The FCC's 'Reasoning' in its ESM Judgment

It only took one further year for the FCC in all but name to abandon the principle of budgetary autonomy. On 12 September 2012, the Court in effect decided that the initial German contribution of €190 billion to the permanent Euro rescue fund, the European Stability Mechanism ('ESM'), and even unlimited German liability for the debts of other Eurozone governments was compatible with Germany's parliamentary budgetary autonomy provided the Bundestag itself authorises liabilities beyond the initial ESM ceiling not even excluding potentially unlimited liabilities.[38]

---

[36] The *Honeywell* principle only relates to the FCC's ultra vires review which the FCC decided it would no longer exercise without a prior opinion of the CJEU. It does not commit the FCC to follow the CJEU's guidance, nor concern the second limb of the FCC's last resort jurisdiction which was clarified in the Lisbon judgment, the FCC's identity review. Under its identity review the FCC reserves the right to examine any EU act for its compatibility with the non-negotiable core of the German Basic Law including the principle of budgetary autonomy. If it is not compatible, as the FCC suggested in its 2014 OMT Opinion, no reference to the CJEU should have been made and the FCC should have declared the programme unconstitutional within Germany.

[37] BVerfG, 2 BvR 987/10 7 Sep 2011, Absatz-Nr (1–142), paras 133–36; also paras 122–29.

[38] BVerfG, 2 BvR 1390/12 vom 12 Sep 2012, Absatz-Nr (1-319), paras 254–76 and esp para. 279. To Germany's agreed and possible future obligations under the ESM must be added the German

In 1993, the Bundesverfassungsgericht decided that the Maastricht Treaty, with its 'no bail-out' clause, strict limits on public borrowing and an independent central bank committed by law to fighting inflation and prohibited by Treaty to engage in monetary state financing[39] adequately ensured that monetary union could not evolve into a fiscal transfer union. In its Lisbon judgment, the FCC affirmed its earlier strict 'no bail out' stance by drawing a red line to protect core areas of national sovereignty beyond which EU integration must not constitutionally advance until the German nation state, by popular decision, is submerged within a newly constituted European nation. Central to national sovereignty, the FCC decided in 2009, is the principle of parliamentary budgetary autonomy, the ability of the national parliaments to shape the living conditions of their populations through democratically accountable tax and social policies. Without budgetary autonomy in this sense, the constitutional principle of democratic self-government and the right to vote enshrined respectively in Articles 20 and 38 of the German Basic Law would be meaningless. With its Euro rescue judgments of September 2011 and 2012 the FCC turned the principle of budgetary autonomy on its head.[40]

B. The Decision to Refer the OMT

On 7 February 2014, following a complaint by a record 37,000 German citizens against the ECB's so-called Outright Monetary Transactions (OMT) programme, the FCC published its considered assessment[41] on whether the OMT was

government's pre-existing guarantees, loans and guarantees to Greece, Portugal and Ireland in so far as they are not absorbed into the ESM, as well as the pro rata cost of 2 haircuts for Greece and, importantly, the Bundesbank's total TARGET2 credit exposure to the Eurozone periphery (€910bn at 31 December 2017). Further account must be taken of any losses Germany may suffer as guarantor for any losses sustained by the ECB's unlimited government and corporate bond buys programmes launched in 2014/15. The apparent much noted limit set by the FCC on Germany's total exposure under the ESM – the €190 bn which the Bundestag can extend by simple majority – thus is no limit at all. In the FCC's opinion, Germany's continuing budgetary autonomy is unaffected even by potentially unlimited liabilities amounting to several times the size of the annual federal budget which varied from €306bn to €329bn from 2012 to 2017.

[39] Art 123 TFEU.

[40] The FCC confirmed the 12 September 2012 ESM decision which, formally, was a preliminary decision on an interlocutory application, in its final ESM judgment of 18 March 2014 (see BVerfG, Entscheidung 18 Mar 2014, 2 BvR 1390/12, Absatz-Nr (1–245)). In addition to affirming that, in principle, even unlimited liability was compatible with the principle of the Bundestag's budgetary autonomy, the FCC went so far as to declare that that principle would not be violated even if the guarantees and unsecured loans to other Euro members factually committed the Bundestag to one and only one 'specific budgetary and fiscal policy' because the principles of budgetary autonomy and democratic accountability through national elections could still be safeguarded if the national parliament transferred far-reaching budgetary powers to 'the organs of a supra- or international organisation'. The decision 'whether and to what extent this is sensible' is a matter for the legislator. (2 BvR 1390/12, Absatz-Nr (1–245) 168.)

[41] BVerfG, Vorlageentscheidung 7 Feb. 2014, 2 BvR 1390/12.

compatible with Article 123 TFEU and Council Regulation (EC) No 3603/93 of 13 December 1993 which provides that the prohibition of direct government bonds purchases by the ECB likewise applies to any attempt to circumvent Article 123 TFEU by other means including secondary market purchases.[42] The FCC opined that 'there are important reasons to assume that [the OMT programme] exceeds the European Central Bank's monetary policy mandate and thus infringes the powers of the Member States, and that it violates the prohibition of monetary financing of the budget'. On this basis, the FCC 'is thus inclined to regard the OMT Decision as an *ultra vires* act'.[43]

The FCC's analysis is comprehensive, clear and convincing in its conclusion that the OMT is incompatible with the ECB's mandate as defined, inter alia, by Articles 123 and 127 TFEU. The FCC reached that conclusion on four distinct grounds: first, a literal analysis of the wording of Articles 123 and 127 TFEU in conjunction with Council Regulation 3603/03; second, a teleological argument based on the underlying purposes of those provisions; third, an economic analysis assessing the effects of the OMT programme and whether the OMT falls under the prohibition of monetary state financing; and, fourth, an assessment of the question of whether the objectives of an EU act (including ECB policy decisions) had to be determined subjectively, in terms of the stated aims, or objectively, in terms of their effects. All these instruments, according to the FCC, agreed that the OMT was unlawful.

Following the FCC's settled position in *Maastricht* and *Lisbon* it would been logical for the FCC to declare the OMT inapplicable within its own jurisdiction and to prohibit the Bundesbank from participating in any bond buys under the OMT or any quantitative easing programme. That the Court refused to do so and instead referred an issue it regarded as clear-cut to the CJEU for further consideration, is not in itself in purely formal terms an act of unconditional submission to the higher judicial authority of the Luxembourg court, but it indicated that while the FCC might bark like a guard dog, when matters get serious it will submit like a lamb.

---

[42] Recital 7.

[43] The Court notes in particular that:

> Art. 123 sec. 1 TFEU prohibits the European Central Bank from purchasing government bonds directly from the issuing Member States. It seems obvious that this prohibition may not be circumvented by functionally equivalent measures. [The] neutralisation of interest rate spreads, selectivity of purchases, and the parallelism with EFSF and ESM assistance programmes indicate that the OMT Decision aims at a prohibited circumvention of Art. 123 sec. 1 TFEU. The following aspects can be added: The willingness to participate in a debt cut with regard to the bonds to be purchased; the increased risk; the option to keep the purchased government bonds to maturity; the interference with the price formation on the market, and the encouragement, coming from the ECB's Governing Council, of market participants to purchase the bonds in question on the primary market.

C. The CJEU's Preliminary Ruling and the FCC's Act of Submission

When the CJEU delivered its requested preliminary ruling,[44] it openly dismissed the FCC's assessment, ignoring the detailed literal, purposive and economic arguments put forward by the FCC, and concluded that, first, 'safeguarding an appropriate monetary policy transmission and the singleness of the monetary policy' was a legitimate monetary policy objective and that, second, for this reason and contrary to the assessment of the FCC, bond buys were legitimate monetary policy and within the ECB's mandate. The CJEU's ruling is poorly reasoned, defies clear Treaty language (Article 127 TFEU) and relevant EU legislation (EU Regulation 3603/03, especially Recital (7)), ignores the patently obvious underlying objectives of these provisions as well as the CJEU's own inconvenient case law on whether the objective of an EU measure must be determined subjectively or objectively, and contains absolutely no economic analysis at all.

Crucially, the CJEU affords the ECB such a wide margin of policy discretion that it in effect exempts the Central Bank from any kind of judicial review and thus leaves it free to take over economic policy functions as and when the bank thinks fit – policy functions which the Treaties largely reserve for the Member States. Since the EU Treaties exempt the ECB from democratic including parliamentary control, the FCC had always emphasised the importance of strict judicial control over the observance of the Central Bank's mandate. Nevertheless, in its final judgment which formally concluded the OMT litigation, the FCC abandoned its earlier detailed objections and consented to making the ECB into the least accountable political institution in post-war non-Communist Europe.[45]

Since the early 1970s, beginning with its *Internationale Handelsgesellschaft* judgment,[46] and culminating in its *Maastricht*[47] and *Lisbon*[48] judgments the FCC, with some non-doctrinal modifications in *Honeywell*,[49] had consistently held that the EU's powers were predicated on the principle of conferral, that the principle of the supremacy of EU law applied subject to that of conferral, and that the German legislature can transfer powers only subject to the Basic Law. If then the Bundestag seeks to transfer powers it is not constitutionally authorised to cede, or if the EU institutions subsequently exercise their powers in a manner incompatible with the Basic Law, it is the FCC and not the CJEU which has the ultimate right to assess and invalidate such an unconstitutional act within Germany just as the CJEU

---

[44] Case C-62/14 *Gauweiler and Others* (16 June 2015).

[45] BVerfG, Urteil des Zweiten Senats vom 21. Juni 2016 – 2 BvR 2728/13 – Rn. (1-220).

[46] *Internationale Handelsgesellschaft von Einfuhr- und Vorratsstelle für Getreide und Futtermittel*, Entscheidung vom 29 May 1974 mit abweichender Meinung (2 BVL 52/71 (also known as *Solange I*), BVerfGE 37, 271 [1974] CMLR 540.

[47] *Maastricht-Urteil*, BVerfGE 89, 155 12. Oktober 1993, 2 BvR 2134, 2159/92 (also known and cited in English as *Brunner v European Union Treaty* [1994] CMLR 57).

[48] *Lissabon-Urteil* BVerfG, 2 BvE 2/08 30 Jun 2009, Absatz-Nr (1-421).

[49] *Honeywell*, BVerfG, 2 BvR 2661/06 6 Jul 2010, Absatz-Nr (1-116).

alone has the authority to invalidate an act of the EU institutions for the EU as a whole.[50]

The problem of *Kompetenz-Kompetenz* spawned some of the finest examples of subtle interdisciplinary and sociologically- and philosophically-informed constitutional reasoning by any court. Yet, when its doctrinally convincing[51] reasoning was put to the test in the OMT litigation by a wily Goldman Sachs-trained central banker determined, in collusion with an inherently integrationist supranational court, to offload the debt of reckless banks and feckless governments onto taxpayers and savers, the German judges lacked what Immanuel Kant called the cardinal value of the Enlightenment and liberal republicanism, 'the courage to follow one's own reason'.

VII. The ECB's QE Programme – A Rerun of the OMT Litigation

Courts rarely admit that they change their mind, that they abandoned a previous position, and they never acknowledge that they ruled the way they did not because it was right but because it was expedient. It comes therefore as no surprise that even after its humiliating climb-down in the OMT litigation; the FCC did not formally abandon its claim to exercise a jurisdiction of the last resort over the EU's treaty-based competences.

That claim has recently been affirmed by the FCC in yet another set of ECB policy-related ultra vires constitutional complaints involving German industrialists, economists and law professors.[52] In essence, the complainants submit that the ECB's Quantitative Easing (QE) programme launched in January 2015 represents a breach of Article 123 TFEU and an arrogation by the ECB of general economic policy powers which the Treaties reserve to the Member States, and that it counteracts the incentives to pursue a sound budgetary policy which the CJEU in its *Pringle* and *Gauweiler* judgments had accepted was a *sine qua non* of the EU Treaty provisions governing the monetary union. After nearly two years of unusually, indeed suspiciously 'thorough' deliberation[53] the FCC once more concluded that

---

[50] As the CJEU has no jurisdiction to interpret the German jurisdiction and is empowered by the Treaties only to interpret EU law and not whether its interpretation also respects the fundamental guarantees and principles of the German Basic Law, the FCC correctly inferred that it can only express a preliminary opinion, and thus at best deliver a provisional answer, in relation to the question of whether an EU act is ultra or intra vires.

[51] eg Arts 46, 60 VCLT.

[52] BVerfG, *Beschluss des Zweiten Senats 18.July 2017 – 2 BvR 859/15 – Rn. (1-137)*; Case C-493/17 *Weiss v Germany*.

[53] The FCC's considered assessment and reference to the CJEU was handed down around 31 months after the ECB launched its QE programme in anticipation of at least another 16 to 24 months before the CJEU would hand down its preliminary ruling, to be followed by around another 9 to 15 months of final deliberation by the FCC to conclude the litigation. Put differently, the FCC has not been in the slightest hurry to reach a conclusion on the legality of a de facto extension of the ECB's powers from monetary to economic policy – an assumption of new powers by the ECU which the FCC itself

the multiple complaints were well-founded and affirmed, as it had previously done in relation to the OMT, that 'there were doubts that the PSPP[54] was compatible with the prohibition of monetary state financing in Art. 127 TFEU'.[55]

In its considered assessment of the QE programme, the FCC once more provided a comprehensive and conclusive legal analysis. The FCC noted multiple Treaty violations but again, as in the OMT litigation, decided to refer further consideration of the matter to the CJEU. Few, if any,[56] expect anything other than a rerun of the OMT saga: self-assertion by the FCC in theory, and submission in practice.

The German FCC, of course, although almost certainly the most influential national constitutional court within the EU, does not speak for other national constitutional courts. Most national constitutional courts have adopted a generally deferential attitude in relation to the CJEU, although this is generally qualified by a theoretical proviso which allows the constitutional court in question either not to accept, or at least not to endorse, the CJEU's claim to *Kompetenz-Kompetenz* over all disputes at the intersection of national and EU law. The FCC's model of theoretical self-assertion and practical submission, however, is not universal. The French, Portuguese and Spanish highest courts have come very close to accepting the supremacy of EU law and the CJEU's claim to *Kompetenz-Kompetenz*, and so, perhaps surprisingly, has the British House of Lords (now the UK Supreme Court) until the UK's intended departure from the EU. At the other end of the spectrum, the Czech, Polish and Danish constitutional courts have asserted their reserve jurisdictions to watch over the principle of conferral both doctrinally and in practice.

In a recent decision, the Supreme Court of Denmark (SCD) in *DI acting for Ajos A/S v The estate left by A* refused to follow the CJEU's ruling in *the Dansk Industri case*. The Court limited the competences of the European Union and the jurisdiction of the CJEU in two steps. First, the SCD emphasised that the Danish Act of Accession to the EEC imposes limits on the direct application of EU law within Denmark and does not cover general principles of EU law except as laid down in the Act as subsequently amended. It concluded that the judge-made general principle of non-discrimination on grounds of age was not covered by the Danish Law of Accession and therefore not directly applicable in Denmark because it did not have its origin in a specific Treaty provision and that, in so far as the

concluded, was likely to be contrary to the EU Treaties and entailed incalculable and irreversible risks of economic dissallocation and risks.

[54] Public Sector Purchases Programme (PSPP), ie the purchase of government bonds by the ECB and national central banks of the Eurozone. The PSPP represents by far the largest part of the ECB's QE which, however, also extends to corporate bonds and so-called asset-backed securities and covered bonds, all of which represent high-risk debt instruments issued by banks or other financial institutions.

[55] BVerfG, Beschluss des Zweiten Senats 18. July 2017 – 2 BvR 859/15 – Rn. (1-137) para 76.

[56] When the FCC officially released its assessment of the PSPP on 15 August 2015, the event was barely registered by the financial markets, and not a single commentator cited in the German and international financial press evinced any serious expectation that, in the end, either the CJEU or, eventually, the FCC could rule the programme unlawful.

principle is recognised in Article 21 EU Charter of Fundamental Rights (EUCFR), Article 51 EUCFR provides that the Charter does not extend the competences of the EU beyond those provided for the Treaties – and Article 6 TEU in particular. Second, the SCD noted that it would in fact exceed its own judicial mandate under the Danish Constitution if it interpreted or disapplied national law on the basis proposed by the CJEU which did not take account of the limiting conditions of the Danish Act of Accession. The decision of the Danish Supreme Court not to disapply national law pursuant to a preliminary ruling by the CJEU is a model application of the relevant provisions of the VCLT and the doctrine of *ultra vires* national review of EU law developed by the German FCC in its *Maastricht* judgment. It led the Danish courts to precisely those conclusions the German FCC should have reached in its Euro crisis decisions had it had the courage to apply its pre-crisis doctrine of the relationship between EU and national law.

The SCD's decision in *DI acting for Ajos A/S* is remarkable in that the SCD chose to refer an alleged breach of EU law by domestic legislation to the CJEU, but then chose not to follow the CJEU ruling by reference to Denmark's terms of accession to the EU over which the CJEU has no jurisdiction. The SCD's ruling thus constitutes a direct challenge to the CJEU's self-assumed *Kompetenz-Kompetenz*. It shows that national judicial dissent vis-à-vis the CJEU is still possible. However, it remains highly exceptional and occurred in a country which is free from historical ideological burdens, not a member of the eurozone and has long been less than enthusiastic about 'ever closer union', and it concerned a legal dispute in which the issues at stake were hardly a matter of fundamental importance to the general direction of EU integration. On the contrary, that direction has not been significantly affected by a rise in national judicial dissent. So far the Danish 'incident' is a local and exceptional (though arguably not entirely unique) event and, notwithstanding its exemplary reasoning which is applicable to many other national supreme courts, there are no signs of a wider judicial revolt.

VIII. Conclusion

The failure of the DCT appears, on the whole, not to have impeded further EU integration. Notably within the eurozone the ECB is now exercising broad-ranging fiscal and economic policy powers which the EU treaty framework reserves to the Member States, whilst the monetary union has been transformed into a transfer and partial fiscal union in which the ECB socialises the costs of both the financial crisis of 2008–09 and the ongoing Eurozone debt crisis and subsidises indebted national governments, reckless financial institutions and investors at the expense of taxpayers, savers and recipients of public salaries and pensions throughout the eurozone. Fiscal policy (ie decisions involving fiscal liabilities including those arising from industrial and bank sector operations by public authorities and indeed of all public expenditure), however, falls within the exclusive competence of national parliaments. The *de facto* transfer of budget-sensitive powers to a democratically unaccountable EU institution occurred in clear breach of the EU treaty framework and national constitutional laws alike, yet was judicially sanctioned both by the CJEU and the FCC which, in practice, accepted the CJEU's claim to be the final arbiter in all disputes about the scope of the EU's powers vis-à-vis those of the Member States.

As it stands, that claim continues to have no other basis than the CJEU's arrogation of a *Kompetenz-Kompetenz* which it does not possess according either to international law or the constitutions of Member States. In these circumstances, the CJEU's arrogation of this sovereign power is, in law, an act of usurpation.

The EU Constitution, even though it was only a treaty in legal terms and did not reallocate national economic policy powers to the Union, would have contributed to legitimating that usurpation. Why? The answer is not legal but socio-psychological for legitimation ultimately resides not in legality but in its perception. The defining feature of the DCT is not its content but its appellation as a 'constitution'.[57] The symbolism of the EU's first constitution as the basis for the exercise of its legal and political authority, which would have been adopted by an unprecedented number of referendums in more than half the Member States, would have had a major impact on the ensuing constitutional conversation including adjudication by the CJEU, the FCC and other constitutional courts. Once ratified, the traditional treaty garb would have been dropped and receded into the historical background by ubiquitous popular, media and official use. If varying interpreting groups – courts and jurists, politicians, administrators and, critically, the media and eventually the general public – refer to, and think, and generally relate to, the EU through a constitutional lens, this inevitably shapes the reality of constitutional understanding.[58] Simply calling it a constitution would have had an effect, not in law but in terms of political rhetoric, public perception and, as Hume astutely observed in his political writings, in relation to the non-rational sources of political allegiance, through sheer force of custom and habit. Elevating the EU's treaty framework to constitutional status would have made it more difficult for Member States to assert their legal sovereignty or to resist calls for further integration whether by amendments to the DCT or judicial stealth. It would likewise have given credence to the CJEU's claim to be the sovereign judicial authority of the EU's sovereign constitutional order and reinforced the reluctance of national constitutional courts to enforce their own constitutions. Over time, the new constitutional conversation would have blurred the tensions involved in the EU's overreach into national policy prerogatives and the CJEU's *contra legem* interpretations of the existing treaties in defiance of both national and international law.

An act of usurpation occurs when political power imposes itself over accepted authority, including constitutional legality. A tension arises between the legality

---

[57] JHH Weiler, 'On the Power of the Word: Europe's Constitutional Iconography' (2005) 3 *International Journal of Constitutional Law* 173, 173.
[58] Ibid, 181.

versus the reality of power. In modern states, however, perception of legality is a major legitimating factor. Political acts perceived to be in accordance with, rather than in opposition to, the existing constitutional framework are more readily accepted because they are perceived as legitimate for as long as the existing legal framework is not discredited, because it is perceived as lacking accepted moral authority or as ineffective and incapable of asserting itself.

At present, the relationship between the EU and Member States is character-ised by at least two prevalent trends. On the one hand, integration has proceeded by stealth, not by legality. The CJEU has articulated certain constitutional claims with no clear basis in the EU Treaties which do not, in fact, generally attack or chal-lenge the legal sovereignty of each Member State.[59] The EU, however, has very little power to impose anything, and certainly not in the coercive manner that is within the power of nation states. The EU only exercises political sovereignty because the Member States have failed to assert their legal sovereignty under national and international law and imposed supranational decision-making on themselves in breach of their own constitutions.[60]

On the other hand, a constitution can confer identity and cohesion only as long as the system it established is perceived as a good or legitimate and effective one.[61] If a constitution fails to exert authority in the real world of politics, not even a constitution perceived as 'good' will be able to confer integrative power on a society.[62] Within the EU, national constitutions are progressively hollowed out by the enduring discrepancy between the legality and reality of sovereign power. In this situation, if this process of 'hollowing out' valid constitutional orders and institutions persists, national institutions will be increasingly perceived as dysfunctional, their legitimating function is eroded and political participation will wane and give way to electoral disenchantment, apathy or increasing popular disaffection.

These ongoing developments essentially open up three options for the future development of the EU. First, integration by judicial and political stealth may continue by persistent Member State acquiescence in the transfer to the EU of further sovereign, including budgetary, powers which, under national constitu-tional law, are the prerogative of Member States. Second, a reassertion of national legal sovereignty based on the self-assertion of national political institutions and renewed respect for the principle of conferral with national judicial oversight. And third, integration by law based on the surrender of national sovereignty,

---

[59] See the brief but interesting remarks by C Bickerton and R Tuck, 'A Brexit Proposal' (2017) avail-able at https://thecurrentmoment.files.wordpress.com/2017/11/brexit-proposal-20-nov-final1.pdf, 25.

[60] See JHH Weiler, 'In Defence of the Status quo: Europe's Constitutional Sonderweg' in J Weiler and M Wind (eds), *European Constitutionalism Beyond the State* (Cambridge, Cambridge University Press, 2003).

[61] H Vorländer, 'Integration durch Verfassung? Die symbolische Bedeutung der Verfassung im politischen Integrationsprozess' in H Vorländer (ed), *Integration durch Verfassung?* (Wiesbaden, Westdeutscher Verlag, 2002) 9–40, 15; also D Grimm, 'Integration by Constitution' (2005) 3 *International Journal of Constitutional Law* 193, 199.

[62] Grimm, 'Integration by Constitution' (n 60) 200.

the acceptance of EU legal sovereignty by express, not merely tacit, consent by national political and judicial authorities. The degree of integration may continue to diverge further within the EU, with the eurozone as an inner core where members increasingly accept the legal sovereignty of common supranational institutions and an outer, less deeply and less broadly integrated membership where the problem of *Kompetenz-Kompetenz*, and of where precisely sovereignty is located, remains largely unresolved because resolution is less vital to the functioning of the EU or at least its inner core.

Where legal and political sovereignty conflict, the political sovereign will seek to legitimate itself by law. If the present process of integration by stealth continues and national constitutions are no longer enforced, they will gradually be perceived as outdated articulations of where powers once lay but no longer lie. They will lose their legitimating function, and a vacuum will arise which will then be filled again. The surrender of national sovereignty by formal transfer may then seem less outlandish and objectionable than it did at the time of the failed ratification of the DCT, which failed because faith in the viability and desirability of national representative democracy was still sufficiently strong. At this point, provided the centrifugal tendencies within the EU can be contained by concerted government and judicial collusion, the idea of an EU Constitution is likely to be resurrected, and no longer in the guise of a 'constitutional treaty'. This point may not lie in the far-away future.

11

Europe's Constitutional Overture

NEIL WALKER

I. A Disputed Legacy

In the summer of 2007, the European Council announced its decision to 'abandon' the 'constitutional concept' it had endorsed so optimistically only four years previously on receiving the draft of a first Constitutional Treaty for the European Union (EU) from the Convention on the Future of Europe.[1] After 'a period of reflection'[2] following the 'no' votes in the 2005 French and Dutch referendums to the (duly promulgated) Constitutional Treaty, and recognising the document's dubious popularity and unratified status in various other Member States, Europe's leaders opted to jettison the brave new world of a supranational constitution and return to the more familiar international law vehicle of a Reform Treaty.[3] The move appeared to pay an immediate political dividend. Agreement was reached as early as the Lisbon summit of December 2007 and, despite further delay occasioned by a fresh referendum defeat in Ireland, the new 'post-constitutional Treaty'[4] was successfully implemented before the end of 2009.[5]

With the advantage of a decade's hindsight, we may be tempted to return a damning indictment of the failed constitutional experiment. We might draw one of two sceptical conclusions. We might view the unsuccessful constitutional project simply as an anomaly – an unnecessary but ultimately insignificant deviation from the tried and tested course of European supranational governance. Or, worse, we might conclude that it did have a significant impact, but a damaging one; that it was a corrosive influence on the future course of European integration. Certainly, the mood that formed as Europe's leaders came to realise that the two failed referendums had dealt a fatal blow to the Constitutional Treaty suggested the

---

[1] German Presidency Conclusions, European Council Brussels, 21–22 June 2007.

[2] Belgian Presidency Conclusions, European Council Brussels, 16–17 June 2005.

[3] Treaty of Lisbon amending the Treaty on European Union and the Treaty establishing the European Community, 13 Dec 2007, 2007 OJ (C 306) 01.

[4] A Somek, 'Postconstitutional Treaty' (2007) 8 *German Law Journal* 1121–32.

[5] See, eg, P Craig, *The Lisbon Treaty, Law, Politic and Treaty Reform* (Oxford, Oxford University Press, 2010).

first view. The abruptness with which the 'Big-C'[6] word was dropped and consigned to the dustbin of unmentionables speaks to a determination to put behind them what many of the Constitutional Treaty's erstwhile sponsors had come to view as an ill-starred adventure. According to this revised understanding, the project had been doomed from the start, although it required the salutary lesson of its failure for the political classes of Europe to appreciate this and to return to pre-constitutional business as usual.

But perhaps the failed constitutional project was no mere legacy-free historical blip. In the alternative sceptical reading, it provides a forewarning of later difficulties, and, more concretely, may even supply an early link in the causal chain that has led the European Union to its current state of political vulnerability and increasing uncertainty over its future. From this perspective, the abortive constitutional initiative marked and in some measure contributed to a downturn in the health of the supranational body politic. The trend in the 20 years preceding the constitutional project had been towards ever deeper integration in an ever-widening European Union, with every new Treaty – The Single European Act, Maastricht, Amsterdam, Nice – a fresh chapter in a cumulative success story. After the failure of the Constitution, however, and notwithstanding the repairs achieved at Lisbon, the European Union encountered a series of fundamental challenges. These began with the sovereign debt crisis and the pressure this placed on the framework of Economic and Monetary Union, and continued through unprecedented problems of mass migration and security to the more remote but real contemporary threat – headlined by Brexit but also present in the rise of nativist Euroscepticism across Europe[7] – to the very sustainability of the Union as a political settlement. In this more pessimistic vision, the failed constitution can be viewed as indicative of a pattern of institutional overreach – and associated political hubris – which risked and has found a severe reaction in subsequent events.

We will return to some of the thinking behind these sceptical positions in due course, but this chapter seeks to offer an alternative and less negative perspective. It argues that the constitutional stirrings which began with the tentative suggestion of the establishment of a Convention by the European Council in its Laeken Declaration of 2001 and continued through to the same body's termination of the process in 2007, rather than being anomalous or necessarily corrosive, *might* instead be regarded as an overture preceding and setting the scene for a more mature constitutional 'performance' in due course. Whether that performance – the conclusion and ratification of a self-styled constitutional settlement – ever comes to pass, cannot, of course, be predicted with any confidence. But the option, I argue, remains a live one, and not – as is implicit in much commentary – something forever foreclosed by the earlier failure.

The plausibility of any such argument depends, crucially, on the combination of two sets of factors. In the first place, there is the question of aptness or ripeness.

[6] N Walker, 'Big "C" or Small "c"?' (2006) 12 *European Law Journal* 12–14.
[7] See, eg, JW Muller, *What is Populism?* (London, Penguin, 2016).

Some who were generally supportive of the idea of a European Constitution in 2001–07 warned at the time, or concluded in retrospect, that the case for such a momentous initiative was just not strong enough in the particular moment.[8] The need was not sufficiently acute, the circumstances not demanding enough of change. While, as we shall pursue below, a better case for ripeness can certainly be made today, we should be wary of the fragility of any such purely 'functional' approach. Like all functional approaches, it argues, *in nuce*, that something should *in fact* happen just because it be would be a good and appropriate thing – a productive or functional outcome – if it were to happen. And, like all functional arguments, it is vulnerable to twin objections: first, the analyst's assessment that its happening would be a good thing might be disputed. And secondly, even if a strong case for the value of such an outcome could be made, that is quite different from, and not necessarily supportive of the claim that the social conditions conducive to such an outcome are actually in place.

That is where the second and crucial part of the argument comes in. This depends on there being an intimate and mutually reinforcing link between the constitutional self-recognition of an entity and its standing as a polity. If, as we seek to do below, we can establish such a connection, it allows us to view the Convention on the Future of Europe in a certain light. Whatever other effects it might have had (including undoubtedly fuelling the flames of certain anti-EU forces), by very dint of its introducing an explicitly constitutional register of thought and discourse, the Convention initiative both reflected and helped foster the development of a more focused way of thinking about the EU as a distinct polity – and so as the object of a common political project amongst its constituents. A written constitution would not have presented itself on the European political agenda in 2001, however tentatively,[9] without an increased readiness to think and talk in in polity-specific and increasingly constitutionally candid terms about a process begun half a century earlier as an interwoven attempt at continental market-building and political rapprochement after the ravages of the Second World War.[10] And the extensive debate over the Constitutional Treaty that ensued certainly reinforced that tendency.

For even though the Convention failed 'in the moment', and even if talk of a written constitution from the EU became scarce for a number of years after 2007,

---

[8] See, eg, D Thurer et al, 'The Union's Legal Personality: Ideas and Questions Lying Behind the Concept' in HJ Blanke and S Mangiameli (eds), *The European Union after Lisbon: Constitutional Basis, Economic Order and External Action* (Heidelberg, Springer, 2012) 147–73.

[9] In the Laeken Declaration the possibility of a written constitution was consigned to an indeterminate future. Following discussion of various heads of reform, the Declaration read that 'The question ultimately arises as to whether this simplification and reorganisation might not lead in the long run to the adoption of a constitutional text'. Bulletin of the European Union. 2001, No 12. Luxembourg: Office for Official Publications of the European Communities. Presidency Conclusions of the Laeken European Council (14 and 15 December 2001) 19–23.

[10] See, eg, J Weiler, *The Constitution of Europe* (Cambridge, Cambridge University Press, 1999) esp ch 7.

the culture of informal constitutional awareness and consideration deepened in the wake of its initiative. Many interested in the EU – practitioners, public and commentators alike – were now more minded to cast their appreciation of the EU's development in constitutional or quasi-constitutional terms where previously they would had been impervious, indifferent or even hostile to such a characterisation. And while this discursive space continued to harbour strong substantive disagreement about the future of Europe, it nevertheless incubated the idea that the European Union was the sort of entity that could be framed and discussed in self-standing, polity-specific terms.

It is this shift, I argue, that allows us to approach the ripeness question differently. For if the constitutional register has become less alien, more familiar, in the context of the EU polity, then it becomes more plausible that the sorts of exceptional political circumstances whose ripeness has provoked a formal, polity-endorsing constitutional response in other entities – typically states – would also do so in the EU.

II. Europe's Constitutional Continuum

A. Beyond Nominalism

Two surface features of the EU constitutional narrative give initial pause to the sceptical argument that the constitutional experiment of 2001–07 was merely an anomalous interlude, or, still worse, a corrosive influence. First, the high level and broad base of political support for the work and output of Giscard D'Estaing's Convention of 2002–03 must be reckoned with. The initiative might ultimately have failed, but that it got so far and gained such momentum requires explanation. Even if the political classes underwent a change of heart after the two failed national referendums, at least some of the reasons why they were prepared to contemplate this *particular* constitutional project in the first place, and were able in due course to garner significant support for it within the broader European public,[11] might stand as factors *generally* favourable to constitutional development in the European supranational context. Secondly, to repeat a point, the abandonment of 'Big-C'[12] documentary constitutionalism was the cue for a greater preparedness to think of the EU as possessing some attributes of a constitutional kind, however we might understand these – informal, unwritten, partial or whatever.

---

[11] See P Norman, *The Accidental Constitution*, 2nd edn (Brussels, Eurocomment, 2005). 17 out of 27 Member States actually ratified the Draft Constitution, 2 (Spain and Luxembourg) after referendums.
[12] Walker, 'Big "C" or Small "c"?' (n 6) 12–14.

What both these features suggest, the second more directly, is that constitutionalism is a fluid idea – a polysemic concept. The development of 'small c' constitutional thinking alongside the decline of 'Big C' constitutional thinking indicates that constitutionalism can mean different things to different people – and often, indeed, different things to the same people in different contexts. Equally, one obvious explanation for the foundering of the initial broad willingness to seek a constitutional solution on the specific terms of the Constitutional Treaty is that for as long as – but *only* as long as – its specific terms are not yet settled, constitutionalism is a broad enough church to win widespread support.

But might this not expose the case against constitutional scepticism as hollow and self-defeating? If all that can be said against the constitutional sceptics and in favour of the spread and resilience of the constitutional idea in the European supranational context is that those operating in that context continue to invoke the term in a myriad of different ways, it is far from clear what the value of such a claim is. If the price of sustainability of the constitutional idea is to be a purely 'nominalist'[13] conception of constitutional meaning, that is surely a price not worth paying. For if constitutionalism is broadened to include just anything that may be considered desirable by way of the regulation of public authority – and that seems to be how it has been treated by some champions of constitutionalism in the EU context[14] – then it may become so diluted that there is effectively nothing left at stake in the debate over whether or not the EU possesses constitutional credentials.

And, this, indeed, is a charge that has been laid by EU constitutional sceptics. They argue that to the extent one can discuss, imagine, represent or even refashion the EU in constitutional terms, these terms bear no meaningful relationship to the fuller project of constitutional formation and government that we typically associate with a written constitutional settlement; that such a fuller project is instead closely – perhaps exclusively – associated with the state tradition of constitutional thought and practice; and that it is an unwarranted (and not necessarily innocent) confusion of meaning to call upon the looser constitutional credentials of the EU in support of its legitimate involvement in the fuller constitutional project.[15]

What are the key assumptions and commitments supporting this deeper sceptical argument about the inappropriateness of a markedly state-centred constitutional tradition to the non-state EU? And how might these be challenged? Here, probing behind the apparent success or failure of particular recent events and initiatives, we come to the nub of the matter.

---

[13] N Walker, 'European Constitutionalism in the State Constitutional Tradition' (2006) 29 *Current Legal Problems* 51, 53.

[14] See, eg, C Joerges, '"Good Governance" in The European Internal Market: An Essay in Honour of Claus-Dieter Ehlermann' EUI Working Papers, RSC 2001/29. Arguments such as those of Joerges may be valuable contributions to the normative debate over the governance of the EU while not being in any way enhanced or moderated by the invocation of specifically constitutional language.

[15] See references at n 34 below.

B. Constitutionalism as a Layered Achievement

The literature on post-national constitutionalism in general – and EU constitutionalism in particular – is replete with binary distinctions that suggest a clear dichotomy between the kind of constitutionalism we associate with the state tradition and the kind attributable to post-national entities. These distinctions find particular favour with EU constitutional sceptics, tending as they do towards treatment of state constitutionalism as the full-blooded variant, and EU constitutionalism – to the extent that the constitutional label is deemed at all appropriate – as its anaemic cousin. Where one is a 'foundational constitutionalism',[16] the other is a derivative or secondary variant. 'Thick' versus 'thin',[17] high versus 'low intensity',[18] full-strength versus 'constitutionalism lite'[19] – these and other nested oppositions form the familiar vocabulary of discussion of the comparative attributes and merits of state and post-national constitutionalism.

According to these binary understandings, state constitutionalism generally refers to the formal settlement drafted in the name of the people (or, in the rare unwritten case, the informal settlement in receipt of popular homologation over time) that establishes and controls the powers of the governing institutions of the state, and to the culture and practice of legal and political self-determination flowing from that settlement. This state-centred idea is treated as the mature version of constitutionalism for two reasons; because it has certain attributes that other forms of constitutionalism are deemed to lack, and because it is the paradigmatic form of constitutionalism we associate with the age of political modernity. Indeed, in many understandings, the modern state and the modern constitution are seen as mutually constitutive and mutually dependent accomplishments; constitutionalism in its modern sense emerges from the social and political context of sovereign state formation and bears its imprint, just as the modern state is defined and distinguished from its premodern predecessors in part through its constitutionally coded legal and political properties.[20]

Beyond the headline labels, what is the basis upon which the binary distinction between the state-shaped model and other forms of constitutionalism is typically drawn? The full constitutional model of statehood is made up of a combination of legal and institutional attributes on the one hand and social and political attributes on the other. Or, in shorthand, we can talk of constitutionalism's

---

[16] N Krisch, *Beyond Constitutionalism: The Pluralist Structure of Postnational Law* (Oxford, Oxford University Press, 2010) ch 2.

[17] See, eg, P Craig, 'Constitutions, Constitutionalism and the European Union' (2001) 7 *European Law Journal* 125.

[18] M Maduro, 'The Importance of Being Called a Constitution: Constitutional Authority and the Authority of Constitutionalism' (2005) 3 *International Journal of Constitutional Law* 373.

[19] J Klabbers 'Constitutionalism Lite' (2004) 1 *International Organisations Law Review* 32.

[20] See, eg, D Grimm, 'The Achievement of Constitutionalism and its Prospects in a Changed World' in P Dobner and M Loughlin (eds), *The Twilight of Constitutionalism* (Oxford, Oxford University Press, 2010); M Loughlin, 'In Defence of Staatslehre' (2009) 48 *Der Staat* 1.

'legal-institutional dimension' and its 'socio-political dimension'.[21] Whereas the legal-institutional dimension is concerned with *authority*, the socio-political dimension is concerned with *community*. More specifically, the legal-institutional dimension refers to the combination and mutual articulation of normative software and institutional hardware – the fundamental rules of political authority and the institutions (executive, administrative, legislative and judicial) – that are constituted through these rules and offer the framework through which, in turn, the rules are extended, adjusted, implemented and adjudicated. The socio-political dimension, for its part, refers to the construction of a sense of a specific political entity with its own societal reference and associated set of interests and conception of the common good.

In its different dimensions, the state constitution operates in a different manner and to different effect. In the legal-institutional dimension, the constitution has a normative design function, supplying both an 'operating manual' for the system of governmental authority and a 'blueprint'[22] of how and to what purposes the statal entity should develop. In the socio-political dimension, the constitution has an expressive function.[23] Through various devices – the mobilisation of support in the constitution-making phase, the investment in the constitutional agreement itself as both token and achievement of a common way of political being, the continuous assertion and refinement of key communal norms and aspirations and the valorisation of key constitutional institutions, the collective memorialisation over time of a litany common events, experiences and accomplishments as part of the constitutional record – the constitution operates as a cultural vector concerned with the process and terms of socio-political integration. The constitution, in other words, nurtures and (through various constitutionally-interested actors) conveys a set of meanings about its particular object – the statal entity which has been constituted or is being (re)constituted – that encourages the audience of those addressed and affected to develop an image of that entity *qua* polity; that is to say, an image in terms of which that audience comes to see itself and sustain an understanding of itself as a community of attachment engaged in a particular form of common political life.

While it is clearly a multi-dimensional and multi-functional affair, important continuities and connections between the legal-institutional and socio-political

---

[21] Borrowing from M. Avbelj, 'Can European Integration be Constitutional and Pluralist – Both at the same time?' in M Avbelj and J Komarek (eds), *Constitutional Pluralism in the European Union and Beyond* (Oxford, Hart, 2012) 381, who in turn abridged my own earlier formulation of four registers – juridical, politico-institutional, popular and societal. See N Walker, 'Beyond the Holistic Constitution?' in Dobner and Loughlin, *The Twilight of Constitutionalism* (n 20) 191–209; see similarly, Dieter Grimm's distinction between the 'normative' and the 'symbolic' functions of constitutions; D Grimm 'Integration by Constitution' (2005) 3 *International Journal of Constitutional Law* 193–208.

[22] T Ginsberg and A Simpser, 'Introduction' in T Ginsberg and A Simpser (eds), *Constitutions in Authoritarian Regimes* (Cambridge, Cambridge University Press, 2013).

[23] M Tushnet, 'The Possibilities of Comparative Constitutional Law' (1999) 108 *Yale Law Journal* 1225.

dimensions and function are acknowledged in respect of the state-based constitutional model. As regards the continuities, in both dimensions two basic but vital aspects associated with the very idea of something being 'constituted' are present; first, that the thing constituted be understood in singular and holistic terms, as an entity defined in terms of the integrity of the whole; and secondly, that the thing has a discrete existence, separable from and independent of other entities.[24] And so, our received idea of a state constitution involves the idea of a 'joined-up' and self-contained legal and institutional order, as well as a distinct sovereign political unit referring to a correspondingly distinct national or multinational society. As regards the connections, just as there are mutual dependencies within the legal-institutional and socio-political dimensions, so too, importantly, there are between them. The norms of the authority system help shape the political community, just as the sense of political community that is conveyed irrigates and lends legitimacy to the authority system. What is more, the link between these various dimensions is not just mutual and ongoing, it is also reflexive. That is to say, in the relationship between authority and community, and between the mechanics associated with the design function of the constitution on the one hand and the sense of the polity conveyed and encouraged by the expressive function of the constitution on the other, we can observe the construction of a sense of a self-recognised collective 'people' engaged in a process of ongoing and adjustable self-government. And while the classical bridging device here is the formal constitutional amendment, the circuit of self-reflection and self-authorisation also connects through the ordinary work and everyday culture of involvement with constitutionally-prescribed democratic institutions and, at one level of representative remove, through judicial interpretation of constitutionally-endorsed text.

So, while a detailed understanding of the operation of the state constitution requires that we break it down into different elements, the overall picture is one that depends on the co-articulation of these elements. Or to adopt a different metaphor, we should think of constitutionalism as a layered achievement – one in which each distinct layer is baked together with and becomes inseparable from the others. Tellingly, however, when we come to look at how the 'thin' European constitution is often depicted in stylised contrast to the 'thick' state constitution, that sense of layered connection appears to get lost, and the separation between the legal-institutional and the socio-political dimensions hardens in a manner that suggests a merely aggregated (and so *disaggregable*), rather than an integrated, understanding of the parts of constitutionalism. For from this perspective the very idea of the EU constitution, either as a matter of 'small c' fact or in 'Big C' prospect, is exclusively or mainly restricted to the legal-institutional dimension.

---

[24] N Walker, 'Reframing EU Constitutionalism' in J Dunoff and J Trachtman (eds), *Ruling the World? Constitutionalism, International Law and Global Governance* (Cambridge, Cambridge University Press, 2009) 149–77.

C. The Thickening of European Constitutionalism

Given the actual pattern of development of constitutional thinking and practice within the European Union, the emphasis on the legal-institutional dimension is in some ways understandable. From the Treaty foundations and early development of judicial doctrine and common governance, Europe's supranational community has been marked by a highly elaborated framework of legal order and institutional architecture; and where explicit constitutional language has been used, it has typically been with reference to that framework.[25] Much of what is understood and supported as the EU's 'small c' *acquis* in the post-2007 world, moreover, continues to reside firmly within the legal-institutional domain. Through a mix of text and judicial construction, most famously in its doctrines of supremacy and direct effect, the EU has long possessed a robust sense of its own legal order as an autonomous, self-contained and in some measure self-enforcing system. Equally, from the outset, it has possessed all the recognised institutions of constitutional self-governance – a compound legislature of Parliament, Council and Commission, a dual executive of Commission and European Council, as well as an independent judicial system centred around the Court of Justice and, more recently, an autonomous monetary system organised around the European Central Bank.

Support for the Draft Constitution, moreover, seemed to draw heavily upon a version of constitutionalism firmly focused on the legal-institutional dimension and its underlying normative design function. The scene was set at the landmark Laeken conference in 2001, where much of the stated motivation of the European Council in pursuing a Convention with a long-term constitutional objective had to do with the consolidating virtues of simplification of legal instruments and re-organisation of the Treaties – virtues that reflected and built upon an understanding of the EU's legal and institutional order as an autonomous and self-contained affair.[26] And if a written constitution promised the formal goods of unity and coherence, it also offered a mechanism of substantive reform – of normative *redesign*. For part of the attraction for those supportive of the Convention was that it simply offered a fresh opportunity – one with the wide consultative basis and accretion of political capital that the solemnity of a self-styled constitutional process and instrument offered – to review the overall framework of governance. It did so at a point where – as the relative failure and attendant frustrations of the Treaty of Nice in 2000 had indicated – the normal Intergovernmental Conference-followed-by-International-Treaty model of reform was providing diminishing returns. The basic operating manual of the EU was becoming more difficult both to implement and to amend – a difficulty that would be exacerbated

---

[25] See, eg, JHH Weiler, *The Constitution of Europe* (Cambridge, Cambridge University Press, 1999); for a detailed tracking of the discursive history, see A Boerger and M Rasmussen (eds), 'Transforming European Law: The Establishment of the Constitutional Discourse from 1950 to 1993' (2014) 10 *European Constitutional Law Review* 199–225.
[26] See n 9.

by the completion of the wave of Central and Eastern European enlargement in 2004–07 – and the pattern of regular revision initiated by the Single European Act was threatened. Against that backdrop, the general strengthening of supranational capacity in both home and foreign affairs together with the extension of Qualified Majority Voting and co-decision in the legislative process that the agreement in the Draft Constitution would have delivered if ratified, represented a significant unblocking of the machinery of governance. So much so indeed, that even parties who did not favour this particular set of outcomes, or indeed any extension of the integration process, were nevertheless drawn into the constitutional debate for fear of otherwise having no say in what seemed like an increasingly rare opportunity to rewrite the Union's operating manual.[27]

It would be a mistake, however, to see the Draft Constitution as no more than a fortified treaty process – and so merely an extended exercise in legal-institutional design. Equally, it would be a mistake to see the consolidation of constitutional discourse post-2007 as only concerned with the legal-institutional dimension. In part, the argument here is conceptual, but, building upon these conceptual foundations, there is also an important empirical aspect.

Let us first address the conceptual foundations. *The key point is that there is no meaningful sense in which we can enter into constitutional discourse without engaging both legal-institutional and socio-political dimensions.* The interpenetration of the layers is more fully developed, and more apparent, in the case of the state, but just *wherever* there is serious involvement in or contemplation of constitutional formation and associated deployment of constitutional language and participation in constitutional debate around a particular polity object, then both design and expressive functions necessarily become engaged. The different design options inevitably convey different visions of political community, and promise different cultural resources from which attachments to that political community may be formed; and the ways in which these projections are or are not internalised by relevant audiences feed back into the development and interpretation of the normative design.

What is more, and of fundamental importance, the very introduction and normalisation of constitutional language is itself a key trigger; it signals the crossing of a key imaginary threshold. To recall, the constitution in the state tradition presupposes and implies an entity 'constituted' as a singular and discrete political object, with its own distinct collective interests and referent society, which in turn are reflexively constructed through and in the name of those who come to see themselves as part of the relevant community of attachment. For two reasons, however, we should not see this kind of framing of the constitutional imaginary as limited to the state tradition. First, as we have argued, these notions of holistic singularity and discrete existence are implicit in the very idea of constitution – they are part of its deeper etymology. Secondly, the fact that these have become

---

[27] See, eg, N Walker 'The Legacy of Europe's Constitutional Moment' (2004) 11 *Constellations* 368–92.

so embedded in the dominant state tradition means that the invocation of constitutionalism in non-state domains, even if the context of that invocation is one of confrontational debate between quite different positions, is bound to invite the same kind of associations. For those who engaged in constitutional discourse in the EU context (in a manner that does not merely *deny* its appropriateness), as, indeed, in other non-state contexts, in so doing necessarily corroborate a sense that the EU is a kind of polity that also exhibits the properties of holism and discreteness, and so is capable of having its own conception of a collective political good – one that is constructed and revised through the very reflexive mode of self-understanding and self-regulation to which their own engagement contributes.

What this conceptual inquiry suggests, therefore, is that it is quite misleading to see the distinction between state and non-state constitutionalism in terms of a rigid distinction between normative design and expression of political community, low and high intensity, 'thin' and 'thick'. Rather, differences in thickness can only be a matter of degree. And all constitutional projects and projections should be seen as situated on a single continuum in which the basic legal-institutional layer is always joined in some measure by a thicker socio-political layer in a process of mutual generation and dependency. And it is by reference to this 'thickening' impulse in constitutional talk and imagination that we begin to establish what was merely posited earlier; namely, the existence of an intimate and mutually reinforcing link between the constitutional self-recognition of an entity and its self-standing as a polity.[28]

If we return to the Draft Constitution, we can now observe some of the ways in which the broader expressive dimension was also engaged alongside the legal-institutional dimension. The idea of a written constitution came to be supported in sponsorship of quite different conceptions of the European polity.[29] On one view, a written constitutional settlement became appropriate as a way of charting a new and higher stage of common achievement in the gradual progression of the European project; or even, and more conservatively, as a way of according 'finality'[30] to the distinct cumulative accomplishment of the supranational form and supplying a token of the successful attainment of a minimal threshold of transnational political community. For others, more ambitiously, it was seen as a platform from which to build on the unwritten constitutional *acquis* toward a fuller political entity with more state-like tendencies, including a still wider and deeper jurisdiction and a more ample framework of democratic representation.[31]

---

[28] See section I.

[29] For a fuller discussion, see N Walker, 'Europe's Constitutional Momentum and the Search for Polity Legitimacy' (2005) 3 *International Journal of Constitutional Law* 211–38, 225–31.

[30] In the well-known formulation of Joschka Fischer, Foreign Minister of the Federal Republic of Germany, 'From Confederacy to Federation – Thoughts on the Finality of European Integration' Speech at the Humboldt University, Berlin, 12 May 2000. This speech is widely credited as a key moment in the mobilisation of political opinion in favour of a 'Big C' constitutional process.

[31] See, eg, J Habermas, 'Why Europe Needs a Constitution' (2001) 11 *New Left Review* 5.

In marked contrast to all these views, however, some positions wary of further supranational expansion also came to endorse the idea of attributing constitutional weight and significance to a new settlement as a way of reining in and containing the process of integration. The (short-lived) conversion of the traditionally Eurosceptic *Economist* magazine to the case for a written constitution, for instance, was contingent upon such a limiting approach.[32] So too, to take another example, was the support of the German *Länder*, wary of the internal competence-creep of national federal government over an expanding set of matters deemed to fall within its 'foreign affairs' European jurisdiction. In these and other cases, a constitutional settlement was affirmed for its capacity, through mechanisms such as the EU Charter of Rights and the competence catalogue, to condition and restrict as much as to constitute supranational governmental authority. Importantly, however, this too involved endorsing not only certain aspects of normative design, but also the symbolic power and cultural force of the constitutional idea in expressing a particular – if more restrictive – vision of the Europolity.

D. The Constitution that Might Have Been

As the unfolding of the Convention demonstrated, the way in which the draft Constitutional Treaty in its expressive function related to the idea of polity vision produced a deep tension between content and form. On the one hand, we have observed how the particular polity visions favoured by different constituencies – evolutional, conservative, transformative and truncated – were quite distinctive. They involve contrasting understandings of the scope and trajectory of the EU polity, and of its appropriate relationship to the existing Member State polities. On the other hand, the very utilisation of a constitutional form of expression implies that each distinct EU polity vision is nevertheless a vision of the EU *as a polity*; that is to say, it is a vision of supranational Europe as the kind of entity that is capable of possessing its own conception of a common interest and a collective good, towards which its members reflexively contribute. On that view, therefore, the very act of involvement in the constitutional debate required a preparedness to put things in common, which if it had led to a successful conclusion – the settling of a common basis for putting things in common – could have provided significant cultural resources for the European project.

Consideration of some of the deeper roots of the constitutional episode allows us a clearer sense of how that successful conclusion *might* have been reached, and how it might at least have been glimpsed in the 'real time' of the Convention. We have already noted how at the legal-institutional level the constitutional debate tended to generate its own momentum, with few constituencies prepared to be

---

[32] See *The Economist* 4 November 2000.

excluded from an increasingly rare opportunity for root-and-branch review of the normative structure of the Union. At the level of socio-political culture, we can see the possibility of a similar momentum-building dynamic – a possibility, moreover, that was closely influenced by the shifting terms and tenor of the normative debate. Since Maastricht's innovative designs in monetary, social, justice and foreign policy, Europe had undergone a period of rapid expansion of competences and regulatory infrastructure as well as of territory – an expansion that had taken the European project well beyond its initial comfort zone of an elite-driven 'permissive consensus'[33] on market-making and the consolidation of peace.

Each of the competing polity visons deployed during the Treaty discussions in its own way represents a response to the fears and hopes associated with that expanding reach and ambition. More specifically, each vision involved a kind of *double engagement* with the challenge posed to the resources of European collective political culture by the exponential growth of the European project. In each case there was a cognitive engagement. The European project was diagnosed variously as an entity in a process of long-term evolution, or which had attained its maturity, or which required a further transformative deepening, or which had reached or even encroached beyond its proper limits. In each case, additionally, there was a practical engagement, an endeavour to provide a treatment appropriate to the diagnosis – *which proposed treatment was itself predicated upon a claim to speak on Europe's collective behalf.* Whether it involved marking and charting incremental progress, celebrating finality, supplying a platform for change, or building a containing fence, therefore, each polity vision invoked the same European 'we'. And in that common invocation lay the opening for a competitive, yet potentially constructive, conversation between parties *already* claiming to speak on behalf of the same collective voice.

In the final analysis, the constitutional project was, of course, *not* successfully concluded. And this speaks to the enduring tension between content and form – to the difficulties for any such symbolic capital-building project to 'get going' in the face of such substantial internal differences. What is more, not only did the general preparedness to engage have to negotiate and overcome the different polity visions – and the different associated cognitive understandings and practical orientations – of all those so generally prepared. It also had to overcome the opposition of those firmly set against the constitutional form itself, and so against the very idea of the EU as an entity capable of developing its own reflexive conception of the common good rather than a dependent product of its Member States.[34]

---

[33] I Down and C Wilson, 'From "Permissive Consensus" to "Constraining Dissensus": A Polarizing Union?' (2008) 43 *Acta Politica* 26–49.

[34] The academic expression of this deeper form of Big 'C' constitutional scepticism comes in various forms. On one view, which is actually quite close to the approval of a written constitution as a mark of evolutionary achievement, the EU is seen as possessing an unprecedentedly organic development and complex richness which cannot be appropriately reduced to and frozen in a single self-contained documentary Constitution. (See, eg, J Weiler, 'In Defence of the Status Quo: Europe's Constitutional

Popular rejection in France and Holland was, arguably, as much if not more about political-cultural opposition from those who believed that *no* form of autonomous constitutional identity for the EU, and so no version of 'we' feeling, could do other than 'steal the clothes' of the Member States and diminish their constitutional standing, as it was about distinctions and disagreement amongst the different constitutional polity visions for the EU.[35]

And so, the expressive dimension of the EU Draft Constitution tells a story both of hope and of disappointment.[36] The hope concerned a boot-strapping exercise in collective self-imagination. The disappointment lay in the failure of this exercise to overcome both differences within the constituency of supporters of a constitutional settlement and the opposition of those set against any such idea. And only to the extent that the hope has left a legacy of possibility might we ever come to think of the failed project as merely the overture to the main performance.

III. Constitutional Possibilities

What, if anything, has changed in 2018? Are we caught in the same bind as a decade earlier? Or do the linked crises of the EU – economic, migration, security and a more basic crisis of political survival – offer some prospect of a constitutional relaunch?

As noted earlier, after the failure of 2001–07 there was little explicit talk of a documentary constitution for a number of years. Constitutional debate, however, kept going through discussion in judicial, political and academic circles of the 'many' aspects of EU's supposedly unwritten constitution – not just the 'juridical constitution' but also the 'political constitution', the 'economic constitution', the 'security constitution' and the 'social constitution',[37] and if not a written constitution,

---

Sonderweg' in J Weiler and M Wind (eds), *European Constitutionalism Beyond the State* (Cambridge, Cambridge University Press, 2003); S Weatherill, 'Is Constitutional Finality Feasible or Desirable? On the Case for European Constitutionalism and a European Constitution' Conweb 7/2002.) Or, in a more uncompromising variation of the sceptical theme, resort to constitutional language by an entity so lacking in the properties of comprehensive political self-authorisation associated with the state tradition is deemed so incongruent that for it to develop a fully-fledged written constitution would be a 'category error' – an exercise in misconceived and wilful self-aggrandisement. (See, eg, A Moravcsik, 'A Category Error' *Prospect* July 2005, 22–26.)

[35] See, eg, S Tierney, *Constitutional Referendums* (Oxford, Oxford University Press, 2012) 156–61; Min Shu, 'Referendums and the Political Constitutionalisation of the EU' (2008) 14 *European Law Journal* 423.

[36] See further M Cahill, 'The Constitutional Success of Ratification Failure' (2006) 7 *German Law Journal* 947; A Phillippopoulis-Mihalopoulous, 'Moment of Stasis: The Successful Failure of a Constitution for Europe' (2009) 15 *European Law Journal* 309–23; N Walker, 'European Constitutional Pluralism Revisited' (2016) 22 *European Law Journal* 333–55; N Gibbs, 'Post-Sovereignty and the European Legal Space' (2017) 80 *Modern Law Review* 812–35.

[37] See, eg, discussion of the many faces of European constitutionalism in K Tuori, *European Constitutionalism* (Cambridge, Cambridge University Press, 2015) esp ch 1.

then at least norms of 'supra-constitutional'[38] standing, a 'constitutional compromise', or an informal 'constitutional settlement'.[39] While much of this talk remained ostensibly within a legal-institutional register, the inseparability of this normative dimension from the expressive dimension and its socio-political register meant that the cultural suggestion of larger constitutional possibilities never disappeared.

Today we detect the stirrings of renewed contemplation of a 'Big C' constitutional initiative, not just in civil society and intellectual settings but increasingly in high political circles.[40] These build upon and feed into a wider re-engagement with the possibility of root-and-branch reform of the Union, exemplified by the Commission's recent White Paper on the Future of Europe.[41] But what prospects are there for a successful new initiative – a mature performance ten years after the fading of the overture?

Constitutional moments that do not involve an entirely new departure, but, as in the EU case, the re-framing and augmentation of an existing political project, would typically bear fruit, and so meet the standard of ripeness, only if the following conditions were met:

1. the current political settlement, or unsettlement, is generally deemed unsatisfactory;
2. a rewind to the state of affairs prior to the existing (un)settlement – the status quo ante – does not command general support, or is not considered feasible; and
3. there is an emerging consensus that the existing situation, deemed both (1) *unsatisfactory* and (2) *irreversible*, and, therefore, unsustainable as it stands, is sufficiently widely and clearly experienced and articulated as a

[38] See, eg, Y Roznai, *Unconstitutional Constitutional Amendments* (Oxford, Oxford University Press, 2017) ch 3.

[39] See, eg, A Moravcsik, 'The European Constitutional Compromise and the Neo-functionalist Legacy' (2005) 12 *Journal of European Public Policy* 349–86; 'The European Constitutional Settlement' (2008) 31 *The World Economy* 158–83.

[40] See, eg, the Sorbonne speech of French President Emmanuel Macron of 26 September 2017 (English version) available at http://international.blogs.ouest-france.fr/archive/2017/09/29/macron-sorbonne-verbatim-europe-18583.html. See also The Ljubljana Initiative, launched by Slovenian President, Borut Pahor: www.up-rs.si/up-rs/uprs-eng.nsf/pages/5D15E0B0A4878677C12580E20041A7E7?OpenDocument; The Rome Manifesto www.united-europe.eu/rome-manifesto/the-manifesto/; The new draft Treaty for the Constitution of the European Union, by Peter Jambrek www.predsednik.si/uprs/uprs.nsf/cc1b0c2e0c8f0e70c1257aef00442bbd/6e9c355dcac33036c12580a0004d8dc2/$FILE/Predlog%20nove%20evropske%20ustave%20The%20new%20draft%20treaty%20for%20the%20constitution%20of%20the%20European%20Union.pdf. And see also the DiEM 25 Initiative, launched by former Greek Minister Yanis Varoufakis in 2015; DiEM (2016) 'A Manifesto for Democratizing Europe'. For general discussion of the state of constitutional ripeness in the EU today, see e.g. M. Avbelj '*Transformation of EU Constitutionalism*' VerfBlog, 2016/6/22, http://verfassungsblog.de/transformation-of-eu-constitutionalism/, DOI: http://dx.doi.org/10.17176/20160622-161220; see also M. Patberg, 'Challenging the Masters of the Treaties: Emerging Narratives of Constituent Power in the European Union' (2018) 7 *Global Constitutionalism* 263.

[41] European Commission, 'White Paper on the Future of Europe' available at https://ec.europa.eu/commission/white-paper-future-europe-reflections-and-scenarios-eu27_en. Discussed at length in M Avbelj, 'What Future for the European Union?' WZB Discussion paper 2017-802, July 2017, https://bibliothek.wzb.eu/pdf/2017/iv17-802.pdf.

shared predicament that invites a common response to overcome the deficit of trust and confidence between constituencies with quite different avowed interests and goals as they might contemplate their capacity to reach a mutually satisfactory agreement to put things in political common.

Today, as the Commission's White Paper itself makes clear, due to the combination of the various crises there is increasing evidence that many constituencies find the present condition *unsatisfactory* (*condition 1*). And, tellingly, the early experience and wider continental reception of the Brexit vote, if anything, has led many other national constituencies, including some who believe that integration has already gone too far or are wary of its so doing, to conclude that the supranational project is nevertheless in practice (if not in theory) *irreversible* (*condition 2*) – that there is no practicable route back to an earlier form of state sovereignty.[42] Yet even if, on these grounds, an emerging body of opinion finds the present state of the supranational project unsustainable in the absence of a new settlement, the sense that this amounts to a *shared predicament that invites a common response* may not be strong enough to overcome the deficit of mutual sympathy required to commit to common constitutional action (*condition 3*).

Here we confront the 'paradox of initiative'[43] which affects, to a greater or lesser degree, many attempts at constitution-making under conditions of social and political division and unsettlement. For the very circumstances which, on one view, make a constitution desirable, namely the absence of the kind of political capital – the sense of common attachment to a political project – necessary to achieve common goods, are also those that prevent the constitutional initiative from being taken in the first place. Otherwise put, without prior common commitment a settled constitutional platform of common commitment cannot easily be generated. Does this boot-strapping paradox mean that we Europeans, as we contemplate of our shared political heritage and future, are fated to live in a time of widespread foreboding – leading, as some authors have put it, to 'despondency and lethargy'?[44] There is no clear answer to this, but let us conclude by considering two sets of factors which may weigh in the balance in favour of the possibility of a new settlement.

First, the constitutional overture of 2001–07, if that is what it turns out to be, not only altered the mood music within the debate over the European future, but also provided an example from which lessons could be learned. In some ways, it was an unplanned and reluctant initiative, on one view merely an 'accidental constitution'.[45] Its origins, as we have said, were in the legal-institutional domain, its wider expressive socio-political dimension for many an afterthought,

[42] 'Brexit has raised support for the European Union' Eupinions trends: policy brief 11/2016 www.bertelsmann-stiftung.de/fileadmin/files/user_upload/EZ_flashlight_europe_02_2016_EN.pdf.
[43] N Walker, 'Our Constitutional Unsettlement' (2014) *Public Law* 529–48, 542.
[44] M Dawson and F De Witte, 'From Balance to Conflict: A New Constitution for the EU' (2016) 22 *European Law Journal* 204, 224, 220.
[45] Norman, *The Accidental Constitution* (n 11).

even if an inevitable and growing supplement. The focus on legal-institutional design produced a document of a length and level of detail largely alien to the state tradition. As well as not *looking* 'constitutional', such a document engaged in a level of normative prescription – and threatened a consequential rigidity of pre-commitment in the framing of the Europolity – that was bound to highlight existing divisions and create new ones. A shorter document could have eased the tension between form and content, with much greater emphasis on the expression of basic agreement to put matters in common, and on the political capital to be secured through that foundational commitment, and much less on the terms of the bargain.

The unplanned and inexplicit constitutional beginning also affected important matters of process. We have already noted how the Laeken Declaration merely hinted at the possibility of a documentary constitutional future. The status of the Convention as 'Big C' Constitutional was self-bestowed on the initiative of Giscard D'Estaing, its President, and it continued to lack the legitimacy of an explicit political mandate from the political leaders of the Member States. Also, no common commitment was made at the outset to a referendum, which caused two significant problems. As referendums were only selectively called, and in some cases after initial hesitation or refusal, this lessened the popular thrust of the initiative and cast suspicion on those national leaders and governments reluctant to put matters to a popular vote. Moreover, referendums were called at different times, and on a national basis and so framed in national terms, which made it difficult to create a pan-European case against the variety of national counter-arguments.[46]

Ten years on, no longer working in virgin politico-cultural soil, any new EU constitutional initiative would and could not be unplanned, and the opportunity to address the structural and processual shortcomings of the first 'accidental' model would exist – indeed could not be avoided. What is more, the intervening years have seen acceleration in the global growth of what some have called a 'post-sovereign' model of democratic constitution-making. A new range of design tools for polities with non-unitary *demoi* have been developed, refined and consciously adapted across different constitutional contexts.[47] Constitutional 'learning' today,[48] therefore, might draw from the experience of other polities as well as from supra-national Europe's own earlier initiative.

Not only, however, might the experience of the previous initiative prove to be salutary for those who would contemplate a second act in the constitutional play. In addition, with regard to the crucial third condition of ripeness, the way in which the problems of Europe manifest themselves and are received today are more likely than a decade ago to give rise to a tangible sense of *shared predicament that invites a common response* through a second such constitution-generative act.

---

[46] See, eg, N Walker, 'A Constitutional Reckoning' (2006) 13 *Constellations* 140–50.

[47] See, eg, A Arato, *Post Sovereign Constitution Making: Learning and Legitimacy* (Oxford, Oxford University Press, 2016).

[48] Ibid, ch 2.

At the time of the previous Convention, and, indeed, partly accounting for its early success, there was very little by way of counterpoint in the constitutional debate. The pressure for change came predominantly from the Europhile side, albeit, as we have seen, it came to incorporate a broad range of conceptions of the polity within that broad church. While the debate remained within the institutions and the Convention itself there was very little to push against, and it was only when it moved to the national sites that the Eurosceptical reaction developed momentum. The constitutional debate, in other words, remained somewhat *dis*engaged and unreflexive. On the one side, there was a prosaic concern with detailed legal-institutional retrenchment or reform with only modest initial effort to capture the popular imagination through the expression and projection of explicit constitutional symbolism or through the connection of any such expression to matters of pressing pan-European concern. On the other side, when Eurosceptical momentum did gain ground, it did so in discrete national silos, typically favouring state-centred understandings of constitutional identity and focusing on state-centred readings of European problems. The *conversation about the constitution,* such as it was, was not really *a constitutional conversation*, but a fractured series of exchanges in which there was little accord either over the framing and weighing of the issues at stake or over the proper constituency for consideration of these issues. There was little sense, in short, of there being a shared predicament giving rise to a common debate about whether, what and how the European people might put things in common.

Today the debate is more closely joined. As we have already noted, against the backdrop of overlapping crises, there is a broader sense of the unsustainability of the current settlement. The discussion and associated lines of disagreement, too, are less fractured into national components, and on both sides argument exhibits a more connected, pan-European quality. For, tellingly, the various contemporary crisis points, although often presented as somehow exogenous to the EU, all concern matters which, as the expanded post-Maastricht agenda has unfolded simultaneously with the slow emergence of a proto-constitutional consideration of supranational Europe as a distinct political entity, have ever more clearly engaged questions concerning fundamental EU interests – and also concerning the type of polity vision most appropriate to the pursuit of these interests.[49] This is most obviously true of the sovereign debt repercussions of the global financial crisis. Debates concerning the mutualisation of debt and the development of a common fiscal policy have become increasingly insistent, and are sharply reflective of differing polity visions in an entity which has enjoyed Monetary Union for two decades. But questions of mass population movement and international terrorism, too, become more salient, their answers more reflective of and more formative of a broader polity vision, in an entity that has already developed many of the features of

---

[49] See, eg, O Cramme and S Hobolt (eds), *Democratic Politics in a European Union under Stress* (Oxford, Oxford University Press, 2014).

a common foreign policy and a shared concern with external borders and internal security. In all of these cases, the sense of having a common stake in finding the appropriate common means to address a common predicament emerges from the close connection between global events, the EU's expanding competence, and the gradual spread of a way of thinking about the EU as a distinct political entity. And the list continues to grow. The treatment of the emergence of authoritarian forms of populism in some Member States and of powerful sub-national independent movements in others might once have been seen as the exclusive preserve of the Member States themselves. But in a supranational regime that claims to be founded on democracy and human rights, and to hold its members to these values, the question of the proper form and level of the EU's response to these democracy-challenging events increasingly takes the shape of a common predicament whose possible solutions again engage different visions of the EU polity.[50]

Of course, the emergence of new stimuli to common polity-defining debate, with such clear constitutional intimations, carries an obvious risk. The stubborn legacy of Eurosceptical concerns that any self-avowedly constitutional status for the EU would be at the zero-sum expense of the socio-political resources of the states makes the task of constitutional construction unavoidably controversial; and this invites the danger of further fragmentation of the supranational edifice, whether in the form of pre-emptive unilateral rejection of any such initiative or in response to its collective failure. Yet that risk should not deflect from the flipside opportunity – from the fact that a more engaged debate on issues of such critical polity-shaping significance also offers the best prospect of developing a deeper and more resilient common constitutional vernacular and commitment. And, as already noted, in these circumstances those agnostic voices who – concerned at the destabilising early consequences of the Brexit response to the 'shared predicaments' of supranationalism – may have come to distance themselves from the exit option, would be left with little choice but for constructive involvement in search of a settled way of political being in Europe.

It is just because the stakes are so high, then, that perhaps today there is more scope than ever before for any fresh batch of conversations about a constitution for the European Union to segue into a reflexively engaged and textually moored constitutional conversation.

---

[50] See, eg, C Closa (ed), *Secession from a Member State and Withdrawal from the European Union* (Cambridge, Cambridge University Press, 2017); G Palombella, 'Illiberal, Democratic, Non Arbitrary. Epicentre and Circumstances of a Rule of Law Crisis' available at SSRN: http://dx.doi.org/10.2139/ssrn.2961940.

12

The European Constitution
and 'the Compulsion to Grand Politics'

RICHARD MULLENDER*

'Civilization is built, history is driven.'[†]

I. Introduction

In 1886, Friedrich Nietzsche dedicated Part Eight of his *Beyond Good and Evil: Prelude to a Philosophy of the Future* to a set of reflections on Europe.[1] The upshot was an exposition that provides strong support for the view that his thinking (like that of Karl Marx) 'looms over twentieth-century Europe'.[2] He saw 'the most unambiguous signs ... that *Europe wants to become one*'.[3] However, he also declared that 'the lunacy of nationality' was producing 'morbid estrangement' between 'the peoples of Europe'.[4] Moreover, he found a distinct politics in each of these features of the scene he surveyed. Nietzsche identified the desire to 'become one' as an expression of 'the compulsion to grand politics'.[5] When he turned to 'the lunacy of nationality', he detected a 'politics of disintegration'.[6] These points made it possible for him to impress upon his readers the cross-pressured condition of

---

* At the conference on 'The Rise and Fall of the European Constitution' that took place in Trinity College, Oxford in September 2017, Dorota Leczykiewicz made a response to an early draft of this essay that proved to be a great spur to reflection. I also owe thanks to Richard Ekins, Gunnar Beck, Kalypso Nicolaïdis, Neil Walker and Alison Young for their respective responses to this draft. James Allan, Nick Barber, Maria Cahill, David Campbell, Dominic Lawson, William Lucy and Patrick O'Callaghan each put me right on important points when they responded to later drafts.

[†] D DeLillo, *Underworld* (New York, Simon & Schuster, 1997) 287.
[1] F Nietzsche, *Beyond Good and Evil: Prelude to a Philosophy of the Future* (London, Penguin Books, 1990 [1886]) 170–91 ('Peoples and Fatherlands').
[2] P Watson, *A Terrible Beauty: The People and Ideas that Shaped the Modern Mind* (London, Weidenfeld & Nicolson, 2000) 38.
[3] Nietzsche, (n 1) 189 [256] (italics in original).
[4] Ibid, 188–89 [256].
[5] Ibid, 138 [208] (italics in original).
[6] Ibid, 189 [256].

Europe at the time he wrote. This is a condition that has continuing relevance to Europe. This chapter identifies 'the compulsion to grand politics' as the practical force that prompted the decision to draft the Treaty Establishing a Constitution for Europe (TCE).[7] Likewise, it uses Nietzsche's analysis to throw light on the decision not to give the TCE legal force following its rejection in referendums in the Netherlands and France. More particularly, this chapter forges tight links between features of Nietzsche's exposition and statements in the draft Constitution's Preface and Preamble. The statements on which we will focus are more expansive than those that appear in the later (2004) version of the Constitution. They thus throw more light on the large ambitions or 'directing ideas' (to use a phrase from Maurice Hauriou) at work within the constitutional project and the process of integration more generally.[8] The adjective 'directing' in the phrase 'directing ideas' is apt. This is because the ideas on which we will focus afford a basis on which to make sense of more particular features of the TCE. Moreover, there are reasons for thinking that these ideas reflect the influence of a more general faculty to which we can apply the label 'the legal imagination'. These points apply to the proportionality principle and the ideal of the social market (each of which we will examine below).

As well as being an aid to analysis, Nietzsche's exposition has relevance to the TCE in two other ways. It supports the view (to which the draft Constitution makes glancing references) that Europe is a civilisation rather than a state-in-the-making.[9] Likewise, it yields a basis on which to argue that Europe has fostered an ideal of community (*politieia*) that has long had its life at the level of the state or nation. As we will see, these points support the conclusion that Europeans should, when considering arguments for integration, apply a principle of caution that may serve to secure state-level contexts that they regard as 'home'. But before we apply Nietzsche to the TCE, we must examine his thinking on Europe.

II. Friedrich Nietzsche on Europe and 'the Compulsion to Grand Politics'

Nietzsche is well known for a full-frontal assault on religion (in which the declarative sentence 'God is dead' features) and for his emphasis on 'the will to power'.[10] He is also well known for his sustained critique of the Jewish faith, Christianity and the egalitarian morality he identifies these bodies of thought as having fostered.[11] Alongside these central areas of concern for Nietzsche, we should set

---

[7] Draft Treaty establishing a Constitution for Europe (Official Journal C 189, 18/07/2003) (TCE).

[8] M Hauriou, 'The Theory of the Institution and the Foundation: A Study in Social Vitalism' in A Broderick (ed), *The French Institutionalists: Maurice Hauriou, Georges Renard, Joseph T Delos* (Cambridge, Mass, Harvard University Press, 1970) 93–124, 114.

[9] TCE (n 7) Preamble.

[10] Nietzsche, *Thus Spoke Zarathustra: A Book for Everyone and No One* (Harmondsworth, Penguin Books, 1969 [1883–1891]) 41 and 136.

[11] F Nietzsche (n 1) 118 [195] and 126–27 [203].

his interest in the condition of Europe. Nietzsche's interest in this topic is apparent in much of his written output and involves him in dwelling on societies in which egalitarian morality on the model he criticises has become part of the social fabric. On his account, this morality has exerted a profound influence on political and legal institutions in Europe by encouraging processes of democratisation and a concern with rights-based legal protection for the individual.[12] Nietzsche's interest in the condition of Europe and the processes of legal and political development at work within its various societies is apparent in *Beyond Good and Evil*. It is at its most obvious in 'Peoples and Fatherlands', a section in *Beyond Good and Evil* that receives surprisingly little attention from Nietzsche scholars.[13]

In 'Peoples and Fatherlands', Nietzsche identifies Europe as a 'civilisation'.[14] He also dwells on relations between France, Germany and the other nation states that feature in his analysis and alerts us to tensions that exist between them. These tensions have many sources but prominent among them is 'the compulsion to grand politics'. Before we probe this phrase, it is important to emphasise that Nietzsche does not write with the commitment to precision that we would find in, say, an analytic philosopher. However, a determination to expose often embarrassing truths is at work in his writing and leads him to characterise his critical onslaughts as exercises in 'vivisection'.[15] This is how he approaches Europe in 'Peoples and Fatherlands' and we can extract from his exposition highly suggestive examples of the compulsion to grand politics. These examples provide the basis for a tentative taxonomy. Nietzsche presents the compulsion to grand politics in a crude form in Bismarckian Germany's determination to assume great power status and to secure a place in the imperial sun. To this end, Germany is ready to deploy military power ('blood and iron') in pursuit of its large purposes.[16] Nietzsche sets alongside this crude example of grand politics a variant that shares its readiness to deploy military force but that is animated by purposes that are (at least in the minds of its proponents) benign. It takes the form of Napoleonic France. Here, Nietzsche recognises that Napoleon and his supporters assumed that France's use of force afforded a means to put politico-legal life in Europe (and elsewhere) on a more satisfactory footing.[17] The compulsion to grand politics in this form provides an example of what the sociologist Pierre Bourdieu has called 'the imperialism of the universal'.[18] Imperialism on this model is about much more than the acquisition of, and control over, territory since it assumes itself to be justifiable

---

[12] Ibid, 126–27 [203].

[13] See, eg, J Young, *Friedrich Nietzsche: A Philosophical Biography* (Cambridge, Cambridge University Press, 2010) ch 21 (which focuses on *Beyond Good and Evil* but does not devote close attention to 'Peoples and Fatherlands').

[14] Nietzsche (n 1) 172 [242].

[15] Ibid, 143 [212] and 174 [244].

[16] Ibid, 187 [254].

[17] Ibid, 177 [245].

[18] P Bourdieu, *On the State: Lectures at the College de France, 1989-1992* (Cambridge, Polity, 2014) 159.

in universal terms. This is because it will, according to its proponents, serve the interests of those who are its objects. To these examples of the compulsion to grand politics, Nietzsche adds a third that has obvious relevance not just in the Europe of the 1880s but also today. He recognises that the egalitarian morality at which he directs his critical fire has spawned a set of 'modern ideas' (including democracy and rights-based legal protections for individuals) that have wide appeal.[19] Moreover, he argues that politicians have fastened on these ideas as a basis on which to secure power within and beyond the borders of the nation state.[20]

As well as giving us the examples that make it possible to work up this taxonomy, Nietzsche contemplates the effects that the compulsion to grand politics seems likely to have in the twentieth century. Here, we can read him as anticipating military struggle on the models of World War One and World War Two. In the first of these conflicts, we see the Germany that Bismarck ushered into existence collide with its imperial rivals. In the second, we see the imperialism of the universal (in its American and Soviet forms) extend its influence across Europe. However, we can also read Nietzsche as being alive to the possibility of an imperialism of the universal that seeks, without resort to violence, to secure the assent of those whose lives it orders. This is a possibility to which his reflections on the years immediately before, during and after the French Revolution lend support. Nietzsche finds in this period of 'transition' practical impulses that express a strong commitment to an egalitarian philosophy of government.[21] For it is at this point in Europe's history that a drive towards democratisation and rights-based legal entitlements for individuals begins to gain moral urgency. Here, the individual who, perhaps more than anyone, embodies the compulsion to grand politics on Nietzsche's second model becomes relevant to our concerns. When reflecting on his life, Napoleon declared that his greatest achievement had not been the masterful deployment of military force in particular battles or campaigns. Rather, it had been his decision to support the specification of the French Civil Code – a body of law that enjoyed the endorsement of those subject to it within and beyond the borders of France.[22]

We can draw out of Nietzsche's account of the compulsion to grand politics another lesson that has relevance to our concerns. As we noted earlier, the Bismarckian variant is cruder (nationalistic but not universalist in orientation) than that exemplified by France under Napoleon. However, it sits at a more recent point on the timeline of European history than Napoleon's France. Thus, when Nietzsche presents us with his Bismarckian example, he challenges the assumption that a teleology of progress is at work in European history. On this reading, Nietzsche is telling his readers that they have no guarantee of progress in their efforts to organise practical life. For retrograde social formations can loom to prominence (as the example of Bismarckian Germany illustrates) and perhaps

---

[19] Nietzsche (n 1) 173 [242] and 182 [251].
[20] Ibid, 138 [208].
[21] Ibid, 177 [245].
[22] CS Lobingier, 'Napoleon and his Code' (1918) 32 *Harvard Law Review* 114, 132–33.

even become (or, at least, seek to become) hegemonic. Nietzsche drives this point home when he observes that, in the Europe of the 1880s, 'warlike' tendencies are becoming more and more apparent.[23]

In this observation, we see Nietzsche's acute sensitivity to the temper of the times in which he lived. The same sensitivity is apparent when he devotes close attention to Germany, France and Britain. He notes that in these three and other European societies, 'atavistic attacks of patriotism' stand in a relationship of tension with the desire to 'become one'.[24] These attacks prompt the Germans, the French, the British and other Europeans to 'cleav[e] to native soil'.[25] Nietzsche sets along-side responses of this sort an opposing tendency towards 'good Europeanism'.[26] He argues that this tendency 'distinguishes Europe' since it leads people in the direction of 'humanisation' and 'progress'.[27] More generally, he identifies 'good Europeanism' as expressing and fostering 'civilisation'.[28] He adds that, even in the increasingly 'warlike' 1880s, this force has become more apparent. Thus we can see in it a 'process of assimilation of all Europeans, their ... increasing independence of any *definite* milieu which ... would inscribe itself on soul and body'.[29] Here, Nietzsche seems prescient, for he talks in terms that anticipate those of the proponents of European integration on the model that finds expression in the TCE.

Prescience is also a feature of Nietzsche's account of life in each of the three countries (Germany, France and Britain) to which he devotes close attention. Germans, he tells us, take pride in their 'celebrated ... Gemüt' (communitarianism on a 'merely national' model).[30] However, he adds that they are capable of developing in ways that mark them out as good Europeans and that make it possible for them to give expression to '*the soul of Europe*'.[31] When Nietzsche turns to France, he identifies it as 'Europe's most ... refined culture'.[32] Moreover, he finds in France 'European *noblesse*' – a commitment to the pursuit of ends that tell a story of 'ancient cultural superiority'.[33] This 'cultural superiority' means that the French 'possess[] a masterly adroitness in transforming even the most fateful crises ... into something seductive'.[34] In England, by contrast, Nietzsche finds a profoundly average and 'unphilosophical' people who have given expression to 'the plebeianism of modern ideas' and 'brought about a collective depression of the European spirit'.[35] These and other such reflections on the practically significant differences

---

[23] Nietzsche (n 1) 138 [209].
[24] Ibid, 171 [241].
[25] Ibid.
[26] Ibid.
[27] Ibid, 172 [242].
[28] Ibid.
[29] Ibid, 172–73 [242] (italics in original).
[30] Ibid, 175 [244] and 178 [245].
[31] Ibid, 178 [245] (italics in original).
[32] Ibid, 186 [254].
[33] Ibid, 185 [253] and 186 [254].
[34] Ibid, 137 [208].
[35] Ibid, 184–85 [253].

between the societies he surveys lead Nietzsche to contemplate the possibility that 'the politics of disintegration' may lie in the European future.[36]

While Nietzsche contemplates this possibility, he identifies the desire within Europe 'to become one' as an implacable force. On his analysis, this desire became apparent with the 'transition ... from Rousseau to Napoleon and to the rise of democracy'.[37] However, the fact remains that Nietzsche dwells on the distinctiveness of Europe's national contexts. This feature of his exposition opens up the possibility of a Europe neither in the grip of a drive towards integration nor in the process of disintegration. This Europe is egalitarian and, as Nietzsche's examination of Germany, France and Britain shows, plural. The Europeans who inhabit this context (in fact, a context of contexts) are not on a grand march towards the same end-state. However, we might describe the civilisation they have in common as something of a pageant. For we find within it a shared commitment to an egalitarian philosophy of government to which they give expression in a variety of ways.

To the extent that this is the case, Nietzsche's account of Europe and his response to it intersects with the work of Alain Badiou (a contemporary French philosopher) on 'the event'. Before we turn to these points of intersection, we must briefly consider what Badiou means by 'the event'. On one analysis, it is an 'explosion' out of a situation that cannot contain it.[38] Thus, while an event's origins lie in an existing state of affairs (or situation), it constitutes a break with it. This means that an event is 'a dissident and inventive rupture with respect to tradition, authority, orthodoxy, rule, or doctrine'.[39] Badiou gives the French Revolution as an example of an event – a moment in European history that was rich in significance for Nietzsche since it featured in the 'transition' he describes in 'Peoples and Fatherlands'.[40] Badiou argues that, in circumstances such as this (a radically altered state of affairs), we should seek to 'think[] the situation "according to" the event'.[41] To this end, we should strive to create conceptual tools that will be faithful to the event.[42] This is because events give inchoate expression to truths that we should try to articulate since they may make it possible for people to escape sets of circumstances that do not serve their interests.

The French Revolution yields a basis on which to explain the broad applicability of Badiou's account of the event to Europe as Nietzsche describes it. For it gave expression, in terms that most saw as radical, to egalitarian impulses already at work within French society and Europe more generally. Time and time again,

---

[36] Ibid, 189 [256].

[37] Ibid, 177 [245] and 189 [256].

[38] G Gutting, *Thinking the Impossible: French Philosophy Since 1960* (Oxford, Oxford University Press, 2011) 174.

[39] J Derrida, *The Gift of Death* (Chicago, Illinois, University of Chicago Press, 1992) 27.

[40] See nn 21 and 37 and associated text. See also A Badiou, *Being and Event* (London, Continuum, 2006), 189–192.

[41] A Badiou, *Ethics: An Essay on the Understanding of Evil* (London, Verso, 2001) 41.

[42] Ibid, 42. See also Gutting (n 38) 179–80.

Europe has been the scene of events that have this explosive or revolutionary quality. The idea of the individual, democracy and socialism, to take three examples, have had the sort of impact Badiou identifies as a feature of the event. These and other such examples (eg capitalism) tell a story of a context that generates cultural artefacts that it consistently struggles to understand, much less accommodate in existing conceptual schemes and institutional frameworks.[43] Nietzsche draws attention to the value of the practices, institutions and other goods that have emerged in this context when he notes '[t]he celebrated European capacity for *transformation*'.[44] His reflections on European civilisation (and, likewise, those of Badiou on the event) should give us pause. We should hesitate before assuming that we have it in our power to fashion a politico-legal-cum-economic framework that can adequately capture and sustain whatever Europe is and could be.

Before we apply Nietzsche's insights to the TCE, we should note a prominent feature of his approach to the subjects he addressed. He was a classical philologist. This discipline fostered in him a capacity for close reading. Thus he could mine textual materials for meaning and squeeze significance out of social formations and processes. Moreover, his capacity to do this extended beyond material that he could reduce to propositional content and encompassed, among other things, mood and psychology. Nietzsche's ability to work in this way is on display in 'Peoples and Fatherlands'. He conveys a sense of Europe as a cross-pressured context of contexts – at once inclined towards, and yet uneasy about, integration. For he presents us with Europeans who are torn between the 'compulsion to grand politics' and countervailing inclinations that he describes as 'cautious and reserved'.[45] Europeans much like those who feature in Nietzsche's exposition loom into view when we examine the context that spawned the TCE. This is a context in which misgivings about integration gave way to the compulsion to grand politics – and the European Council set the scene for an effort to transform a 'fateful' crisis into 'something seductive'.

III. From Nice to Giscard's Convention

By the time the former French President, Valéry Giscard d'Estaing, and those around him, began working on the European Constitution, the process of integration had been unfolding for half a century. This meant that the European Union (EU) already had a constitution in the sense of the treaties that placed its operations on a legal footing. However, after the intergovernmental conference in Nice in 2000, a document that would identify the EU as a state became a practical necessity in the minds of many prominent proponents of integration.

---

[43] Z Bauman, *Europe: An Unfinished Adventure* (Cambridge, Polity Press, 2004) 124.
[44] F Nietzsche, *The Gay Science* (Cambridge, Cambridge University Press, 2001) 24.
[45] Nietzsche (n 1) 171 [241].

The Nice conference had made apparent sources of acute tension in the EU and had led *Nouvel Observateur* to conclude that '[t]he delegates all went to the Cote d'Azur ... to despoil a corpse'.[46] The whiff of decay that this and other such comments suggested prompted the European Council to establish a constitutional convention with the aim of breathing life back into the project of integration.

The Constitution that emerged from this Convention sounds a fateful note in its (non-authoritative but illuminating) Preface by declaring that the EU has reached 'a turning point in its existence'.[47] The Preface also emphasises the momentous tasks that the Convention has taken on. It has had to draw up 'proposals' that will make it possible 'to bring citizens closer to ... European institutions' and 'the European design'.[48] Likewise, it has had to point the way forward on the 'organis[ation] of politics ... in an enlarged Union' and on the development of the EU as 'a stabilising factor and ... model in the new world order'.[49] To the large ambitions on display in these statements, we must add those that appear in the Constitution's Preamble. The Preamble states that 'the peoples of Europe are determined to transcend their ancient divisions and ... forge a common destiny'.[50] To this end, the Convention has sought to 'draw[] inspiration from the cultural, religious and humanist inheritance of Europe'.[51] Here, the text suggests a process of rational reflection that has made it possible for the participants in the Convention to extract from European history material with which to establish just and enduring practical arrangements. More particular provisions within the Constitution reinforce this impression. This is true, for example, of measures that have to do with the coordination of economic and employment policies and with the interests of consumers. Here, the TCE sounds an ambitious note by identifying a 'social market economy' as one of the EU's objectives.[52] This understanding of the market is ideal in orientation. For it has to do with defensibly accommodating the interests of all those affected by the market's operations (and thus bespeaks a commitment to the ideal of distributive justice).[53]

While the Constitution gives expression to these and other large ambitions, it also exhibits some (albeit limited) attentiveness to the practical difficulties that will be involved in turning Europe into a state. Giscard and his colleagues sound a faintly communitarian note when they tell us that the peoples of Europe 'remain[] proud of their national identities and history'.[54] This prompts the question as to how the Constitution will accommodate these identities and the histories that

---

[46] JG Gillingham, *The EU: An Obituary* (London, Verso, 2016) 136.
[47] TCE (n 7) Preface.
[48] Ibid.
[49] Ibid.
[50] Ibid, Preamble.
[51] Ibid.
[52] Ibid, Art 3.
[53] D Brack, 'David Owen and the Social Market Economy' (1990) 61 *Political Quarterly* 463, 463–64.
[54] TCE (n 7) Preamble.

play a role in sustaining them. The Constitution offers a rather glib answer to this question. Europe, we learn, will become, 'united in its diversity'.[55] This response reveals the Convention to be grappling with a state of affairs that we can describe as cross-pressured. At work within Europe, we find both the impulse to integrate and practical forces (national and historical) that threaten to limit or stymie this process.

Large ambitions of the sort we have been considering find expression in a general guide to action that features in the TCE: the proportionality principle. This principle restricts the range of circumstances in which the EU can act in pursuit of ends that serve the public interest. Where significant interests countervail against the EU's plans for social improvement, it must demonstrate that it is necessary to override them in order to secure or advance the ends it has in view.[56] These points reveal proportionality to be a mediating principle. It accommodates and affords a means by which to reach decisions that concern two types of practical impulse. The first type of impulse is consequentialist since it assesses activity (concerned with pursuit of the public interest) by reference to the outcomes it will, or is likely to, produce. The second type of impulse is deontological and assumes certain goods or states of affairs (here considerations that tell against pursuing the public interest) to have intrinsic value. As well as accommodating these two types of impulse, proportionality gives sequential priority to consequentialist considerations that serve the public interest. However, it qualifies its commitment to the pursuit of these ends by making it possible for those who consider their interests to be under threat to raise objections (thus putting the Union to proof of necessity).

This brief account of proportionality's main features tells us much about the way in which the EU goes about its business. Where it can satisfy proportionality's necessity requirement, the interests of individuals must yield. This point is relevant to a further feature of the TCE. This is its commitment to the protection of human rights.[57] While the Constitution makes much of this commitment, proportionality affords a basis on which to limit or override the rights-based protection that individuals enjoy.[58] These points support the conclusion that a species of moral philosophy to which we can apply the label 'qualified consequentialism' informs the EU's operations. This label is apt since the EU prioritises the pursuit of outcomes that have the purpose of advancing its integrationist agenda while making limited concessions to those who bring countervailing considerations to light.[59] These are points we can press further by drawing on Nietzsche's account of 'the compulsion to grand politics'.

---

[55] Ibid.
[56] *Internationale Handelsgesellschaft* [1970] ECR 1125, 1146, per Advocate-General Dutheillet de Lamothe.
[57] TCE (n 7) Art 7.
[58] Ibid, Title VII, Art II-52.
[59] R Mullender, 'Theorising the Third Way: Qualified Consequentialism, the Proportionality Principle, and the New Social Democracy' (2000) 27 *Journal of Law and Society* 493, 500–06.

IV. Grand Politics in a Cross-pressured Context

The compulsion to grand politics is apparent in the fateful note Giscard and his colleagues sound in the TCE's Preface. Europe has reached a 'turning point' and must bring its citizens closer to 'European institutions'. Likewise, the compulsion to grand politics finds expression in the TCE's Preamble. The peoples of Europe are, the Preamble tells us, 'determined to … forge a common destiny'. The word 'destiny' conjures up the image of an end-state towards which Europeans must move. The Preamble identifies this end-state as attainable when it refers to an 'inheritance' that will make it possible for Europeans to 'transcend their ancient differences'. To talk in these terms is to sound a progressive note (as Europe's peoples leave behind the disagreements of the past). This progressive note also rings out in the Preface. For it identifies transcendence as promising not merely a state but a global 'model'. Here, we can see the compulsion to grand politics on the third model we drew out of Nietzsche's exposition. As a global model, grand politics in Europe will not be narrow and nationalistic in the way Nietzsche illustrates by reference to Bismarck. Neither will it deploy force in pursuit of its aims (on the second (Napoleonic) model Nietzsche describes). Rather, it will seek to secure the endorsement of citizens, and the emulation of others, by advancing and/or promoting their interests.[60] Here we can ascribe to the TCE a service conception of authority. This is because it identifies as the route to endorsement and authority Europe's ability to pursue ends in which citizens have an interest and that would be less secure in more parochial (state-level) contexts.[61]

The compulsion Nietzsche describes is also apparent in the TCE's institutional detail. It is on display in the proportionality principle. As we noted earlier, this principle is attentive to the particular concerns of individuals. Hence, it requires those who apply it to adopt (to use a phrase from the philosopher Thomas Nagel) an agent-relative standpoint.[62] But those who apply it must also consider the public interest. Here, they fall under an obligation to adopt (to draw on Nagel again) an agent-neutral perspective.[63] For the public interest encompasses all EU citizens. Thus when a measure satisfies proportionality's necessity requirement, the EU can identify it as benefiting the individual whose particular interests have to yield. This makes it possible for the EU to identify pursuit of the public interest as proceeding on an egalitarian basis. However, as the EU goes about its business in this way, its operations take on an implacable appearance that makes talk of 'ruthlessness' (in a sense specified by Nagel) apt. Nagel describes public bodies as ruthless in circumstances where they exhibit a 'heightened concern' for the outcomes they

---

[60] M Burleigh, *The Best of Times, The Worst of Times: a History of Now* (London, Macmillan, 2017) ch 8 (on the EU as an 'empire of virtue').

[61] On the service conception of authority, see J Raz, *The Morality of Freedom* (Oxford, Clarendon Press, 1986) 56 and 59.

[62] T Nagel, *The View From Nowhere* (New York, Oxford University Press, 1986) 152–54.

[63] Ibid.

seek to pursue and attenuated interest in action-oriented constraints (including the particular concerns of individuals).[64] 'Ruthlessness' gives us an analytic tool with which to bring into focus an aspect of grand politics that led Nietzsche to describe the state as 'the coldest of all cold monsters'.[65]

Just as Nietzsche helps us to bring out the grand politics at work in the TCE, he also helps us to gain analytic purchase on the Constitution's cross-pressured condition. This condition is apparent in the limited response it makes to Europe's cultural diversity. Nietzsche looks more closely at this state of affairs than does the TCE. Unlike Giscard and his colleagues, he does not make the assumption that those who participate in particular cultures will be able to transcend their differences. While Nietzsche is not a proponent of communitarianism, he recognises the practical significance of 'community' when he places emphasis on local sources of value, meaning and identity. Thus he gives us pause as we contemplate the TCE's integrationist agenda. His exposition has the same effect when it draws attention to features of European history that mark it out as an 'event' in Badiou's sense. Likewise, it has this effect when it identifies Europe as a 'civilisation'. A civilisation is a commodious social formation: a context in which a range of broad ideas can find expression in a variety of ways.[66] In Europe, we can include among these ideas an egalitarian philosophy of government, and recognition that the practices of law, politics and economics afford means to foster just social relations in ways that invest people's lives with significance.

These points make it possible to draw a sharp distinction that is relevant to our concerns. We can set against the compulsion to grand politics at work within the TCE three considerations that may prompt a cautious response to arguments for integration. These considerations are Europe's cultural diversity and its character as both an event and a civilisation. Moreover, we might challenge the agenda of integration by identifying these considerations as investing a principle relevant to our concerns with normative force. This is the principle of caution. Two of the considerations that make this principle a significant guide to action (cultural diversity and the understanding of Europe as a civilisation) lend it a conservative appearance. This is because they find in existing states of affairs reasons for rejecting a large plan that (according to its proponents) promises social improvement (European integration on the model of a state). Rejection of the TCE on grounds such as these calls to mind the outlook that John Rawls captures in his 'conservative' 'maximin' decision rule. For 'maximin' appeals to those who take the view that 'a bird in the hand is better than two in the bush'.[67] However, to the extent that Europe is an event of the sort Badiou describes, it seems problematic to describe it as 'conservative' (if this means determined to stick with 'the way we now do

[64] T Nagel, *Mortal Questions* (Cambridge, Cambridge University Press, 1979) 82 and 84–85.

[65] Nietzsche (n 10) 75.

[66] N Elias, *The Civilizing Process: Sociogenetic and Psychogenetic Investigations* (Oxford, Blackwell, 2000) 1.

[67] S Freeman, *Rawls* (Abingdon, Routledge, 2007) 167–80.

things around here'). Hence, it seems better to describe the principle of caution as having to do with prudence (rather than progress on the qualified consequentialist model on display in the proportionality principle). For it directs our attention to considerations that promise stability, cooperation across borders, and innovations that (while not invariably benign) have consistently yielded benefits to Europeans and people more generally.

Cautiousness on the model we have been considering yields a basis on which to forge a link with 'home' as Roger Scruton has recently described it. Scruton maps out a European future in which the first-person plural of 'we' bulks large at the national (rather than the supranational) level.[68] In the section below, we will contrast the future contemplated in the TCE with an alternative that has affinities with Scruton on 'home' (and, likewise, Joseph Weiler on '*Heimat*').[69] While very different, each of these views instantiates the civilisation we are examining.

V. European Civilisation Now

A. Integration as Inventive Rupture

European integration is a project that calls on those who participate in it to engage in a species of transcendence. They must embrace an identity that carries them beyond their local commitments. While 'transcendence' is a rather grand word, its use makes sense in the context of a civilisation that has the character of an event and in which 'inventive rupture' is a feature of practical life. Its use is certainly apt when we contemplate the EU's response to the rejection of the TCE in the French and Dutch referendums. While the EU decided to abandon the Constitutional Treaty, its commitment to the project Giscard had sought to move forward has remained strong. This commitment finds expression (albeit on a more limited scale) in the Lisbon Treaty. This is an aspect of the EU's operations on which Nietzsche is, at least, suggestive. In order to explain why this is the case, we must return to the period of 'transition' (before, during, and after the French Revolution) on which he dwells. As we noted earlier, Nietzsche identifies this as a period in which egalitarianism found expression in commitments to democracy and law as a way of protecting individual rights. We can see the practical outlook he describes in the Declaration of the Rights of Man (1789). Likewise, we can see it in Napoleon's Civil Code (1804). In both the Declaration and the Code, we can find intimations of what some commentators call 'superlegality'. They mean, by 'superlegality', the use of law in ways that have the purpose of giving expression to the foundational

---

[68] R Scruton, *Where We Are: The State of Britain Now* ((London, Bloomsbury, 2017) ch 3.
[69] Ibid, ch 4, and JHH Weiler, 'United in Fear – The Loss of *Heimat* and the Crises of Europe' in L Papadopoulou, I Pernice and JHH Weiler, *Legitimacy Issues of the European Union in the Face of Crisis* (Baden-Baden, Nomos Verlagsgesellschaft, 2017) ch 15.

or 'directing ideas' at work in a particular social formation. This is a point that we can apply to the TCE. As Giscard and his colleagues make clear in the Preface and Preamble to the Constitution, it is their aim to capture the practical impulses that lie at the foundation of social life in Europe.

If this analysis is correct, there are reasons for thinking that the TCE is a document in which the legal imagination is at work. This faculty (in common with imagination generally) makes it possible for those who possess it to conjure up images or visions in the mind's eye.[70] The legal imagination enables its possessors to contemplate norms, institutions and, indeed, entire social frameworks that are 'made of law'.[71] All of this may be true and, yet, invite the response, 'Why should we associate the ability to think along these lines with "superlegality"?' The large ambitions on display in the TCE yield a basis on which to answer this question. One of these ambitions has to do with using law in ways that will make it possible for Europe to transcend its past and progress towards a 'model' state. Here, we find a vision that appears to assume that Europeans can converge on an ideal end-state or optimal social formation. To the extent that this is the case, it gives expression to the assumption that models of human association (such as we find in France, Germany and the UK) are commensurable (amenable to ranking on a common scale). Alongside this assumption we should set the service conception of authority that appears to inform the TCE. Giscard and his colleagues claim to be able to deliver goods in which all Europeans have an interest. This is apparent in, for example, the TCE's commitment to the protection of human rights. Here, the Constitution stakes out positions that give expression to 'objective list theory'. On the account offered by Derek Parfit, theory on this model identifies goods in which all people have an interest (insofar as they promote their welfare).[72]

In staking out these ambitious positions, the TCE is, at once, an expression of and an appeal to 'good Europeanism' as Nietzsche describes it. In both the Constitution's Preface and Preamble, we find 'directing ideas' that tell a story of people who have resolved to put parochialism behind them and forge a common – indeed, a 'model' – future. Moreover, they find in the richness of European culture the means to take this bold step into a better future. However, there are reasons for thinking that the 'good Europeanism' Nietzsche describes may foster atavistic responses of the sort he also brings into focus. The EU, notwithstanding its decision to abandon the TCE, has (as the Lisbon Treaty makes plain) continued to pursue its integrationist ends and to expand its reach (by welcoming new Member States). However, as it has struck down this path, it has elicited responses that have made apparent the density of European culture. A culture, and the history from which it has emerged, are dense in circumstances where they are thick with practical

---

[70] S Blackburn, *The Oxford Dictionary of Philosophy* (Oxford, Oxford University Press, 1994) 187.

[71] P Bobbitt, *The Shield of Achilles: War, Peace and the Course of History* (London, Allen Lane, 2002) ch 14.

[72] D Parfit, *Reasons and Persons* (Oxford, Oxford University Press, 1984) 4.

impulses – some of which are benign and some of which are retrograde.[73] In recent years, we have seen the rise of populism in Europe and, in this development, we can find support for the conclusion that it is a culturally dense context. For populist rejection of 'Europe' (in, for example, France, Hungary and the Netherlands) has brought with it a readiness to embrace invidious discrimination on a model at odds with the egalitarian spirit of European civilisation.[74] Developments of this sort may prompt the conclusion that the nation state is a context that we need to transcend as a matter of urgency. However, Scruton on 'home' and Weiler on '*Heimat*' lend support to an alternative view (whose roots lie deep in the history of the civilisation we have been examining).

B. Staying Close to Home

When we examine the EU's Member States (and, more particularly, the nations that nestle within some of them), we find forms of life that are rich in social capital (cooperative practices that serve people's interests). Prominent among these practices are law, politics and economic markets that, in each case, operate on an at least incipiently egalitarian basis. In combination, these practices have given expression to forms of life that have become sources of value, meaning and identity and that, in the minds of many, take on the appearance of 'home'. Moreover, these forms of life were (in earlier, less refined forms) grist to the mill of universal history as Kant and Hegel wrote it. Each of these philosophers found, in the Europe of their day, signs of a growing commitment to an egalitarian philosophy of government with universal moral appeal.[75] Hence, we might (in common with Kant and Hegel) find in these forms of life world-historical achievements. If this analysis is correct, European civilisation emerges as a complex politico-legal-cum-economic ecology. It takes the form of long-lived, ramifying and morally appealing cultural artefacts that merit attentive, respectful responses. Responses of this sort might, for example, involve those who wield power in Europe (both at state- and supranational level) exhibiting caution vis-à-vis these sources of value. For just as they might be shattered by war, they may be imperilled by large social engineering projects (of which the pursuit of 'ever closer union' is an example). However, it is far from obvious that the proponents of integration have shown such caution.

In one respect, though, the proponents of integration have honoured a European tradition with historical roots that we can trace back into classical antiquity. Seminal contributions to Western political philosophy (most obviously, those of Plato and Aristotle) identify law and politics as components of a broader

---

[73] Cultural density is a feature of actually-existing community (*Sittlichleit*) in GWF Hegel, *Elements of the Philosophy of Right* (Cambridge, Cambridge University Press, 1991) 189–98 (Pt III, [142]–[156]).
[74] I Krastev, *After Europe* (Philadelphia, Pennsylvania, University of Pennsylvania Press, 2017) 45–46, 100–01 and 108.
[75] F Fukuyama, *The End of History and the Last Man* (London, Penguin Books, 1992) ch 5.

category, '*politeia*'. *Politeia* is an ideal that finds in law and politics means to the end of community.[76] Moreover, community on the model *politeia* brings into view presupposes economic activity of a sort capable of sustaining law, politics and community life more generally. The effort to use law, politics and economics in ways that sustain the life of a community has been an abiding feature of practical life in Europe. If we think of the long-lived effort to do this as the stuff of a tradition, it becomes easy to see Europe as its bearer or heir. To the extent that this is the case, Europe has sought to pursue on a more general basis a project that has proceeded more locally (eg in the EU's member-states).

The instantiations of *politeia* we are considering may merit attentive, respectful responses for a further reason. Each of these constellations of value is part of the European present that the TCE was supposed to transcend. But, as we noted earlier, incommensurability (the inability to rank goods on a common scale) may preclude efforts to shake off the dust of the past and move into a better future. This is a point that we can develop by reference to Isaiah Berlin's account of value pluralism. Berlin recognised that an array of goods serve human interests. Thus he was an objective list theorist. However, his contribution to objective list theory is modest by comparison with that on display in the TCE. While he identified a range of goods that serve human interests, he argued that the problem of incommensurability makes it impossible to move to an ideal end-state.[77] Berlin's response to this problem is to point to 'the general pattern of life in which we believe' as a guide to action for those whose task it is to accommodate such goods.[78] Like Berlin, the TCE takes account of Europe's cultural diversity. However, it prioritises the pursuit of union. Giscard and his colleagues justify movement in this direction on grounds that are ultimately cosmopolitan and utopian: a European state will provide a 'model' for the world. If Europeans one day take up residence in such a context, it seems most unlikely that they will find a home (in the sense of a 'general pattern of life' in which they believe).

VI. Conclusions

Nietzsche helps us to bring into focus a practical force at work within the TCE and the EU more generally. This is the compulsion to grand politics. We see it in a Constitution that provides an example of 'superlegality'. For it gives expression to a group of directing ideas. These ideas find expression in its Preface, Preamble and the proportionality principle. Likewise, they find expression in the Constitution's commitment to the social market, a service conception of authority, objective list

---

[76] V Harte and M Lane (eds), *Politeia in Greek and Roman Philosophy* (Cambridge, Cambridge University Press, 2013) 3–4.

[77] I Berlin, *The Crooked Timber of Humanity: Essays in the History of Ideas* (London, Pimlico, 2003 [1998]) 80–84.

[78] I Berlin, *Four Essays on Liberty* (Oxford, Oxford University Press, 1969) 63.

theory and the ideal of distributive justice (see Table 1). As well as helping us to identify these directing ideas, Nietzsche also brings into view practical impulses at work within the EU's Member States that may stymie the pursuit of integration. Here, he, like Giscard and his colleagues, shows himself to be alive to Europe's cultural diversity. But unlike the group that gave us the TCE, he looks hard at these impulses and recognises that they may lead Europe in the direction of disintegration. Moreover, he recognises that movement in this direction may be the result of a 'good Europeanism' that assumes too readily that integration is a practical possibility. Nietzsche also encourages us to think of Europe not as a state-in-the-making (the view to which Jean Monnet and those who have followed his lead have cleaved) but as a civilisation. On this point, he is, at most, suggestive. While this is the case, we have been able to develop the point he makes in two ways. We found in Alain Badiou's writings a basis on which to argue that Europe is an 'event'. Over and over again, Europeans have been able to step beyond the institutional frameworks and modes of thinking that have shaped their lives. Thus we can find in European history support for the view that 'there is more in us … than there is in the … institutional worlds we make and inhabit'.[79] For this reason, a constitutional project that shows every sign of wanting to propel Europe towards an optimal end-state seems questionable. For it threatens to abridge the legal-cum-political-cum-economic context of contexts of which it is but one highly ambitious (and narrowly focused) manifestation.[80] We found an alternative to the end-state contemplated by Giscard and those around him in the ideal of *politeia*. This ideal provides a basis on which to explain how Europeans can use law, politics and economics in ways that express a common – civilisational – commitment to an egalitarian philosophy of government. But, at the same time, it affords them the breathing space to do so in a range of ways that are attentive to the particular patterns of life (to use Berlin's phrase) in which they believe.

To work along these lines would be to give up large ambitions of the sort the compulsion to grand politics fosters. It would also make apparent a willingness to act in accordance with the caution principle. This principle enjoins us not to put at risk the practical achievements brought forth by European civilisation. To the extent that this is the case, it encourages us to embrace an agenda that Nietzsche does not propose. However, it is an agenda that can draw strength from his 'Peoples and Fatherlands' (and his meditations on Europe more generally). For he alerts us to the possibility of a Europe that is neither integrating nor disintegrating. This is a Europe neither in the grip of compulsion nor atavism. It has an enduring, commodious character. This makes the application of the term 'civilisation' to it apt. It is the fruit of concerted human effort extending along a lengthy timeline. However, it does not hold out the prospect of movement to a model end-state. In light of these

---

[79] R Unger, *What Should Legal Analysis Become?* (London, Verso, 1996) 185.

[80] For an argument running on the theme that when we abridge a 'tradition' with the aim of capturing its 'truth', we 'inevitably' lose its 'full significance', see M Oakeshott, *Rationalism in Politics and Other Essays* (Indianapolis, Indiana, Liberty Fund, 1991 [1962], expanded edn) 30.

points, we might draw the conclusion that Nietzsche and the drafters of the TCE have at least one thing in common. They provide support (in very different ways) for the conclusion that civilisation is built and history (when we understand it in fateful terms) is driven.

Table 1 The TCE, 'the Compulsion to Grand Politics' and Superlegality

'The compulsion to grand politics': This compulsion finds expression in a body of 'directing ideas' that make apparent a commitment to 'good Europeanism' on the model Nietzsche describes.		
Qualified consequentialism (which (generally) gives sequential priority to the pursuit of outcomes that serve the public interest and, in the case of the EU, to the pursuit of European integration.	The proportionality principle (which facilitates the pursuit of integration by making it possible to override countervailing considerations).	A 'model' end-state that meets the requirements of a service conception of authority, objective list theory and the ideal of distributive justice (which finds expression in, for example, the social market).

13

Recollections from and Reflections on the Making and Failure of the European Constitution

GISELA STUART*

Giving the final speech of the day is never easy. It's doubly so if your first speaker was Giuliano Amato. You just know that the end will be nowhere as good as the beginning.

Giuliano and I worked together on the Convention on the Future for Europe which produced a 'Draft Treaty Establishing a Constitution for Europe' – which eventually became the Lisbon Treaty. I worked with him on the 13-member drafting body – grandly called the Praesidium. The Convention was composed of representatives of the Commission, the European Parliament, Member States and national parliaments. Together with John Bruton, the former Irish Prime Minister who went on the become the EU's Ambassador to the US, and Lojze Peterle, the former Slovenian Prime Minister who became an MEP in 2003 and continues to be one, I was one of three representatives of national parliaments.

That put me in a very unusual position. I was not there as a UK government representative (that was mainly Peter Hain and, for some matters, Patricia Scotland) but it was generally assumed that my views reflected those of the UK government. Looking back, I was also that rare creature that never was, has been or became a representative of any of the EU institutions.

I was answerable to the UK Parliament. For Westminster, this was uncharted territory. For the first time Parliament as an institution was directly involved in drafting a treaty. The House was swift to adapt and set up a joint committee of both Houses. The House of Commons found me an office and the budget for two members of staff to support my work. The UK Parliament was the first one to have its own office in the European Parliament and their support was invaluable. I had to work across Whitehall in a way you rarely ever do, even as a Cabinet minister. And it enabled clerks from the UK Parliament to be involved with government processes in a way they had not before.

* This is a lightly edited text of the closing remarks delivered in Oxford in September 2017.

The 13-strong Praesidium would set out the draft papers for the whole Convention, which embraced over 200 people, and set up working groups. In the final stages of the 15-month-long negotiations, when the members of the Praesidium were allowed to bring a legal advisor into the closed meetings, I chose 'Speaker's Counsel' rather than a Foreign Office lawyer.

This did not go down well with the Foreign Office. I wanted someone who could (and did) give me advice that had a longer historic perspective than that of the current administration. That is when I discovered how some ideas which were dismissed in the Maastricht negotiations, or meaningless compromises struck then, made their reappearance. Equally, some things remained strictly off limits, like the European Parliament meeting in Strasbourg. When the Praesidium discussed clause by clause which decisions should move from unanimity to quali-fied majority voting, I suggested, in the spirit of European cooperation that the location of the European Parliament should move to qualified majority voting. Valéry Giscard d'Estaing simply looked at me, told me 'very amusing Madam Stuart', and moved on to the next item.

As a parliamentarian there were three points which I thought were essential for the Commons to agree on anything the Convention would come up with:

- One – the removal of the phrase 'an ever closer union'.

- Two – a clause which would provide for powers to return from the centre as well as going to the centre.

- Three – a clause which would spell out how a country could leave the EU.

These were not government priorities. Tony Blair was a pro-European Prime Minister, not for reasons of history and nostalgia but for long-term strategic considerations. New member states were joining and he wanted them to see the world the way the British did. In countries like Poland, Hungary, the Baltic States, Romania and Bulgaria our embassies worked closely with their representatives on the Convention. Global capabilities, commitment to liberal markets and strong defence were what mattered.

We worked for the best part of 15 months. I don't think I've ever worked so hard, or learnt so much.

This conference is about the 'The rise and fall of the European Constitution'. It seems to me as if most people think that its fall was a bad thing, but it is worth examining this assumption. The first question which requires an answer in this story is 'what was the problem to which we thought a Constitution would provide the answer?' Closely followed by the second question of 'what were the problems which led the European Council to set up the Convention?'

The Laeken declaration reflected some of the 'unfinished business' enshrined in the compromises of the Nice Treaty. It called for simplification of the Treaties, greater precision in the delimitation of competences whilst respecting the princi-ple of subsidiarity, and establishing the legal status of the Charter of Fundamental Rights and the role of national parliaments. But the declaration went further and posed 60 questions – which among other things were meant to bring the European Union closer to its people.

If the Convention had been more level-headed about the problems and its solutions we may have produced something more enduring and balanced.

Early hints of our overstretched ambitions could be gleamed from the books we were reading. Joseph Ellis' *Founding Brothers: The Revolutionary Generation* – an illuminating study of the intertwined lives of the founders of the American republic, John Adams, Aaron Burr, Benjamin Franklin, Alexander Hamilton, Thomas Jefferson, James Madison and George Washington – was a favourite.[1] Closely followed by Gore Vidal's *Inventing a Nation: Washington, Adams, Jefferson*.[2]

Maybe we should have been reading up instead on the 1902 US coal strike when Theodore Roosevelt's response to the crisis significantly extended the President's constitutional role. Roosevelt rebuffed criticism by noting that the 'constitution is made for the people, not the people for the constitution'.

In the end, we did not come up with a proper answer to the two questions noted above. It's not that we didn't try, we just didn't succeed. It was the fundamental failure to create accountability with checks and balances, which led to my personal rejection of the project – something which incidentally did not occur until the final days of the Convention. This may also explain my advice to Brexit negotiators. Watch out for the last 72 hours. All sorts of things you thought were agreed fall and new demands appear out of nowhere.

During its stages of metamorphosis, the Convention on the Future of Europe tadpole did turn into a frog, but alas no princess came to kiss it and turn it into a princely constitution. The text was rejected in several national referendums, and in the case of the UK – despite the promise by all the main political parties in the run-up to the 2005 general election to have a referendum – that promise was never kept. There was an early hint of the flawed compromise in the very title of the document: 'A Treaty to establish a constitution', ie the nation states and not the people were speaking. That wouldn't have been fatal, but unlike the Founding Fathers who elegantly dealt with the fact that not all states had yet signed up, so rather than listing the states came up with 'we the people' – they found a people and we didn't. There was no and still is no European *demos*. To paraphrase Roosevelt – we made a constitution but we failed to create 'a people'.

I'd argue that the UK's decision to leave the EU in the referendum in 2016 has to be seen in the context of that failed Constitutional Treaty as well as the Maastricht Treaty opt-outs. We weren't going to join the single currency and we were not going to be part of a free travel area (ie Schengen). Once the Euro was introduced the 'creative ambiguity' of that position was stretched beyond its limits, and continues to be so.

---

[1] J Elllis, *Founding Brothers: The Revolutionary Generation* (New York, Vintage, 2002).
[2] G Vidal, *Inventing a Nation: Washington, Adams, Jefferson* (New Haven, Yale University Press, 2003).

Giuliano Amato understood the proper purpose and functions of a constitution more than many of us. Towards the final stages of the Convention he posed a question to the Presidium. He said, 'You have to decide if you want to make buns or babies'. He went on to explain that when you make buns you start with the organic reaction of yeast, sugar and flour, but then you bake it and the shape is fixed. Babies on the other hand are truly organic, they grow and adapt. Giuliano firmly came down on the side of babies.

That is not an entirely new notion. Coleridge in 1830 in *On the Constitution of the Church and State* argued that for the balance of harmony, alteration and cultivation, the state needs the means to change if it is to survive.[3] Giuliano made the opening line of his argument more memorably, but intellectually he is an equal to Burke and Coleridge. Over the 15 months of working with him I learnt to appreciate that his supreme skill is to find innovative, elegant and creative solutions to legal and political problems which aren't the lowest common denominator but are creative and new. I sometimes wonder what would have happened if the Laeken declaration had not been drafted under the leadership of Guy Verhofstadt and if Amato rather than Giscard had chaired the Convention.

Giscard d'Estaing was a man in search of his destiny. He once told us 'what we had to do if we wanted them to build statues of us on horseback in the little villages we came from'. He was right about coming from a little village, but the last time I sat on horseback in my little village was when my father sold the last horses for ploughing and we purchased a tractor.

I don't subscribe to the view that history is just one thing after another, just a string of decisions and events. I think there are broad causal relationships as well as recurring power struggles which play out on national as well as international levels.

It is worth recalling the context of the Laeken declaration and the Convention. The 1990s were a decade of blissful optimism. Everything was possible. The Cold War had come to an end. The Berlin Wall been torn down. For the first time in its history, the boundaries of the German state were concurrent with the notion of 'Germaness'. The Soviet Union had collapsed and liberal market economies were seen to prevail. Military interventions in the former Yugoslavia and Sierra Leone were successful. And New Labour had even put an end to economic 'boom and bust'.

The Convention did not just include the 15 existing members it also embraced the 11 accession countries, as well as representatives from Turkey. Some of the accession countries like Poland were already members of NATO, and for most of the others NATO membership at that time seemed at least as, if not more, important than EU membership.

Bravely, we proclaimed that ideologies no longer mattered and we had entered the age of 'technocratic governance'. Democratic inconveniences would be

---

[3] ST Coleridge, *On the Constitution of the Church and State* (London, Routledge & Kegan Paul, 1976).

outweighed by the promise of a better tomorrow. British voters may have had no idea who their MEP was and what they did and that they were elected on the most undemocratic proportional representation system of closed party lists – as long as we continued to be better off, there was no need to worry. Herbert Morrison thought 'socialism is what a Labour government does' whilst his grandson Peter Mandelson subscribed to the view that Labour does what works.

The structures and founding principles of the EU were made for just that age. No more destructive battles of ideas. Ideologies would be replaced by the promise of future prosperity, economic well-being and sound bureaucratic governance.

There is just one problem. As a system it fails to inspire, lacks the capacity to motivate and adapt and, above all, it displays a glaring democratic deficit.

The EU did try to address this by creating a directly elected European Parliament. Step-by-step the Parliament's powers increased. Alas the voters responded by ever lower turnouts. There is no sign that pan European political parties are about to emerge. And outside Brussels no-one thinks that the nomination of a *Spitzenkandidat* for the Council President, agreed on over a succession of congenial political family dinners, makes up for this.

European elections continue to be fought on national issues and the European *demos* stubbornly refuses to emerge.

This is not the topic for today but I'd argue that the European Parliament has done more to prevent the emergence of a *demos* than any other institution. It did not take root in national frameworks. A double mandate of national MPs serving as EU MPs as well would have given a democratic anchor. The European Parliament as an institution was the only group which overcame factional interests during the Convention and resolutely worked for an increase in its powers. Institutional self-interest overcame all other divisions. It is still a complete mystery to me how the UK government, in particular, came to agree to a Convention which gave the European Parliament such a powerful position. But I digress.

In this spirit of new world optimism, it did not seem unreasonable to gather and try to create a European nation. Or at least put down further building blocks for such a notion.

And then came the attack on the Twin Towers in New York in September 2001 followed by the decision to invade Iraq. The UK sided with the US, France to everyone's surprise did not join and Germany's position was summed up by Joschka Fischer announcing in the UN meeting that he 'was not convinced'. The Convention was in session when the Labour Foreign Secretary Robin Cook gave his resignation speech from Cabinet in Spring 2003. The Member States of the European Union, with or without a constitution, did not have a common foreign policy position. The EU did not have a foreign policy, because the interests of the Member States were too diverse to agree on anything. But they blamed it on the absence of EU institutions.

But whatever happened in the world, and with or without a *demos*, there were other pressing matters. Since the introduction of the single currency, new arrangements were needed and changes had to be made.

Giscard was right about two things. If we were to move to an EU model which was sustainable the Commission needed its 'own resources', ie an independent funding stream rather than having to rely on Member States agreeing on how much much to give to give to the EU. He also thought that new ways had to be found to ratify future treaty changes. The 'People's Congress' was an idea much supported by the French. Government ministers, national parliamentarians and European parliamentarians would gather to agree and ratify treaty changes on behalf of the nation states. Theoretically he was right, but politically he failed. Neither idea was carried forward. Or as the spell-check on my laptop put it, every time I typed in 'Giscard', it corrected it to 'discard'.

The problem of the need for its own resources has not only not gone away, it has intensified since the introduction of the Euro. Mervyn King the then Governor of the Bank of England in his book *The End of Alchemy* touches on the mutual incompatibility of democracy, national sovereignty and economic integration.[4] The creation of money requires a sovereign and the EU as an institution has not yet faced up to the logical consequences of that fact.

It is worth reflecting on what the British Government's priorities were in the process.

As ever there were lots of things we were determined should not happen, and then they did. From the creation of a Foreign Minister to the incorporation of the Charter of Fundamental Rights. However, there was a positive agenda too. Tony Blair was clear that the Council of Ministers required a more permanent structure.

He argued that as the Commission and the European Parliament were working on four-year cycles, so the Council required greater stability than the six-monthly rotating Presidency provided. He proposed a President of the Council. The idea was ridiculed and dubbed the ABC plan – the retirement plan for Aznar, Blair and/or Chirac.

Just before Christmas 2002, Tony Blair told me that 'this was the most important thing the government had to focus on'. When I queried this by suggesting that Iraq might just be slightly more important he replied that 'Iraq was going to happen whatever we did now, but shaping Europe was something we could and had to do'.

I mention this simply as a reminder that the notion that the UK could never get anything done at EU level is simply wrong. We could, when we tried. We just rarely did.

As an aside, I found it intriguing that in a speech in 2016 Jean Claude Juncker suggests a merging of the President of the Commission with the President of the Council, ie a weakening of the Member States.

During the Convention, I chaired a working group on the role of national parliaments. My aim was not to make national parliaments a new institution in the EU architecture, but to create a platform where they could become the guardians

---

[4] M King, *The End of Alchemy* (London, Little: Brown, 2016).

of the principle of subsidiarity and proportionality. We suggested a 'red card' system to be administered by a reformed COSAC (the Conference of Parliamentary Committees for Union Affairs), ie one where the MEPs no longer had a role. This failed because the MEPs refused to be shifted and, more irritatingly for me, the British government did not support the proposals.

I even recall being told by a Commissioner of the name of Michel Barnier, who also served on the Praesidium, that the idea of a red card was an insult to the Commission. It suggested that they could ever come up with anything so unreasonable that national parliaments could conceivable object. As an aside, I have always found Michel Barnier a very straightforward Gaullist, with all that political description entails.

I could not but respond with a wry smile when David Cameron, 13 years later, conjured up the brilliant idea of a 'red card for national parliaments' as part of his negotiations.

The proposed Constitution did not contain an exit clause, a clause for which I had argued. Any exit clause was opposed by most countries, but some argued that as the Vienna Convention on Treaties was open to interpretation we should provide legal clarity. The assumption was that the UK would have the greatest difficulty ratifying the Constitution, so the exit clause became an expulsion clause. It provided for 'any country not having ratified the Constitution within two years being asked to leave'. Little did they think it would be France and the Netherlands which rejected the Constitution in their national referendums before the British could even get round to asking anyone. The 'expulsion' clause became Article 50 in the Lisbon Treaty. It was never meant to be invoked. Just another one of those little things in the EU which once thought of, one couldn't get rid of.

Constitutions are a reflection of the rules by which a people chose to be governed. They are about power and as such require checks and balances. My basic objection was the absence of those checks and balances. A European Parliament which was given the same status as the other institutions, which had not anchored itself in a pan-European *demos*. A court that had as its stated duties to further deepen integration and lacked mechanisms to achieve a balance in the nomination processes. And the absence of workable procedures for powers to be challenged on grounds of subsidiarity. And not least, no processes which would allow powers to be returned from the centre.

In December 2003, the Fabian Society published *The Making of Europe's Constitution*, which outlined my concerns and misgivings.[5] The government was irritated but in reality had to acknowledge that it, at least privately, shared my major concerns. I didn't explicitly call for a referendum on the Constitution then, but asked for at least a free vote by MPs. By 2005, the three major political parties promised one in their election manifestos. Once the Constitution had become the Lisbon Treaty the promised referendum vanished into thin air.

---

[5] G Stuart, *The Making of Europe's Constitution* (London, Fabian Society, 2003).

Those elected by the people, time and time again, were afraid of the people when it came to the subject of Europe. The spell was broken on 23 June 2016, in a manner and with consequences we are still trying to comprehend.

We shouldn't have been surprised. The outcome was the logical consequence of the Maastricht opt-outs and David Cameron's failure to negotiate real changes. We were not part of the Euro. We were not part of the common travel area. And in the long run these 'opt-outs' would have had to be part of a permanent structure of the EU which acknowledged that some countries are part of the single currency and others are not.

If David Cameron had not called the referendum we would have gone on for fair bit longer but his decision crystallised a state of affairs that had existed for at least more than 20 years.

The conceit of a two-speed Europe, same destination but arriving at a different pace, was no longer possible once some countries had a single currency. With the UK leaving, only Denmark has an opt-out. All other countries, including Sweden which rejected the Euro in a referendum, are under a legal obligation to join. Let's see what Poland does, or will by then the EU have finally acknowledged the need for change?

It is not inconceivable that historians will conclude that the real aberration was the period between 1973 and 2019, ie the UK's membership of a European mainland institution which had as its clear aim political integration.

What will happen next?

The UK is leaving the EU.

This should not be seen as a controversial statement – but in many quarters it still is.

Allow me to quote Anthony Barnett, the first Director of Charter 88 and the co-founder of openDemocracy:

> Brexit must be respected as a conscious judgement by people of the way they are governed and not 'explained' as if it was a mental disturbance. Any judgement made on the fate of the future of one's own society and its government will be rooted in its history – for we are historical animals.

The sooner both sides realise that it is our joint task to find a good way forward the better. There do not have to be winners and losers – indeed that language itself sets wrong parameters.

But there are choices to be made.

The Euro countries will have to converge more closely. Their battle will be about fiscal transfers. The UK will have to take a hard and honest look at some of its structural problems and take action to overcome them. It is in neither the UK's nor the EU's interest not to reach a mutually beneficial agreement. That is what our voters expect from us. The UK and the EU will have to fight for their place in the world and that will mean that we will have to spend more on defence, as we can no longer rely on the US to do it for us.

The UK will have to decide which international battles it wants to fight and stay out of others altogether. A greater focus on the navy is inevitable – because, to state the obvious – we are an island.

Breaking the spell of the European dream does not mean turning it into a nightmare. It means waking up, acknowledging the good things which have been achieved and then adapting to the changing world around us. Our international institutions aren't up to dealing with the global flows of goods, finance and people. But we have a chance to create new ones.

This referendum is the first time since the introduction of the franchise when significant sections of the elites are refusing to implement the decision of the ballot. Saying that we can leave the EU, but stay in the Single Market are perfect examples of what the Greeks would have called sophistry. Not implementing the decision to take back control of our borders, laws and trade deals would have a profound effect on the state of democracy in the United Kingdom. It would empower the very extremists that the referendum has so effectively side-lined.

It was a privilege to have been part of the Constitutional Convention, just as it was an honour to chair the official Vote Leave organisation. The Constitution may have failed, but the Eurozone in particular, will need to change radically. The UK has voted to leave and that means a re-assessment of external as well as internal relationships. But rather than taking about regrets and missed opportunities we can and should show that we have the courage to shape the future.

'Tomorrow is another day!'

INDEX

Lightning Source UK Ltd.
Milton Keynes UK
UKHW020045191220
375408UK00004B/238